Helping Families Build Assets:
Nonprofit Homeownership Programs

*For Mary Ann
Best wishes,
Peter Werwath*

Peter Werwath
Senior Program Director
The Enterprise Foundation

Assisted By
Kathleen Colquhoun

THE ENTERPRISE FOUNDATION

Columbia, Maryland

We wish to thank the following organizations for their generous support, without which this study and its publication would not have been possible.

AT&T Foundation
The Annie E. Casey Foundation
The Chase Manhattan Bank
The Lewis and Dorothy Cullman Foundation
Fannie Mae Foundation
GTE Foundation
NationsBank

ENTERPRISE RESOURCE CENTER
Diana Meyer, Director
10227 Wincopin Circle, Suite 500
Columbia, MD 21044-3400
410/964-1230
410/964-1918 Fax
http://www.enterprisefoundation.org

Library of Congress Catalog Card Number: 96-90879
ISBN 0-942901-99-1

In memory of James W. Rouse

who believed that vision and hard work
will bring low-income people
into the mainstream of American life

ABOUT THE AUTHOR

As a Senior Program Director for The Enterprise Resource Center, and in other positions at The Enterprise Foundation, Peter Werwath has helped launch and expand affordable housing programs in 28 cities around the country. In this work, he has helped design and fund homeowner assistance programs in Chattanooga, Tennessee; Santa Fe, New Mexico; Fort Worth, Texas; Miami, Florida; and rural areas of Maine.

Mr. Werwath is author or editor of a number of professional publications on affordable housing, including *The Housing Production Manuals*, *Loan Processing for Low-Income Borrowers*, and *A Consumer's Guide to Home Improvement, Renovation and Repair*. Recently, he has compiled and edited hundreds of case studies and model documents for The Enterprise Resource Center's on-line database. He is a faculty member of the Affordable Housing Institute at the Harvard School of Design.

Prior to joining Enterprise in 1983, Mr. Werwath directed housing and code enforcement programs in Lewiston, Maine, was a building renovation contractor in Maine, and founded a nonprofit community newspaper in Boston. He is a native of Missouri and attended Washington University in St. Louis. He lives with his wife and three of his children in Newcastle, Maine.

CONTENTS

PROGRAM MODELS AND BEST PRACTICES

CASE STUDIES

FOREWORD

Homeownership is a uniquely American value. Almost universally, Americans, regardless of race, creed, color, or income, strive to own their own home and control their domain. Homeownership helps to stabilize families and communities. Even more importantly, however, a home is often the single asset that helps a family to accumulate wealth and get out of poverty, permanently. It is from this vantage point that we have written this book, *Helping Families Build Assets: Nonprofit Homeownership Programs*. This book provides a menu of the best practices that communities have used to design and implement successful, nonprofit-sponsored homeownership programs, including special financing tools, home buyer training and counseling, and important partnerships that should be encouraged.

The past fifteen years have shown us that the for-profit, real estate development sector cannot profitably create homeownership opportunities for low-income persons. Stand-alone, nonprofit programs, like the eleven highlighted in this book, were created to fill this void. While their programs differ in parts, they all consistently do one thing: help to make low-income families homeowners. If we want to make the American dream available to all, we must work together--local governments, community nonprofits, financial institutions, and other partners--to create a new system that brings hope and homes to families throughout the nation.

Reynard Ramsey
President & Chief Operating Officer
The Enterprise Foundation

ACKNOWLEDGMENTS

We wish to thank the executive directors and other staff members of the nonprofit organizations that are the subject of the book. Without their many hours of compiling information, responding to queries, and reviewing manuscripts, this book would not have been possible. Our thanks to:

Jamie Blackson, Project Manager, Famicos Foundation
Sue Carlisle, Manager, single-family program, Dallas Affordable Housing
  Partnership
Phile Eide, Executive Director, Jackson Metro Housing Partnership
Ed Ellis, Executive Director, Liberation Community, Inc.
Leigh M. Ferguson, President & CEO, Chattanooga Neighborhood Enterprise
Bert Green, Executive Director, Habitat for Humanity of Charlotte
Kenneth Gross, Vice President for Lending, Chattanooga Neighborhood Enterprise
Julie Gunter, Director, Dallas office, Dallas Affordable Housing Partnership
Rosalind Magee-Peychaud, Executive Director, New Orleans Neighborhood
  Development Foundation
Pam Nelson, Director of Community Services and Family Development, Garrett
  County Community Action Committee
Cassandra Palmer, Executive Director, NorthRiver Development Corporation
Sr. Marilyn Ross, R.S.M., Executive Director, Holy Name Housing
  Corporation
Cynthia Swopes, Director, Omaha 100
David Vlaming, Operations Manager, Santa Fe Community Housing Trust
Sharron Welsh, Executive Director, Santa Fe Community Housing Trust
James G. Williams, Executive Director, Famicos Foundation
Duane Yoder, Executive Director, Garrett County Community Action
  Committee

In addition, these individuals should be recognized for their tireless and creative efforts to help low-income families buy homes. The success of these programs also reflects well on the efforts of their colleagues in the public and private sector, members of their governing boards, and their low-income clients, who work so hard to overcome daunting barriers to homeownership.

Others deserve credit for their help with this book. Diana Meyer, Director of The Enterprise Resource Center, was a thoughtful and thorough reviewer of the study and editor of the manuscript. Ben Hecht, Director of Housing Services for The Enterprise Foundation, read the manuscript and made a number of helpful suggestions. Heidi Most, Assistant Director for Program Development in the National Center for Lead-Safe Housing, an Enterprise affiliate, provided detailed information on the best ways for nonprofits and home buyers to deal with lead paint issues.

Catherine Hyde, Enterprise's Publications Director, advised on editing and directed the production process. Steve Judd designed the cover. Missy Zane was a patient copy editor, and Sherri Dietrich a thorough proofreader and second copy editor.

Kathleen Colquhoun deserves special thanks for her tireless, cheerful, and invaluable help over a five-month period with the research, writing, word processing, and graphic design.

INTRODUCTION

The 11 case studies in this book were researched and written in order to discover how each home buyer assistance program operates and what can be learned from a comparative analysis. It is our intent that these detailed analyses will help those who are starting new home purchase assistance programs, or those who may want to fine-tune existing programs.

From the case studies and the analytical chapters that precede them, we hope readers can learn three things:

▶ The best practices of successful home buyer assistance programs.

▶ How programs must be shaped by their unique environments--their markets, demographics, available funding, the inspiration of their founders, and other factors.

▶ How individual leadership and partnerships among organizations contribute to success.

One of the clearest lessons is that nonprofit organizations cannot, and do not, go it alone in this work. Every successful program described here involves one or more important partnerships--whether local government, state government, federal agencies, lenders, for-profit businesses, local foundations, national support organizations such as The Enterprise Foundation, or individual volunteers. Therefore, this book is also intended to

inform those in other sectors of the industry, keeping in mind that some lenders and local governments operate similar programs without the involvement of nonprofits.

In addressing best practices, *Helping Families Build Assets* attempts to answer these key questions.

▶ **What financial products work the best for clients with low incomes?** What kinds of affordable first mortgage products are available? What kinds of subsidies, if any, are needed to finance very low-income, low-income, and moderate-income buyers?

▶ **What client services are most effective?** What approaches to counseling, training, home inspections, and other services best prepare low-income people for homeownership?

▶ **How can nonprofits best organize themselves to do this work?** How do effective organizations market themselves, screen clients, and help them through the home buying process? How are they managed and staffed, and how are the organizations and their boards of directors structured?

▶ **Where can the money be found?** How do organizations obtain operating funds, and how do they raise the capital for making loans and undertaking housing development?

▸ **Who are the most important partners?** How do institutions such as banks, local governments, state governments, foundations, and others fit in?

Still, trying to copy proven practices is no guarantee of success. Personal energy, skills, and leadership are also critical factors. Therefore, where possible, the case studies show the contributions made by executive directors, other staff members, public officials, clients, and other individuals. All determine how the programs started, how they operate, and what they produce.

In short, the book focuses on services to low-income buyers, financing, organizational issues, and human resources--and how all these components must respond to local conditions.

A Focus on Client Services, Not Housing Development

Since there is already a great deal of literature on the subject of housing development, the process of building or rehabilitating homes for sale is not described here in depth. Instead, we were more interested in how the organizations serve low-income families' needs--how these clients are first contacted, screened, trained, helped with selecting their homes, coached on closing sales contracts, advised on mortgage financing, given other financial assistance, and assisted if problems develop after the purchase.

Therefore, project descriptions are limited to the features and sizes of the homes, their sales prices, and any attached special financing.

How the Research Was Done

The research for this book consisted of a nine-month study of 11 locally based nonprofit organizations that help low-income families buy homes. Initially, 40 organizations among the 700 that are affiliated with The Enterprise Foundation were identified, along with several other nonaffiliated groups located in cities where Enterprise works. From this initial list of possible case studies, we selected only programs that were helping with 15 or more home purchases a year. For the most part, the programs had operated for at least four years, but we intentionally picked a few startup programs as well.

These 40 organizations were asked to send documentation of their programs. Fifteen organizations replied. The final selections were based on these criteria:

▸ Completeness of the documentation and the follow-up telephone interviews.

▸ Representation of as many major variables as possible, such as various approaches to homeowner training, financing, and housing development, or location in different kinds of markets (urban, inner-city, rural, low-cost, high-cost, etc.).

Most of the information presented in this book was self-reported by the organizations through their written materials and telephone interviews. It was beyond the scope of this study to verify facts with on-site visits and interviews with funders. However, many of the organizations provided audited or independently compiled financial statements, which verified much of the key financial data.

It should be acknowledged here that the author worked with six of the organizations at different times during the 1980s and 1990s. Thus, the case studies of programs in Chattanooga, Cleveland, Dallas, Fort Worth, Jackson, and Santa Fe benefited from some personal experience and knowledge--typically gained during the startup phases of the programs.

Respondents were asked to send annual reports, budgets, financial statements, production reports, organizational charts, business plans, strategic plans, program descriptions, policies, procedures, and forms. All the cooperating organizations were generous in providing candid and factual information--most importantly, internal financial and production reports. About half of the organizations supplied detailed business plans. A few declined to share detailed financial statements.

For each case study, the sources were cross-checked among themselves and with the results of interviews. As a result, a number of inconsistencies and ambiguities were resolved, so that Enterprise has high confidence in the data.

In addition, 1990 census data was used to describe the backdrop of each city. While this information is seven years old at this writing, it is still the most reliable source of comparative information about the cities. In some instances, in which this data was clearly outdated, more current information was provided by the cooperating organizations. For population figures, 1992 estimates by the Census Bureau were used, except where noted.

Where to Look for More Information

For each case study, one or more contact names and addresses are given. If you wish to contact the organizations, we suggest that you do so judiciously and with specific questions or document requests in mind. Program staff were very generous with their time, but none of the organizations has staff time to spare.

Those wanting more details on housing development and finance can look to numerous other sources. For example, *Enterprise On-Line* offers how-to information, model documents, and reviews of books that cover many aspects of housing development. This information is available through the Handsnet on-line service, through the World Wide Web at www.enterprisefoundation.org, or through The Enterprise Resource Center at the locations described on the title page. The Center's library has copies of a number of model documents from the 11 programs we examined.

Who Should Read the Book?

This book was designed for the following audiences:

▶ Personnel and board members of nonprofit organizations that currently operate home purchase assistance programs or wish to do so.

▶ Officials of local, state, or federal government agencies that administer similar programs or fund nonprofit-sponsored programs.

- Community reinvestment officers, loan officers, and others who work for lenders or secondary market institutions that are concerned with financing home purchases for low-income borrowers.

- Builders, real estate agents, credit counselors, foundation officers, and others who work with (or would like to work with) home buyer assistance programs.

- Analysts and researchers from industry and academia, who are welcome to draw their own conclusions from the case studies.

How to Use This Book

Chapters 1 through 5 consist of analysis and conclusions drawn from the case studies. This is the only part of the book that readers may wish to peruse from start to finish. It includes findings that should be of interest to anyone involved in the business of helping low-income families buy homes.

Chapters 6 through 16 are the case studies. Near the beginning of Chapter 1 is a matrix that serves as a road atlas for these profiles of home buyer assistance programs. It shows which elements are represented by each program. For example, Program A may offer only counseling, training, and low-cost second mortgages, while Program B offers the same services but is also trying to revitalize an inner-city neighborhood by acquiring, renovating, and selling homes.

The matrix should serve as a pointer to the case studies that are of interest, or specific program elements (such as new home construction) that are described in more than one case study.

Tools for Business Planning

Certain detailed information in the case studies should be of particular interest to those developing business plans for similar operations. Pertinent data includes:

- Analyses of the market conditions each program responds to.

- The marketing strategies used by these successful organizations.

- Detailed descriptions of the services and financial products offered, rates and terms, and fees charged, if any.

- The criteria used to determine which clients get help--including incomes, geographic restrictions, credit standing, employment, minimum cash required for purchase, housing payment ratios, and other loan underwriting criteria.

- Descriptions of other key policies and procedures.

- Lists of staff positions and, in many instances, descriptions of staff roles and responsibilities.

- Size, composition, and roles of boards of directors.

- Annual administrative costs and the sources of revenue used to pay them.

From the study, it was clear that each program is carefully tailored to the market conditions, funding resources, government policies, and other characteristics of its city or county. Therefore, we do not presume any program we described is *the* solution--completely replicable in other locations.

Instead, we invite you to compare the 11 programs and their markets, and to form your own opinions about which financial products and services, and which approaches to doing business, might work best where you live or work.

Challenges and Rewards

In listening to staff members of the programs talk about their work, it was obvious that helping low-income people buy homes is often a difficult process. Some clients simply fail to get steady employment, earn adequate incomes, or clean up their credit. There are no guaranteed sources of affordable homes, low-cost capital for secondary financing, or funds to pay a staff. Program staff members work long hours--often at low pay or for no pay--to ensure that low-income families have the resources to buy homes.

On the other hand, it is hard to imagine more rewarding work. Those we interviewed spoke with well-deserved pride about the homes they renovate or build, the success of their training and counseling work, the innovative financing they are able to offer, and the benefits to low-income families.

Since home buyer assistance programs are a growing movement, it is likely that many more people working for nonprofits, government agencies, banks, and real estate companies will experience these challenges and rewards. Even when things are most difficult, as they often are when new programs are starting up, we hope that the professionals in this business stay energized by the ultimate goals--helping low-income families find decent homes, build assets, and become more economically self-sufficient.

P.W.

Program Models And Best Practices

1. Major Findings and Recommendations

Major Goals of Purchase Assistance Programs

In taking a critical look at programs helping low-income home buyers, the first question we asked was: "What are the major goals that effective programs try to accomplish?" While there are a number of other goals that programs set for themselves, we saw these as the primary ones, and the ones that were most measurable:

► Clients buying homes in significant numbers, as measured by homes purchased per year.

► Helping clients with lower incomes, as measured by the average income, percentage of median income or other standard--recognizing that the lower the income the more families need subsidies to buy homes.

► Helping people who could otherwise not attain homeownership, as indicated by the volume of special financing used to fill gaps between what families can afford and what they would otherwise afford in the open market.

► People staying in the homes and building assets, as measured by reasonably low delinquency and default rates.

► Impact on revitalizing distressed neighborhoods, as evidenced by homes being built and rehabilitated, other visible improvements, and a rising homeownership rate.

► Cost effectiveness--reasonable costs for the goods and services delivered.

Those are major goals, but certainly, there are others just as worthy. Some of the programs try to increase family self-sufficiency. Through volunteer work and sweat equity, the one Habitat for Humanity program we examined tries to build permanent bridges between middle- and upper-class people and very low-income people.

The fifth goal, cost-effectiveness, is the only one that is not an output--that is, something that directly helps low-income people or neighborhoods. This has to do with the amount of subsidies used, the benefits of those subsidies, and the amount of overhead for goods and services produced. We feel it should be in the top five because the other four goals are almost always attainable if there is enough grant money--particularly federal grants, which are the major sources of both subsidies and overhead dollars. In these days of federal budget cutting, grants will be in shorter and shorter supply.

Secondary Measures of Success

If those are the major goals, there are secondary measures that give indications of

Goals and Functions of Programs Studied: A Comparison

	Charlotte: Habitat	Chattanooga: CNE	Cleveland: Famicos	Dallas: DAHP	Fort Worth: Liberation
MAJOR GOALS					
Assist low-income buyers	X	X	X	X	X
Help with non-housing issues	X	X	X		X
Revitalize target areas	X	X	X		X
Control future appreciation					
SPECIAL FINANCING					
Down payment grants	n/a	by others	n/a	by others	by others
Deferred payment loans	n/a	X		X	X
Amortizing 2nd mortgages	n/a	X			X
Tax-exempt bond financing		X			by others
Below-market 1st mortgages	X	X	X	by others	by others
OTHER SERVICES					
Prequalifying for financing	X	X	X	X	X
Home buyer training	X	X	X	by others	X
Financial counseling	X	X	X	by others	X
Prepurchase inspections	n/a	X	X	X	X
Help with sales contracts	n/a	X	X		X
SOURCES OF HOMES					
Houses on the market		X	X	X	X
Purchase/rehab by sponsor		X	X		X
New homes by sponsor	X	X	X		X
OWNERSHIP OPTIONS					
Fee simple	X	X	X	X	X
Land trust					
Lease-purchase			X		X

Garrett County, MD CAC	Jackson: Metro Partnership	New Orleans: NDF	Omaha: Holy Name	Santa Fe: Housing Trust	Toledo: North River	
						MAJOR GOALS
X	X	X	X	X	X	Assist low-income buyers
X	X	X	X	X	X	Help with non-housing issues
n/a	X		X		X	Revitalize target areas
				X		Control future appreciation
						SPECIAL FINANCING
		by others	by others	X		Down payment grants
X		by others	by others	X	X	Deferred payment loans
	X				X	Amortizing 2nd mortgages
		by others		X		Tax-exempt bond financing
by others	X	by others		by others		Below-market 1st mortgages
						OTHER SERVICES
X	X	X	X	X	X	Prequalifying for financing
X	X	X	by others	X	X	Home buyer training
X	X	X	X	X	X	Financial counseling
X	X	X	n/a	X	X	Prepurchase inspections
	X	X	n/a	X		Help with sales contracts
						SOURCES OF HOMES
X	X	X		X	X	Homes on the market
	X		X	X	X	Purchase/rehab by sponsor
X			X	X	X	New homes by sponsor
						OWNERSHIP OPTIONS
X	X	X	X	X	X	Fee simple ownership
				X		Land trust
	X					Lease-purchase

how well programs are achieving their primary goals. These include:

- The number of clients trained and counseled

- Low delinquency and default rates

- Keeping housing affordable for future buyers

- Helping families solve problems and gain more self-sufficiency

- Quality of prepurchase training and counseling

- Quality of homes

For the last three measures, it was difficult for us to determine with certainty how well programs are performing without conducting site visits and client surveys, both of which were beyond the scope of this study. Nonetheless, the chapters following are filled with examples of, and advice on, the best policies and practices that local organizations use to get the best performance in these areas.

Goals and Functions of the 11 Programs

The recommended practices described in this book are a menu, not a recipe. Different financing mechanisms (explained in Chapter 4) and different approaches to training, counseling, and other functions must be analyzed and then accepted or rejected. The tables on the previous two pages give a quick overview of the variations we found in financing mechanisms and program

functions, held up against the major goals each program is trying to achieve. All of the programs aim to assist low-income home buyers. And they all train and counsel families, and prequalify them for financing. But after that, the programs diverge a great deal.

Two Replicable Models

We found that two programs--Habitat of Charlotte and the Neighborhood Development Foundation (NDF) in New Orleans--are fairly transportable models in every aspect of their program operations.

Habitat of Charlotte is an excellent model of inner-city home construction using sweat equity, socially motivated volunteers, and a revolving loan fund capitalized with grants and contributions. The program is replicable where: 1) land or older homes can be obtained for new construction or rehabilitation; 2) many volunteers can be recruited; 3) the potential for raising large amounts of grants and contributions is high; and 4) there is no desire to leverage conventional financing with grant dollars (one credo of Habitat programs is to not charge interest).

But this model is not for everyone. While many non-Habitat organizations put volunteers to work in many ways, most choose to use conventional builders for construction. Most programs want to involve lenders and will not commit to relying exclusively on grants and loan repayments to finance homes.

NDF has a complete, time-tested, and effective approach to home buyer training and counseling and assistance in negotiating purchase contracts. It offers no grants or and counseling and assistance in negotiating purchase contracts. It offers no grants or low-interest loans but helps low-income buyers get conventional financing and subsidies from other sources. The NDF program appears to be highly replicable in any market large enough to produce 200 or more successful low-income home buyers in a year, and it might be scaled down to work effectively with 100 buyers a year.

But it is doubtful that the NDF program could work nearly as efficiently if limited to one or several small neighborhoods. Nor could such a program compete well in a market where a similar organization was offered subsidies.

However, NDF's approach to counseling and training seems to be widely replicable. For example, the Santa Fe Community Housing Trust modeled its training and counseling program after NDF's. But unlike NDF, the Housing Trust engages in extensive real estate development and provides special financing assistance.

While the Habitat and NDF models are widely replicable, no one would claim that they are the solution for all low-income home buyers. A more significant finding of the study was that local market conditions, demographics, funding environments, and philosophies determine what program models are needed and adopted. There are no "one size fits all" solutions.

Effective Financial Assistance

As indicated in the chart on the preceding pages, the programs studied typically mix and match a unique set of financing tools for their clients. Chapter 4 and the case studies describe these mechanisms in great detail. Here are some conclusions about what works.

Convincing lenders to offer high loan-to-value (LTV) first mortgage products: The plain vanilla affordable loan programs offered by banks, thrifts, and secondary market institutions like Fannie Mae typically allow 95 percent or 97 percent LTVs, and this is highly beneficial to low-income buyers. These liberal standards are very helpful where small amounts of secondary financing are given to clients, and where low property values lead to appraisal problems. All other factors being equal, these loans can work where clients' incomes are relatively higher, home prices are very low, and first mortgage lenders have confidence in the specific housing markets in question. But there is a limit to the benefits of high LTV loans, as explained next.

Using higher amounts of non-conventional financing in low-valued markets: Subsidy financing, whether amortizing loans or soft seconds, is clearly a key to enabling lenders to finance low-income buyers where property values are relatively low. The programs in these kinds of markets used the largest percentages of non-conventional financing--namely, in Cleveland, North Omaha, North River in Toledo, and the Polytechnic area of Fort Worth. In all the cases except Cleveland, this resulted in lower LTVs for lenders (no conventional first mortgage financing is used in Famicos' program in Cleveland). Even lenders that offer high LTV products seem to appreciate a higher comfort level in these markets.

Using soft second mortgages to bridge large affordability gaps: In all kinds of markets, soft second mortgages (due only on resale) are essential where a client's income is simply too low to afford even the lowest-priced housing. To the extent that these soft seconds reduce the first mortgage amount, they also reduce the total housing payment. Most first mortgage lenders in this study allowed a maximum 33 percent of income for the housing payment, and 38 percent for all installment debt. For many low-income and very low-income families, these underwriting ratios are more critical barriers than loan to value ratios, since they limit the absolute amount of money that can be borrowed. Amortizing second mortgage loans, even at low interest rates, do not cure this problem.

Not making underwriting ratios too high: Sometimes, first mortgage lenders are willing to use very high underwriting ratios so buyers can qualify for higher first mortgage amounts--we found ratios as high as 35/50. We feel that ratios over 33/38 are not advisable. Most programs we examined try to keep the ratios at or below 33/38. Some aim for a more affordable 28/36, the ratios used with conventional loans.

Using amortizing loans to recycle subsidy funds where possible: One of the surprises of the study was how four programs--in Chattanooga, Jackson, Fort Worth, and Toledo--effectively use amortizing second mortgage loans for some or all of their secondary financing. In these markets, existing homes are available in the range of $25,000 to $50,000, making them affordable without deep subsidies even for very low-income families. The amortizing

loans have the obvious benefit of recycling subsidy funds. Nonetheless, all but one of these programs also use grants to write down project costs and soft seconds for more expensive homes, typically new homes on infill lots. The underlying strategy is to provide just enough subsidy, but not too much.

Using stronger resale restrictions in appreciating markets: In Santa Fe, the one rapidly appreciating market we examined, land trusts and shared appreciation devices are used to let families build assets while still allowing the program to recapture and recycle subsidies for the benefit of future buyers. This technique is widely used by government agencies and nonprofits in more expensive housing markets, and we feel it is wise, given the large amounts of subsidy capital needed to operate home purchase assistance programs in those markets and the scarcity of subsidy dollars. Conversely, we found that in markets with flat or slowly appreciating housing prices, few if any resale restrictions appear to be necessary. In these places, it is desirable and possible for subsidies to be repaid on a monthly basis (through an amortizing second mortgage) or at resale, so long as buyers still build equity.

Not forgiving all the debt on soft second mortgages: Following the wishes of local governments that pass through HOME and CDBG funds, several programs that offer soft second mortgage loans forgive them over a period of five to 15 years. In other words, the debt goes away. Since subsidy funds are scarce, and several other programs we examined are collecting repayments on resale of the properties, we believe that these forgiveness policies are generally not advisable.

There is one notable exception. It makes sense to forgive some of the debt when: 1) the total financing package exceeds the market value of the property, as is the case in many inner-city markets; or 2) the amount of the subsidy is only a few thousand dollars or less, as is the case with many closing cost assistance programs.

Streamlining the processing of tandem loans where possible: In some programs, clients must go through a triple underwriting process: with the nonprofit program sponsor, a conventional lender, and with the local government agency that provides the subsidy. We recommend that government agencies delegate as many underwriting and inspection functions as possible to their nonprofit partners. On the other side, nonprofits must assure compliance with federal Housing Quality Standards and income limits and do a quality job of underwriting the subsidies. There appear to be many opportunities for streamlining the process of obtaining tandem conventional-subsidy loans.

Asking banks to help process secondary financing: One highly streamlined program--in Dallas--has the largest annual number of home purchases of nonprofit-sponsored programs that we know of (400) and remarkably little staff (five people). When clients apply for first mortgage loans, the 15 members of a lender consortium take applications for soft second mortgage loans that are originated by a nonprofit-sponsored program. However, only about one-third of the clients receive counseling and training.

As a result, at the time of our survey, the nonprofit lender and the partner banks were looking for ways to improve those services.

Reducing delinquency and default rates with better collections work: The delinquency and default rates we found in the programs examined were typically much higher than average, and high even when compared to low-down-payment FHA loans. While the figures were not alarming, a number of techniques for improving performance in this area are recommended in Chapter 4. In particular, nonprofits and conventional lenders should set up better systems for early intervention and communication. What is most lacking seems to be timely collections work, not post-purchase counseling.

Factors Affecting Numbers of Home Buyers Assisted

As described, the number of buyers helped in a given period of time is a primary measure of the effectiveness of a program. Among the programs examined, there was a wide range of output--from 17 up to 400 homes purchased by clients. As we said, this is only one measure of success --one that often competes with other goals such as revitalizing neighborhoods.

Still, it is useful to look at the factors that appeared to increase the numbers of low-income families that bought homes. We identified the following characteristics of higher-output programs:

Working in larger markets: As common sense would dictate, it appears to be easier to work in a large market than to target a

BUYER INCOMES, COSTS, STAFFING AND OUTPUT OF THE PROGRAMS

	Average Client Income	Typical Home Price	Typical subsidy per home	Buyers Per Year	Number: Housing Staff	Annual Overhead Costs
Charlotte: Habitat	$14,000	$47,000 N	$47,000 at 0% interest	31	14	$519,000
Chattanooga: CNE	$24,000	$45,000 E	$5,000 E	281	42	$2.35 million*
Cleveland: Famicos	$18,000	$35,000 E	$35,000	25	15	$405,000*
Dallas: DAHP	$24,000	$63,000 E $75,000 N	$15,000	400	5	$300,000
Fort Worth: Liberation	$14,000	$35,000 E $52,000 N	$15,000 E $15,000 N	30	6	$257,000*
Garrett County: CAC	$21,000	$70,000	$14,000	17	2	$2.4 million*
Jackson: Partnership	$17,000	$40,000	$8,000	73	4	$190,000*
New Orleans: NDF	$22,000	$59,000	None	209	5	$300,000
Omaha: Holy Name	$15,000-$30,000	$35,000 E $80,000 N	$18,000 E $28,000 N	40	14	(2 orgs) $260,000
Santa Fe: Housing Trust	$24,000	$94,000 E $110,000 N	$12,000 E $20,000 N	271	6.3	$330,000*
Toledo: N. River	$23,000	$25,000 E $75,000 N	$6,000 E $42,000 N	17	5	$236,000*

"Typical subsidy" means any project write-downs or below-market-rate financing

E: existing homes

N: new homes

* Includes costs of major functions unrelated to home buyer assistance

small one. The four citywide programs we examined--in Chattanooga, Dallas, New Orleans and Santa Fe--each helped between 209 and 400 home purchasers in a 12-month period. In contrast, the seven neighborhood-based programs helped between 17 and 40 home buyers a year. This is not to say that citywide programs are better, but they do get more low-income clients into homes. Neighborhood-based programs have other agendas--like revitalizing neighborhoods and combatting poverty--that involve difficult tasks such as buying and renovating homes for sale, building new homes, and undertaking other human development and community development activities.

Obtaining large amounts of subsidy funding: Two of the three highest-producing programs--in Dallas and Santa Fe --offer their buyers generous deferred payment second mortgages. This appears to be appropriate, since the programs operate in two of the highest-cost housing markets we looked at. One of them --the Santa Fe Community Housing Trust-- also develops homes and uses grants extensively to write down project costs. Both organizations use millions of dollars of subsidy funds each year to make homes much more affordable than those purchased without financial assistance. In Dallas, the program has strong City support and a large annual allocation of HOME funds. In Santa Fe, the organization has no certain source of subsidies, but aggressively seeks them from such sources as the State HOME program, private grants, and special Congressional appropriations.

Getting through startup stages and program modifications: It took between two and five years for the 11 programs to hit their stride. The one program still in its startup stage added more and better financing tools in its second year and expected to more than double its output in its second year.

The table on the preceding page illustrates the great variation among programs in buyer incomes, program costs and program output.

Recommended Counseling and Training Practices

Local programs make their own decisions about how much training and counseling to offer and how much hand-holding they will do throughout the purchase and loan application process. These decisions are based on market characteristics, resources for overhead, goals for homes purchased per year, and a number of other factors. Nonetheless, we found that one fairly standard approach to marketing, intake, screening, counseling, training, and providing secondary financing seems to be effective in many situations--it is summarized here.

There are some caveats: This full-service approach costs $1,000 to $2,000 per client, is tailored to the needs of low- and very low-income clients, and may not be needed by all clients. Some are readier to buy than others, and should not be "run through hoops" unnecessarily. With those caveats, these are the recommended practices.

Rely on clients and partners to market the program: Most program managers told us that word-of-mouth advertising brings in most of their clients. Happy clients appear to be the best marketing tool. Several of the programs, distinguished with more longevity and higher numbers of clients served per year, stay in close touch with former clients through newsletters and post-purchase programs such as maintenance training. Lenders and real estate brokers are also very useful in marketing programs.

Have minimum entrance requirements: For new clients, workshops and group counseling sessions open to all comers should not be the point of entry. Programs should do some basic screening over the phone and require clients to bring pay stubs, tax forms, and other documentation to a meaningful intake interview, where an on-line credit report should be reviewed and some preliminary prequalification for financing should occur. Some programs may go farther by advertising minimum income requirements, home prices in the market, and available subsidies. This avoids wasting the agency's time and frustrating clients who clearly cannot buy homes at this time. However, no program should refuse to talk to unqualified clients, who might be encouraged to meet the qualifications by various efforts.

Get to people early in the home buying process: Most of the programs studied, along with many experts in the affordable lending industry, believe the best point to intervene with counseling and training is before clients start looking for homes.

Prequalify and counsel clients in the intake interview: Initial prequalifying and counseling should occur in the intake interview. From this point on, some programs continue to work with very marginal clients, but most do not. Some programs offer training with more life skills and budget counseling for these marginal clients but most do not.

Screen out unqualified clients early on: Most programs for which data was available lose two to four clients for every one who applies--usually not far into the process. Where homes are being bought on the open market with conventional financing, realistic screening is a service to lenders and real estate brokers and keeps program costs down by reducing the counseling workload. One could argue that this is creaming the market, but minorities and very low-income people appear no more likely than others to be screened out, unless their incomes are simply too low to afford homes.

Do not turn people away, give them a plan: Almost every program we studied does not turn away unqualified people. Verbally or in writing, they are given advice or a plan for getting ready for homeownership.

Offer classroom training after, not before, intake and initial counseling: Most programs offer training primarily to clients who are close to qualifying for conventional financing. This means most clients are goal-directed and highly motivated, adding good spirit and peer support to the workshops of 20 to 40 prospective home buyers. While most programs do not refuse training to anyone, they do not market the training to clearly unqualified clients.

Require about eight hours of group training: The best use of group training sessions is to impart knowledge that every home buyer needs and to inspire clients to improve their finances and become astute real estate buyers. Most programs offer two three- or four-hour sessions that must be attended consecutively. Common subjects include the home purchase process, family budgeting, dealing with credit problems, qualifying for a loan, inspecting homes, closing purchase contracts, applying for loans, maintaining the home, and other responsibilities of home ownership.

Do training early on, and counsel clients separately: To avoid duplicating the benefits of the training sessions, most personal counseling should occur during and after the training. Group training sessions are not the place to counsel people individually (as has been tried in some programs which are not described in this study).

Make one-on-one counseling available through the purchase process: Most programs offer advice on negotiating purchase contracts and are a helpful go-between with conventional lenders. Most help with home inspections and offer advice on needed repairs.

With older existing homes, adopt better approaches to lead hazard abatement: Based on the information we received, none of the programs studied appears to emphasize lead paint abatement. Chapter 3 describes recommended practices.

Lease-Purchase Arrangements

Our study examined four lease-purchase programs. Two--in Jackson and Fort Worth --operate on an ad hoc basis and involve only a few families who rent rehabilitated homes while they prepare to qualify for conventional purchase financing. One, in Garrett County, was started with five newly built homes leased to very low-income families and probably will not be continued. The fourth is operated by Famicos, the Cleveland Housing Network, and other affiliated nonprofit housing organizations. The Cleveland program may well be the largest lease-purchase program in the country, taking in over 300 families a year.

From the detailed information about these programs provided by the sponsors, we conclude the following:

▶ Lease-purchase arrangements appear to be inefficient if undertaken on a small scale by an organization that does not already maintain residential properties and collect rents or loan payments from tenants or home buyers.

▶ The lease-purchase approach appears to offer no benefits if families can be prepared for outright ownership within a year or so. There are two exceptions: 1) when the lease-purchase program reduces home prices or financing costs in a way that could not be duplicated by an outright sales program; and 2) when the organization is willing and easily able to help a family that needs a home but is not ready to buy.

The Importance of Partners

Every program we looked at is operated by a freestanding nonprofit organization. That is the bias of the study. We intentionally did not examine programs solely sponsored and operated by government agencies, housing finance authorities, or lenders.

Eight of the 11 programs focus primarily on housing. As is typical, the one rural program is operated by a multipurpose community action agency. Two organizations--not coincidentally in two of the lowest-income neighborhoods found in the study--offer a variety of social services besides housing assistance.

Private lenders: Except for the one Habitat for Humanity program, all of the programs examined would not exist without private mortgage lenders and secondary markets. In one city, lenders appeared to be particularly reluctant to make affordable housing loans, and a nonprofit organization, Chattanooga Neighborhood Enterprise, filled the gap by becoming the nation's largest nonprofit originator of first mortgage loans. But in other situations, all of the programs are designed around the available first mortgage products from conventional lenders and mortgage brokers.

HUD, local governments, and state government agencies are equally critical to the success of most programs. Mostly acting as conduits for HUD funds, local governments are the largest single source of capital for secondary financing and overhead expenses. In smaller cities and rural areas, state agencies that pass through HUD funding fill that role or complement it.

Local governments offer important support for real estate development projects in the form of write-down grants and sometimes help with property acquisition and infrastructure. In inner-city areas, they sometimes provide tax-foreclosed lots and houses at little or no cost. But this appears to be a complicated process and is used less widely than purchases of lots and marginal homes in the open market. In one high-cost market, the local government asked for developer contributions of affordable homes or land--a useful resource. Several cities in the study provide ongoing general funds to local home purchase assistance programs for operating costs, project development capital, or secondary financing.

Foundations and other private contributors provide very important help in paying overhead costs. Foundations and other grant-makers are the sources of the most flexible capital--helping to capitalize revolving loan funds and funding the early, high-risk costs of development projects through loans or grants. After foundations, lenders are the major source of grants.

Credit counseling agencies are partners with many programs in helping clients clean up serious credit problems. This help is provided on an as-needed basis, apparently for a minority of clients.

Homebuilders are important partners with the two citywide programs we examined. One, Dallas, is a moderate-cost city. Costs in Santa Fe, on the other hand, are high. In both places, the housing market was tight enough at the time of the study that new home construction was beneficial. In inner-city areas, **rehabilitation**

contractors are more important allies, since housing vacancies tend to be higher, renovation of homes helps revitalize the neighborhoods, and new construction typically requires much deeper subsidies. (New construction costs more than twice as much as buying and rehabilitating homes in many of these areas.)

Real estate brokers are essential partners in most programs that help buyers find and finance existing homes--as was primarily the case in Dallas, Santa Fe, Garrett County, Jackson, New Orleans, Chattanooga, and Toledo. Most of these programs constantly reach out to brokers to make sure they know about the training, counseling, and any special financing. Brokers, in turn, can save time and effort by directing low-income clients to the nonprofits, which can prequalify buyers, help them determine a price range they can afford, and help put together the financing package.

The Importance of Affiliations and Leadership

In analyzing the 11 programs, we found that formal affiliations with lenders, religious ministries, and others were influential factors in the formation of nine organizations. They continued to exert an important influence over how eight of the programs operated at the time of our study.

In each of these cases, it is doubtful that the programs would have started at all without the backing of other established, committed organizations--whether for-profit, nonprofit, religious, or governmental. In the other programs, less formal but substantial backing from the same kinds of institutions made the startup possible. So we conclude that these kinds of institutional affiliations are essential to the success of startup programs.

All but one of the organizations we studied do more than help low-income home buyers. Many develop and operate rental housing. Some operate rent subsidy or emergency assistance funds for the homeless. One works with small business development and job training.

Clearly, one of the most indispensible ingredients for success is personal leadership. Chapter 5 describes how mayors, other public officials, program founders, executive directors, and other committed individuals moved programs from concept to reality.

Benefits of Spin-Offs

Only one organization, Liberation Community, which operates eight separate housing and social service programs with a staff of 15, is considering a tighter focus. It recently expanded into two distant neighborhoods and started a construction job training program modeled after the YouthBuild program. Facing more citywide competition for federal funds (which are passed through the city government), Liberation is considering spinning off two new neighborhood-based community development corporations and its job training division.

Spin-offs have worked well for two organizations. Holy Name in Omaha, the citywide lender consortia already described, spun off a separate community development corporation to develop for-sale and rental housing in a neighborhood across town.

Staff Sizes and Diversity of Functions

As we explain in Chapter 5, staff sizes of the organizations studied range from a low of four people to a high of 42. Programs with larger staffs take on staff-intensive functions such as in-house construction, origination of first mortgage loans, and lease-purchase programs.

But even smaller organizations like the Santa Fe Community Housing Trust, which has only six staff members, have found ways to take on many different kinds of roles, handle many clients, and manage tens of millions of dollars a year in development and financing. The Housing Trust accomplishes this by using highly specialized outside firms and individual contractors.

Staff Efficiencies

As described in Chapter 5, one rough measure of program efficiency is home purchases assisted each year, per staff member. Among the programs we looked at, this ranged from four to 80. To our knowledge, no industry standards exist for measuring whether a program's output is reasonably efficient. When and if efficiency measures are developed, they need to take into account the following factors.

▶ **The number of products and services provided by a program can vary enormously.** The New Orleans Neighborhood Development Corporation focuses on training, counseling, help with sales contracts, and assistance with mortgage financing--so it offers a good benchmark for that group of services. But other organizations build homes, develop land, provide secondary financing, and even operate a number of programs unrelated to homeownership.

▶ **Programs focused on one or several low-income neighborhoods are likely to produce fewer home buyers per staff member.** Each of these programs we studied was involved in housing development, which is particularly difficult in distressed, inner-city areas on a scattered-site basis. Conversely, programs that work citywide--as in Dallas, Santa Fe, Chattanooga, and New Orleans--have higher outputs, as does the only program we looked at that develops tract homes, again in Santa Fe.

▶ **There are trade-offs between staff costs and the possible benefits of undertaking labor-intensive tasks.** Scattered-site rehabilitation is more labor intensive than new construction. But in the inner-city programs we examined, acquiring and renovating homes costs about half as much as new homes, requires much less subsidy, and improves dilapidated properties.

Overhead Costs and Funding

Administrative costs of the 11 organizations ranged from $190,000 a year for one organization with the least employees (four), to $2.34 million for CNE in Chattanooga, which has 42 employees.

The other six ranged from $257,000 a year to $519,000. In these figures, we included all staff costs and associated overhead, but left out all direct expenditures on loans to clients and real estate development. In some cases, the budgets include costs not associated with home buyer assistance programs, since those could not be separated out.

Salaries and contract services are by far the major expense of these organizations--as they should be. The major outputs of the programs are human energy that helps clients and, in some cases, creates new or renovated homes. The expenses of producing the organizations' products--loans made and homes sold--do not and should not show up as administrative costs.

It is difficult to draw conclusions about the appropriateness of these overhead costs within an in-depth evaluation of each program, which we did not set out to perform. Where the information was made available, most of the organizations spent between 71 percent and 86 percent of their overhead on salaries, benefits, payroll costs, and professional services.

Sources of capital for loans and real estate development are discussed in Chapter 5. But regarding overhead, most programs funded their overhead in the following ways.

▶ Most rely heavily on grants. Local governments, lenders, and foundations are major sources.

▶ Fees and program income typically generate less than 20 percent of the

funding for overhead costs. A few programs charge clients training and counseling fees (between $200 and $1,100 paid with the home financing), but this reimburses only a small portion of the cost of services. Loan repayments and interest income generate significant income for several organizations, but are often restricted for use in making more loans.

Forming Your Own Conclusions

This chapter includes the findings and conclusions we identified as most widely applicable. We have made recommendations regarding financing products, best practices for training and counseling, organizational structures, and overhead funding.

Each of these issues is treated in more depth in the following three chapters. Following those, the 11 case studies give real world examples of how successful programs operate. If you disagree with some of our conclusions, the information is there to form or refine your own point of view.

2. Tailoring Program Models to Meet Local Needs

Virtually every attempt at creating cookie cutter housing programs has failed. We have learned that housing programs--including homeownership assistance programs--cannot be cloned like McDonald's franchises. For example . . .

▶ Decades ago, most policy makers and practitioners assumed that a national, one-size-fits-all public housing policy could solve our housing problems. Today, the very concept of public housing has been called into question, and there is strong support for letting local authorities find their own destinies.

▶ When the Neighborhood Reinvestment Corporation was congressionally chartered in 1978, its local Neighborhood Housing Services (NHS) affiliates were cast in pretty much the same mold--with standard products, procedures, and organizational structures. Nearly 20 years later, diversity is more the rule among the hundreds of chapters.

▶ At HUD, the "reinvention" team talks of consolidating its 70-plus categorical programs into three or four block grants, so local jurisdictions can design their own programs. The success of this bottom-up approach is exemplified by the CDBG and HOME programs.

All these changes have come, at least in part, from the realization that cities' housing markets and community development needs are all different. One city may need new construction, while another has homes crying out to be renovated. In some, existing home prices are within the reach of many low-income families, while in others deep subsidies are required. Some markets have great quantities of single-family homes, while others are densely built with multifamily housing.

But it is fair to ask whether there aren't some successful and replicable models of home purchase assistance programs--ones that can help newcomers to the field avoid reinventing the wheel. After all, haven't conventional home purchase loans been standardized like McDonalds' hamburgers, despite the differences among housing markets? And hasn't that benefited home buyers everywhere with better access to financing and lower rates? So why can't home buyer assistance programs be standardized?

The answer is that many *practices* can and should be more standardized. But it is simply a fact that effective *program models* vary widely from place to place. Special home purchase assistance programs exist precisely because standard financing products are not reaching everyone, especially minority and low-income families. And the reasons they do not work vary from place to place. Here are some examples from this study of why program models must vary considerably from place to place.

Unique reasons for being a nonprofit first mortgage lender: Until recently, most Chattanooga lenders were very reluctant to market home purchase loans in inner-city neighborhoods. As a result, Chattanooga Neighborhood Enterprise became, in effect, a nonprofit mortgage company, originating market rate first mortgage loans and subsidized second mortgage financing. In most other cities in this study, that model is not needed because for-profit lenders are ready to do business in low-income markets.

Where deferred payment loans make sense and where they don't: The Dallas Affordable Housing Partnership and the Santa Fe Community Housing Trust both offer substantial second mortgage financing for which no repayments are due until resale of the home. In contrast, the Jackson Metro Housing Partnership and NorthRiver Development Corp. offer second mortgage loans that have to be repaid over 10 or 20 years. The programs in Dallas and Santa Fe are not spendthrifts--the existing homes they finance cost one-and-one-half to two times as much as those being financed in Jackson and Toledo. Even though recycling of subsidy financing is desirable, in expensive markets, it is more difficult for a low-income home buyer to make a monthly payment on a first *and* second mortgage.

Types of Housing Markets Represented

The types of housing markets represented in this study vary considerably. By housing market, we mean the primary market that the program is directed toward--either a county, a city, a neighborhood, or group of neighborhoods. The markets fall into five categories.

1. A high-cost citywide market: In this study, Santa Fe represents the highest-priced market. Aside from the below-market priced homes produced by the Santa Fe Community Housing Trust and several other local nonprofits, minimum home prices are $90,000 to $130,000 for existing and new homes, respectively. The program is not geographically targeted because low-income residents are not concentrated in specific neighborhoods. Of all the markets in the case studies, this one bears the most resemblance to growing suburban areas and gentrifying urban areas.

2. A moderate-cost citywide market: As in Santa Fe, the Dallas Affordable Housing Partnership (DAHP) operates its programs citywide, without targeting neighborhoods. DAHP home buyers pay the second-highest home prices of the 11 programs studied. Prices range from $50,000 to $80,000 for existing and new homes. The market is typical of many stable urban and suburban markets with homes built, for the most part, between the 1950s and 1970s. Upward pressures on prices are moderate. Two other programs studied--Chattanooga Neighborhood Enterprise and Holy Name in South Omaha--operate in part in this type of market but put most of their emphasis on blue collar neighborhoods with older housing stocks and lower housing prices.

3. Stable blue collar areas: The Chattanooga program, the Jackson Metro Housing Partnership, the New Orleans Neighborhood Development Foundation, and Holy Name's South Omaha program focus primarily on this kind of neighborhood. The first three programs work citywide, and the last targets a large area containing many neighborhoods. The Jackson program limits home sales prices to a maximum of $47,000, effectively targeting its second mortgage loans to low-income but not highly distressed areas. (It should be noted that the Chattanooga, Jackson, and Omaha programs also target very distressed areas for special redevelopment projects.)

In these markets, prices for decent, existing homes range from $35,000 to $50,000. Financing sales of existing homes--either as-is or renovated--is a major activity in these markets. Also, construction of new "infill" homes is seen as a method of revitalizing these areas and, in some cases, attracting lower-middle-class families.

To some extent, Habitat for Humanity of Charlotte and Liberation Community also work in these kinds of markets, but most of their efforts are in poorer neighborhoods. The NorthRiver neighborhood in Toledo, although statistically very low-income, has seen an influx of blue collar families due to the success of the housing program there.

4. Very low-income neighborhoods: When many people think of cities and affordable housing programs, the image of very low-income neighborhoods comes to mind. Built somewhere between the early 1900s and the 1950s, they have been victims of years of disinvestment. Due to the loss of major employers, the middle class has moved out. Poverty, crime, and drug use are major problems. Some homes are abandoned and boarded up. Where homes were torn down, vacant lots abound. Most homes need rehabilitation, but the costs in our case studies were fairly modest--$25,000

to $40,000. Limited new construction is also occurring, with costs of $60,000 to $80,000 per home. But new construction is harder to finance than in blue collar neighborhoods, because the monthly payments must be kept lower.

In this study, the programs that address these kinds of markets focus on one or more small, defined neighborhoods--such as the Famicos Foundation in Cleveland, Liberation Community in Fort Worth, NorthRiver Development Corporation in Toledo, Habitat for Humanity of Charlotte, and Holy Name's program in North Omaha. The Jackson and New Orleans programs operate in these kinds of areas, but finance most of their home buyers in more stable blue collar areas.

5. Rural areas: In this study, Garrett County, Maryland, is typical of many rural markets far removed from cities. Housing is reasonably affordable, but as in many inner-city neighborhoods, the number of very low-income families is high due to a weak job base. But Garrett County has not experienced disinvestment and deep economic distress, so home prices are more in line with those in moderate-priced urban markets. Thus, as in Dallas and Santa Fe, the gaps between a low-income family's ability to pay and the market prices of housing are wider than in the blue collar neighborhoods that were examined.

Obviously, the study did not examine all types of markets. Very high-cost markets such as New York, San Francisco, and Honolulu were not represented. Core cities with very old and densely built single-family housing such as Baltimore's and Philadelphia's were not included. Nor were places such as Washington, DC, where small multifamily buildings are being converted to cooperatives and sold to low-income home buyers.

With home buyer programs in those places, one would expect to find higher per-unit home costs, along with more use of project write down grants and soft seconds to make the homes affordable. However, other features of the programs studied should be transferable to those places.

How Financing Tools Are Chosen

Aside from the markets they work in, the most striking differences among the programs studied are the variations in financing mechanisms, in terms of both first and second mortgage financing. And these variations strongly influence the overall design of programs.

For example, programs that provide direct financing to clients (as in nine of the 11 examples) need staff and operating systems to process, underwrite, and collect loans. They need more investment capital, and therefore more sophisticated financial management systems. Those that originate first mortgages need systems for selling loans to secondary markets.

Nonprofits that got involved in housing development often did so because project write down grants and soft second mortgages for buyers were available from local or state government, or in rural areas, the Department of Agriculture.

In Chapter 4, we examine in detail how these numerous financing mechanisms work. But here, it is important to note how the choice of financing tools is strongly influenced by local environments. For the organizations in this study (and presumably many similar programs), the following factors determined which financing tools were chosen or rejected.

Factors Affecting the Choice of Financing Tools

► Availability of subsidy funds from public and private sources--primarily HUD and the Federal Home Loan Bank System

► Existing home prices

► Housing development costs

► The private lending climate

► Public policies and political philosophies

► The scale of the program

Let's look at how these factors affected how the 11 organizations studied chose financing tools, and often decided to mix and match them. We identified seven major kinds of financing tools, as follows:

1. Conventional first mortgage financing: For primary home purchase financing, every program except Habitat for Humanity relies on traditional first mortgage loans. Banks, savings and loans, and mortgage companies typically provide these loans at market rates, with a few lending at below-market rates. Less frequently, nonprofits originate some but not all of the first mortgage loans in their own programs-- as in Chattanooga, Omaha, and Fort Worth.

2. Nonprofit-originated first mortgage loans: In only two programs did nonprofits originate the first mortgage loans--CNE in Chattanooga and the lender consortium, Omaha 100 (the first mortgage lender for Holy Name clients). This program model has limited application for two reasons. First, it appears not to be needed where individual lenders are aggressively promoting affordable first mortgage products and even competing for community investment business. For this very reason, DAHP in Dallas stopped originating first mortgage loans. Second, this approach requires more skills and overhead that--to be used efficiently--must be spread over larger scales of operation than most nonprofits can attain. CNE originates about 160 first mortgages a year, and the Omaha group aims for 100 loans.

3. Nonconventional first mortgages: Habitat of Charlotte, like most Habitat affiliates, provides 100 percent financing at zero percent interest, using grants, individual contributions, and loan repayments to fund the loans. This is a matter of deeply ingrained principles--the Habitat philosophy is to not charge interest, even though some of its clients could undoubtedly qualify for conventional financing piggybacked with subsidies.

4. Down payment and closing cost grants: Disregarding this study for a moment and taking into account all programs in which secondary financing is used, the most minimal and most widely used forms of financing help are grants or forgivable loans of $1,000 to $5,000 per client. For our purposes, we will call these "down payment grants." If loans, they are typically forgiven over five years. This is a useful tool in almost every market. Nearly everywhere, this device is funded primarily by Community Development Block Grant (CDBG) funding (which has special rules for this kind of purchase financing) or grants from the regional Federal Home Loan Banks through their Affordable Housing Program.

In almost every case we studied, this level of assistance is not sufficient to qualify the typical low- and very low-income home buyer being served by the programs, and is often piggybacked with other secondary financing. Our study looked only at more comprehensive, nonprofit-sponsored programs, which tend to target families that need more financial help. Down payment grants, standing alone, appear to help only the high end of the low-income spectrum and moderate-income families. This being the case, the Chattanooga program challenges the notion that this help should be in the form of grants--for families with incomes over 80 percent of median, it loans up to $2,500 in down payment and closing cost assistance and charges six percent interest.

5. Soft second mortgages: We found soft seconds in two kinds of places. First, they are used in citywide or countywide markets where the prices of existing homes average over $60,000 (Dallas, Santa Fe, and Garrett County). Second, they are used in connection with inner-city redevelopment programs where the costs of rehabilitated or new homes range from $35,000 to $80,000-- as in Omaha, Fort Worth, Toledo, and Chattanooga. The loans typically range from $10,000 to $15,000 and are most often funded with federal HOME dollars.

In every case, these loans are used to bridge the gap between incomes and housing prices. In the inner-city areas, the housing costs are sometimes less expensive but the incomes are commensurately lower. Certainly, there are other markets where soft seconds would be useful, or are just coming into use (as in New Orleans). This is a very capital-intensive form of assistance--helping 100 home buyers typically takes over $1 million in grants. Therefore, the availability of funds is highly dependent upon the policies of local and state government regarding the desired uses of HOME funds. Soft second mortgage programs often compete with affordable rental projects and less costly down payment grant programs.

In some cities (such as Santa Fe, Omaha, and Dallas), buyers have to pay back these loans when the home is sold. In Garrett County, the loans are forgiven over a number of years. The City of Dallas is revisiting its policy for funding the loans of the Dallas Affordable Housing Partnership and considering forgiveness terms. Liberation Community in nearby Fort Worth is moving in the other direction--asking the City to stop forgiving the loans and make them repayable. The differences are philosophical rather than practical--some push for efficiency and recycling of funds, and others are more focused on converting the subsidy to owner equity.

6. Subsidies with a payment book: One of the biggest surprises of this study was how some organizations are able to help very low-income families buy existing homes, and get their subsidy back over time--with interest. This was found to work in extremely low-income target neighborhoods in Cleveland, Charlotte, Toledo, and Fort Worth, and also in less targeted programs in Jackson and Chattanooga.

These examples defy the conventional wisdom that very poor buyers cannot pay back their subsidized financing and need deferred payment loans. Interest rates range from zero percent (Habitat in Charlotte), three percent, six percent, and up to market rate. The benefit, of course, is that subsidies are recycled, and the programs need fewer infusions of grant dollars. The key to using amortizing loans seems to be the availability of very low-cost new homes or existing homes that can be acquired and renovated very inexpensively--costing in the range of $35,000 to $45,000. In some places, the flip side of neighborhood decline and disinvestment is that homes sell very cheaply.

7. Grants to write down new home costs: Some of the major subsidies to low-income home buyers are less obvious than the ones just described. In Santa Fe, Toledo, and Omaha, public funds are used to write down the costs of land, infrastructure, and construction in new home developments. In Santa Fe, these subsidies are needed to reduce the highest development costs found in this study, and the write-downs are sometimes even piggybacked with soft seconds to make home prices affordable. In Omaha and Toledo, new homes cost less to build, but the incomes of buyers are sometimes lower than those of the Santa Fe clients. Homes in those inner-city areas also appraise for less, making write downs almost a necessity to attract mortgage lenders and buyers.

In Santa Fe, great efforts are made to recapture these write downs through additional liens on the properties or even shared-appreciation mortgages. The purpose is to forestall windfall profits and recycle subsidies when homes are resold. But in the other markets, windfall profits are unlikely because property values are relatively lower and not appreciating rapidly as in Santa Fe.

What Determines the Scale of Programs

Skill, luck, and entrepreneurial spirit clearly affect whether programs work or not. In our study, we intentionally picked programs that work. But they operate on very different scales, helping between 10 and 400 home buyers a year.

Assuming skilled people are operating the program, environmental factors clearly are the biggest determining factor in the scale of operations. And the most influential factor is the size of the target market. Market size, in turn, directly affects the program design. As described in Chapter 1, neighborhood-focused programs tend to have much smaller output than citywide programs. And they tend to focus more on redevelopment and housing rehabilitation because those have a more visible and stronger affect over the long-term on neighborhood revitalization.

Three secondary factors decide whether a program will be neighborhood-based or operate in a wider market area. These include local government funding policies, community-based development philosophies, and market realities. In the business plan of a for-profit organization, all these factors would be part of a market analysis. Strangely, with nonprofits, these factors are often barely noticed, or like the air we breath, they are taken for granted. Nonetheless, together, these three environmental factors have an enormous influence on program design.

Size of the target market area: Programs that target inner-city neighborhoods get involved in property acquisition, construction, and home sales because homes are substandard and reconstruction helps revitalize the neighborhoods. Because property values are low, marketing and financing require more work. These labor- and capital-intensive tasks limit the output to 20 or 30 homes a year at most. On the other hand, the programs that work citywide help between 209 and 400 families a year. Larger markets make it easier to achieve high output. They have more existing homes that do not need renovation. Typically, buyers are free to find any decent home they can afford in any area.

Local government funding policies: The major factor appears to be the willingness of a government agency (as in Dallas) to provide the large subsidy pools needed for citywide programs--trading bigger production numbers for a lack of neighborhood targeting. And bigger visions often beget more money. Groups like CNE in Chattanooga, DAHP in Dallas, and the Santa Fe Community Housing Trust started off deciding to help large numbers of families in a number of different ways. Then they wrote business plans to achieve those goals. When one or more programs started working well, more public and private financing flowed their way.

Community-based development philosophies: On the other hand, some local governments, local foundations, and national foundations strongly support neighborhood-based revitalization strategies built around community development corporations

(CDCs). Cleveland, Toledo, and Fort Worth offer the best examples of this strategy. In effect, the local governments have chosen to work with more groups, accepting lower output per group and often higher per-unit subsidy costs as a trade-off for achieving more targeted and difficult community redevelopment.

On the other hand, the CDC movement has shaped government policies in some cities. For example, many of the CDCs that are allied with the influential and respected Cleveland Housing Network started as activist neighborhood groups that demanded the City, lenders, and foundations reinvest in distressed residential neighborhoods. The result, in Cleveland, is that most special funding for housing development is directed to neighborhood-based organizations or the Housing Network, which works in alliance with those kinds of organizations.

But citywide and neighborhood-based programs are not mutually exclusive. The neighborhood-based Holy Name organization in Omaha cloned another CDC in South Omaha and helped to start the citywide loan consortium. Famicos targets three neighborhoods in Cleveland but is willing to work outside them. CNE in Chattanooga and the Santa Fe Community Housing Trust work citywide--and develop projects that benefit specific low-income neighborhoods.

Market realities: Obviously, behind all these policy choices are some market realities. In cities where the cities have invested in CDCs as an approach for community revitalization, many neighborhoods are still very distressed and impacted with poverty, despite some improvements over the years. But growing places with low unemployment and low vacancy rates--like Santa Fe--simply need new affordable housing anywhere in the city and do not have significant distress in inner-city neighborhoods. As a result, the Housing Trust has become a land developer--its staff spends much more time with engineers, site planners, and zoning officers than any other group profiled in this book.

But in Dallas, since there is an adequate supply of moderately priced homes, the DAHP program is not involved in land development or home construction. And private sector builders are more adept at building low-cost homes than in Santa Fe. Builders have just started putting up $70,000 to $80,000 homes to respond to the new demand created by the DAHP program. In Santa Fe, unless the Housing Trust or another nonprofit group is the land developer, new home prices start at $130,000, and because for-profit builders could not produce lower-priced homes, nonprofits got involved.

Similarities in Program Practices

This chapter has focused on the differences among the cities and housing markets examined in the study, and the effects these differences have on the program models that developed--and more particularly the financing products used and scales of operations.

Yet, programs that help low-income home buyers have much in common when it comes to day-to-day operations. For example, the way programs find, counsel, and train clients is remarkably similar in almost every case we looked at. The best of these practices are the subject of the next chapter.

3. Best Practices for Counseling and Training

In this study, one of our primary goals was to determine what works and what doesn't. To do so, we reviewed the output of the 11 programs in terms of both quantity and quality. We looked for approaches that seemed most efficient and effective in helping low-income families get decent homes at a low price with low-cost financing.

Naturally, we were also concerned that the clients who buy homes have an excellent chance of staying in them without experiencing problems with delinquencies and unexpected home repair needs.

"What works" is covered in this chapter and the two that follow it. Chapter 4 describes the many ways in which nonprofits can provide special financing and the most-used sources of capital for making loans or undertaking housing development. Chapter 5 describes effective organizational structures, the benefits of affiliations, approaches to management and staffing, administrative costs, and sources of administrative funding.

This chapter describes the best approaches to counseling and training clients, along with some of the typical problems that are encountered in working with clients and other agencies. These specific topics are covered:

▸ Effective ways to market programs

▸ Tested procedures for intake and screening

▸ Methods of providing one-on-one financing counseling and using related tools such as credit reports and mortgage scoring

▸ Standard curricula and methods of delivering group training to home buyers

▸ Helping clients with home inspections and negotiating home purchases

Marketing That Works

Word-of-mouth advertising through former clients, real estate agents, and lenders (in that order) are the most effective marketing tools. Therefore, using newsletters, seminars, meetings, and brochures to reach those partners makes lots of sense. Staff can be used efficiently to train these no-cost marketers in periodic seminars.

For more general outreach, all the programs surveyed have staff members who give talks to community groups. One high-output counseling program arranges lunch-time meetings at the work places of major employers with low-wage workers, many of whom qualify for the program. Simple brochures are absolutely critical--especially ones that tell clients what documentation to bring to the first interview. When needed, these are printed in other languages.

Several of the programs send newsletters to their clients who have bought homes and other program supporters. Most of the programs have found they can get free media coverage by staging events and creating opportunities for feature stories.

Still, most program managers in this study said that satisfied former clients are their best advertising. The experience of one program suggests that they can help market programs in more ways than one.

"Clients are our most important resource," said Sharron Welsh, executive director of the Santa Fe Community Housing Trust. "When we started, we had training and counseling for clients before we had second mortgage money or homes for sale. We asked them for help all the time, and they gave it. They helped design the homes. They showed up at public hearings for our development projects or funding requests to the City. They agreed to buy homes before they were built. And they tell their friends about the program. Without them, we would be nowhere."

Marketing to Catch Clients Early in the Process

In their marketing strategy, managers have to decide at what point in the home buying process they want clients to come in. Will the program try to identify them before they begin serious house hunting or apply to buy a home from the program? Or do they want to become involved with the client after this process is underway?

Most programs try to capture clients for screening, qualifying, and home buyer training before they get very far in the home purchase process. "Think preparation, not house," a seasoned staff member, Fred

Johnson, advises new clients in the New Orleans program.

Recently, HUD sponsored a high-level conference on home buyer education. In a published report, *Financing the American Dream*, one of the findings was:

"The most desirable way to prepare home buyers is through counseling provided before any sales contract is signed. About 80 percent of affordable housing loan applicants have not had that counseling prior to signing a contract on a house."

Many prospective first-time home buyers have not thought over all the pros and cons of home ownership. They don't know how to shop for a home or inspect a house for problems. They don't understand about sellers' brokers and buyers' brokers, or making offers, or purchase and sale contracts. They don't know how to calculate the amount of financing they qualify for, or what special financing may be available.

Clients who come to programs after selecting their homes may not have factored in commuting costs. Or they may not strike the best deal for either the home or financing and end up paying too much. Most important, when they consider all the factors, they may not be ready to buy a home. These and other issues can lead to delinquencies in mortgage payments and ultimately defaults.

Relying on real estate brokers or lenders to market the program may mean that clients are sent to the program late in the process, and then probably just to get special financing. Most experts agree that training and counseling can accomplish little at this stage.

But astute brokers and loan officers realize that training and counseling programs can save them a lot of work if they refer clients earlier in the process. They often see clients in the preliminary stages of the home hunting process, when they are browsing or inquiring only in general about home prices and financing. If they know a local nonprofit-sponsored home buyer program is good, they might say, "Why don't you go to Program X before you look at too many houses. Find out what you can afford. Find out about their special financing."

There's no question about it: Reaching clients early in the process is difficult. Most programs insist that clients finish classroom training before getting special financing, but sometimes, highly qualified low-income buyers walk in the door after identifying a good home that they can afford. This creates problems. Waiting to be scheduled for training can delay the purchase for several weeks or even months, and home sellers often will not wait.

With clients who walk in ready to buy, some program managers say they try to be flexible. Of course, one way to lessen these problems is to focus on recruiting clients directly, before they have approached brokers or lenders. Unquestionably, home buyer training can increase skills and confidence in dealing with these professionals, so the educational value added is probably highest for clients who are not yet involved in selecting a home.

Effective Client Intake and Screening

Most programs use their own trained staff to screen clients into several groups:

▶ Those not nearly ready for homeownership

▶ Those needing serious credit repair

▶ Those who prequalify for a bank loan, either with or without a subsidy--or are close to prequalifying

Finding out which category a client falls into should not be left to chance or hearsay about family income and debts. Effective programs require clients to bring in good data on income, debts, and assets. They also pull a credit report. This information is discussed in an interview lasting less than an hour.

Typically, according to many program managers, between 50 and 75 percent of prospective clients are culled out at this point because of having extremely low incomes, family instability, major financial problems, or lack of strong interest in solving the income or credit problems.

Careful Income and Credit Screening

Unless larger problems loom, the client's income and credit report are the most important matters discussed in the interview. Accuracy in calculating incomes of all prospective co-borrowers is absolutely essential. A miscalculation can unfairly toss out a candidate for special financing, or just as bad, prequalify someone whose income is too high to qualify for a subsidy.

Credit reports must be examined in detail, preferably in the first interview with the client. A recent study of its loan portfolio by the Mortgage Guaranty

Insurance Corporation (MGIC)--a major provider of private mortgage insurance, found that clients who make very low down payments and have two or more adverse items on their credit reports are 20 percent more likely to become delinquent on their loan payments. Those with no credit histories were 70 percent more likely to become delinquent.

Credit scoring ranks a prospective borrower in terms of his or her relative risk of defaulting on consumer debt. Only one organization in the study, Chattanooga Neighborhood Enterprise, reported using this evaluation tool regularly. With this technique, the credit reporting company assigns a numeric rating to the client's credit quality. MGIC has found that affordable housing loan clients with credit scores of less than 620 are nearly two times more likely to become delinquent on their loans than clients with credit scores over 660.

Mortgage scoring is a more sophisticated tool that takes into account the credit score and other factors such as the type of property, LTV ratio, debt-to-income ratios, cash reserves, an applicant's years on the job, and regional economic data. The data forecasts the likelihood of a default. This technique is becoming part of automated underwriting, a computerized system by which quick mortgage decisions can be made automatically from data inputs.

While some nonprofit housing organizations and advocacy groups fear that these scoring systems discriminate against low-income and minority home buyers in subtle ways, others (mostly on the private lending side of the industry) say it will give them a fairer shake. Secondary market and mortgage insurance institutions like Freddie Mac and PMI Mortgage Insurance Company are promoting automated systems.

One of the weak points of some nonprofit-sponsored programs is that they cannot afford to pay for staff with the skills to act as shadow loan underwriters. Having staff with these underwriting skills is critical to screening out completely unqualified buyers, and helping others obtain mortgage financing.

The new automated underwriting systems may begin to fill this gap. Home buyer assistance agencies will be able to do mortgage scoring for clients as dry runs for the credit checks that will occur at banks. Ideally, this should occur in the intake interview--when the mortgage score would be obtained along with on-line credit reports that are now commonly used by nonprofits. Rather than screening people out, the agency can play what-ifs with variables such as loan-to-value, cash reserves, and credit repair to determine the best advice and assistance for each client.

CNE, which uses credit scoring when it originates first mortgage loans, has a loan delinquency rate of 2.1 percent (below average for the mortgage lending industry) and an extremely low default rate. So while the technique is still controversial because of concerns about discrimination, it is worthy of more investigation and experimentation.

The Need for Financial Counseling

MGIC's loan delinquency and default statistics point up the reasons for careful financial counseling. In a survey of affordable housing loans insured by that agency between 1985 and 1990, the effects of layered, or cumulative risks were studied. These were some key findings:

▶ 95 percent loan-to-value (LTV) loans were 2.3 times more likely to default than 90 percent LTV loans.

▶ 95 percent LTV loans were 3.6 times more likely to default if underwriting ratios were over 33 percent of income for housing payments, and 38 percent of income for all installment debt.

▶ When loans were made in that last category *and* borrowers had adverse credit findings, they are 6.6 times more likely to default than 90 percent LTV mortgages, which translates to a default rate of about 13 percent [our estimate, not MGIC's].

Most of the programs studied offer 95 percent, or even 97 percent LTV loans, when the first and second mortgage loans are combined. With a minority of their clients, lenders in some of the programs studied liberalize their ratios to as high as 35/50. And many clients have two, three, or more black marks, such as late payments, on their credit reports.

Fortunately, in the programs studied here, the default rates range from zero to about five percent and average less than two percent in our unverified survey--not an alarmingly high figure considering that many clients in the programs have credit problems, some use high LTV loans, and some were underwritten with ratios over 33/38. This implies that education, counseling, and screening are working to counteract credit risks. Special financing

makes monthly payments more affordable and, in some cases, leaves clients with more cash reserves than they otherwise would have had. The MGIC sample from the 1980s included few, if any, clients who had benefited from this kind of assistance.

But the findings of the MGIC study raise a question that could not be answered definitively by this study: *Do the programs lessen delinquency rates by screening out less qualified clients, by improving credit worthiness, or by both means?* Our suspicion is that screening out unqualified clients is more important than anyone admits. While it is an article of faith that education can change families' money management habits for good, no study has proven that theory.

Screening out clients on the basis of credit reports sounds a bit cruel and, on the surface, implies that no help was given at all. Thus, we found staff members of the nonprofits were reluctant to discuss the topic. The New Orleans program was the only one to provide reliable records in this regard. In 1995, the program screened 761 clients, trained 455, and ended up with 209 home buyers, a ratio of 3.6 intakes for every home purchased.

These figures do not take into account a higher and unknown number of prospective clients who screened themselves out when they read or heard about the program's requirements for income and debt documentation, training, and counseling. It stands to reason that, all other things being equal, individuals who seek out a program such as this are more responsible and more interested in self-improvement.

Effective Counseling Techniques

Among the programs, there was some confusion in the use of the terms counseling and training. As does most of this industry, we define counseling as assistance from one or more trained professionals who advise clients in private meetings or over the phone. Counseling is individually tailored help. Training consists of workshops where groups of prospective home buyers receive general information and, often, motivation from inspirational talks and the encouragement of peers.

Furthermore, counseling is not just credit counseling or budget counseling. It can, and should, involve advice and referrals on family problems, house hunting, home inspections, negotiation of purchase contracts, and the mortgage application process. This can be accomplished by one very skilled counselor, a staff of several specialized counselors, or a mix of staff counseling and referrals to other agencies. The organizations that offer the most client services use referrals frequently but have one counselor who stays with the client throughout the process, almost as a case manager.

In a group training session, a participant may complete the exercise of calculating what mortgage amount is affordable or what the monthly family budget should be. But clearly, these sessions cannot deal with serious impediments to home buying--for example, a recent bankruptcy, serious credit flaws, or a spouse who is a spendthrift or is abusive. In a full-service counseling program, these and many more serious issues will come out and, if possible, will be resolved.

Resolution may take months or years, but may not involve much work from program staff. Several program managers noted that many clients were helped simply by identification of their barriers to homeownership in the first interview. They went away for months, or longer, without ever attending training sessions and came back to the program only when the problem was solved.

Many programs refer clients with serious credit problems to Consumer Credit Counseling, a nationwide organization with local offices in larger cities or regions, or to similar credit counseling agencies. Unlike the programs that are advertised on late-night television, these nonprofit-sponsored programs help repair bad credit the old-fashioned way--by controlling spending and getting rid of debt. The agencies can also be go-betweens with creditors and help negotiate workable repayment schedules for delinquent accounts.

Based on this study, we conclude the following about the best practices for counseling:

Start early: Financial counseling should begin in the intake interview, and that intake should be thorough, screening out clearly unqualified clients, as described in the section on intake and screening.

Limit training to prequalified clients: Only clients with adequate income and employment history, who are close to prequalifying for a bank loan, should be sent on to training.

Discourage house hunting early on: House hunting should be discouraged until late in the training process--probably about two months after the initial intake--because of the realities of scheduling training.

Help with home inspections and purchase contracts: Once house hunting has started, a counselor should be ready to advise on home inspections and negotiation of the purchase contract.

Plan on spending up to 20 hours per client: A thorough counseling process will require about 10 to 20 person-hours of in-house work and a variable amount of credit repair counseling by an outside agency in order to get a client to closing. Clients who do not close on home purchases (often two or three times as many as those who do close) will still require between one and 20 hours of assistance, as they may get discouraged or be disqualified at any point along the way.

Keep services flexible: Clients should not be forced through a cookie cutter counseling track. Needs of clients will be very different, and some will need little help at all.

Screen out unmotivated clients: Clients who do not pay their bills and show no inclination to change those habits should be screened out early. If they somehow hide their problems or squeak through to get a loan, they are almost certain to default.

Assume clients know something about money management: Good clients should be given some credit at the outset for good money management. Many people could not live and raise children on less than $25,000 a year in take-home pay, a figure that is typical in most programs.

Don't smother clients with advice: Clients should not be smothered with advice but given the information, tools, inspiration, and encouragement to achieve goals they have set.

A few programs studied--such as Habitat's in Charlotte, Liberation's in Fort Worth, and Famicos' in Cleveland--stretched farther than others in counseling and training marginal clients. Those groups provide intensive financial counseling and even life skills training--both one-on-one and in group workshops.

Because some or most of their clients cannot obtain a bank loan in the foreseeable future, Liberation and Famicos offer lease-purchase arrangements running from one year to 15 years. Famicos offers some family counseling over the entire 15-year lease period of its typical clients.

These extra measures obviously raise the cost of putting the average client into a home and keeping them there. Not wanting to pay those costs, most programs practice a form of benign neglect, hoping some of these marginal clients will shape up on their own and come back some day.

What is the "right" way depends on the goals of the program. Those wanting to revitalize declining neighborhoods through homeownership programs will inevitably end up providing more counseling, and ideally, purchase and support mechanisms for non-bankable clients. But programs that aim to help the most clients in a city or area will logically focus their scarce resources on the low-income clients who have the best chances of buying a home.

We think the Neighborhood Development Foundation in New Orleans has an exceptionally effective approach to client intake, screening, counseling, and training. As explained in the case study, their approach is to inspire clients to help themselves and offer some tough but supportive guidance. The program saves its hand-holding for clients who are trying to solve problems and getting ready to buy homes. Its simple but effective policies, procedures, and operating systems are described in detail in the case study.

Home Buyer Training

Almost every program we studied requires that clients complete group training workshops. These typically range in length from two to nine hours and comprise one or two separate sessions held during weekday evenings or on Saturdays. Programs involving secondary market loans that are sold to Fannie Mae or Freddie Mac have approved training curricula comprising about seven hours in two or three sessions.

Habitat of Charlotte's training is the most extensive, requiring 25 hours of attendance in 15 separate sessions held once or twice a week. Since the organization relies on volunteers for financial counseling, it integrates individual counseling sessions with set times and places into its training schedule. Otherwise, the logistics of scheduling counseling with many clients and many counselors would become overwhelming. No other organization pre-schedules its financial counseling.

In programs that offer special financial assistance, completion of training is one of the qualifying requirements for grants or low-interest loans. Only DAHP in Dallas allows clients to complete a take-home training manual instead of attending training,

and DAHP wants to upgrade its training and counseling component if it can find the resources.

In most cases, the curricula of home buyer training workshops include the following topics.

Pros and cons of buying a home
Tax consequences of a home purchase
The importance of the home's location
Financial responsibilities of home
  ownership
Formulas for calculating affordable home
  prices from income
Estimating down payment and closing
  costs
Family budgeting
Reading credit reports and clearing up
  credit problems
Looking for homes and working with
  brokers
Prepurchase home inspections by the
  buyers
Professional home inspections
Real estate contracts
The mortgage loan application process
Special financing programs that may be
  available
Dealing with credit denials
Obtaining hazard insurance
Closing costs
Real estate closings and loan closings
Home maintenance
Dealing with financial crises after the
  move-in

Typically, volunteer real estate brokers, loan officers, and others help program staff members teach the courses. Many excellent training manuals are available and include sample forms and documents. Fannie Mae's was widely used as a model by the organizations in this survey, but most organizations customize the sample documents to reflect local markets and business practices.

Typically, before Fannie Mae or other secondary market agencies will buy loans with liberalized underwriting, they must approve the program. This involves a review of the training design, the counseling involved, the form of financial assistance provided (if any), and the legal form of any second mortgage documents used.

A few organizations, such as Habitat of Charlotte and Famicos in Cleveland, integrate stress management, avoiding substance abuse, and other self-improvement topics into their training curricula.

Lack of Training and Counseling on Lead Paint Hazards

In reviewing the training curricula of the various programs, we found little or no mention of lead paint hazards in older homes. When some or all of the home buyers will be considering the purchase of older homes, information on identifying the hazards and abating them should be included. In these markets, it is our recommendation that training sessions include the following:

▸ Information on the health effects of lead exposure.

▸ Advice on the latest regulations concerning disclosure of lead-based paint and lead-based paint hazards during real estate transactions of pre-1978 housing.

▸ Advice on how buyers might identify potential lead hazards.

▸ Information on the dangers of disturbing lead-based paint during renovation (which can actually increase hazards dramatically).

▸ Home buyers who are considering purchasing buildings with rental units need to be aware that their renters must also be informed of the presence of lead-based paint or lead-based paint hazards and given an informational booklet.

Lead poisoning is the number one environmental health hazard for children in the United States. An estimated 1.7 million children (nine percent of children under age six) have elevated blood lead levels. Hispanic and African American children living in low-income, inner-city neighborhoods characterized by older, deteriorating housing are the most at risk. The primary cause of childhood lead poisoning is deteriorating lead-based paint and lead-contaminated dust and soil in older housing.

Even low levels of lead exposure can have very serious health consequences, leading to loss of intelligence, learning disabilities, and behavioral problems such as hyperactivity and aggressive behavior. Because the damage can be irreversible, it is important to correct lead hazards before they create harm.

Counselors should give their clients a copy of the EPA booklet *Protect Your Family From Lead In Your Home*, which explains how to identify lead hazards. They should also discuss lead safety issues when discussing conditions to look for in buying a home. Potential home buyers should be concerned if the home was built before 1950 and particularly if it has deteriorated paint.

If a home was built before 1950, it is likely that it contains lead paint. For houses built after 1950 but before 1978, there is a fair chance that lead-based paint is present. The mere presence of intact lead-based paint does not necessarily present a hazard. If the property was well maintained and managed, lead-based paint poses few health risks. Of more concern is lead-based paint in deteriorated condition, or intact lead-based paint that is disturbed during renovation or repairs.

Buyers who can afford to should consider hiring certified risk assessors. The risk assessor will evaluate the home for lead hazards and draw up a plan for their remediation. The inspection will cost approximately $250 to $300. If this is not possible, and buyers are using a home inspector, the inspector should be asked if he or she has the capability to perform a less thorough check for lead hazards.

If the home buyer has determined that lead-based paint hazards are present, typical treatments should involve at least treating defective surfaces (using lead-safe painting or covering techniques) and cleaning with lead-specific detergent. Homeowners untrained in lead-safe techniques should not undertake these repairs themselves. Hazards could be substantially increased if lead-based paint is disturbed in an unsafe manner.

Local or state funds may be available to pay for lead hazard control, and acquisition/rehabilitation funds may also be available through HUD's FHA 203(k) program.

The National Center for Lead-Safe Housing is developing a training module for inclusion in homeowner counseling programs. For more information, call Heidi Most at 410-992-0712 for further information.

Help with Home Selection

Eight of the 11 programs studied help clients find and finance existing homes, and account for the great majority of home purchases in the study. The big producers-- DAHP in Dallas, CNE in Chattanooga, NDF in New Orleans, and the Housing Trust in Santa Fe--collectively help over 1,000 families a year buy existing homes. Two of the 11 programs studied--in Dallas and New Orleans--rely almost exclusively on existing homes for sale in the open market.

Nine of the programs build new homes or renovate older ones for sale to their clients at below-market prices or with subsidized financing. This development activity accounts for about 250 homes sold in all the programs. Six of those developer organizations also help to finance existing homes in the market.

As a result of this development activity, about one out of five clients in all the programs studied are, in effect, a captive market--attracted to the training, counseling, and financing programs by the chance to get access to decent homes that are priced far below the market. While they are getting a bargain, usually their choices are very limited. When qualified clients come to the top of the list and a house of the right size is available, more often than not, they select that home. The site selection, design, and construction are handled by the nonprofit organization and its professional contractors. Usually, homes are built or renovated only

---

in neighborhoods targeted for revitalization, or in Santa Fe's case, in its new subdivisions.

The Santa Fe Community Housing Trust asks its counseling-training clients to participate in focus groups to help design homes and allows slight customizing of design. Habitat of Charlotte's clients pick the sites for their new homes from a short list of available lots. But most programs build or renovate homes "on spec," meaning no client is identified at the time the property is acquired, built, or repaired. This agency-driven development keeps costs down and speeds up the development process.

With existing homes, the choices are much broader. Only the Fort Worth and Toledo programs restrict purchases to their target areas, which respectively have about 9,000 and 12,000 residents. Six of the organizations let buyers scout the entire city or county for affordable homes--restricted only by what they can afford and the program's maximum purchase prices, if any.

Helping clients select existing homes on the market requires more effort. While the amount of help varied widely among the organizations in this study, the following appeared to be the best practices:

Pre-selection training: Most organizations have as part of the training curriculum some preparation for the home selection process. Workshops cover topics such as location of homes, relative costs of commuting, using real estate brokers, possible problems with lead paint, and how to judge whether homes need major repairs.

Help with home inspections: Most organizations either have inspectors on staff, or help clients hire qualified home inspectors. Some of the programs pay for this service, and others require that buyers pay for some or all of the cost at the loan closing.

Help negotiating home purchases: Several organizations give clients advice on making offers and putting special conditions in offers, such as requiring deficiencies found during the inspection be remedied. NDF in New Orleans encourages clients to make offers on its special form of purchase and sale agreement, which includes some extra buyer protections (and an agreement that the buyer will pay NDF's fee for assistance). While some organizations expressly avoid offering this help, we feel it is advisable when nonprofits have staff with skills to give this advice, particularly in markets where help with negotiations can reduce purchase prices and better ensure that repairs are done.

Factors Affecting Selection of Existing Homes

When programs are designed to help purchase existing homes, several kinds of policies can greatly affect home selection:

▶ Maximum price limits

▶ Formulas for available subsidies

▶ Lead hazard abatement standards

▶ Other housing quality standards

Maximum purchase price policies are primarily used to prevent families from using subsidies to "buy up." In some programs--like the Jackson Metro Housing

Partnership--a strict $45,000 price limit effectively targets home purchases to low-income areas where the City and the Partnership want homeownership to increase. Obviously, maximum price limits relate to market prices of decent homes, what buyers can afford, and production targets. When DAHP in Dallas raised its price and income limits, program output increased greatly.

When HOME funding is used for second mortgage loans, as is common, HUD sets the price limits for each metropolitan area and county. Usually, this limit is higher than most low-income families can afford, so the most effective limits we saw were more conservative ones set by the local programs or their local governments.

Ten of the 11 programs studied offer some form of special financing that usually raises the price a family can afford to pay--from a few thousand dollars up to $20,000 in a few cases. Thus, it is all-important that clients know what they can qualify for when they go house hunting, sign a purchase contract, or apply for a mortgage.

Help with Home Inspections

All of the programs examined that help with purchases of existing homes either require prepurchase inspections or strongly encourage them. A few programs have staff members who inspect houses before purchase, and other programs rely on professional inspectors who work for a set fee.

When the program's home buyers have very low or extremely low incomes, the cost of inspections can become a big issue. Most programs arrange for the cost to be paid out of the loan closing. Some programs pay for inspections if the prospective buyer does not purchase the home. Costs of inspections range from a low of $95 in Santa Fe (where inspectors offer the program a steep discount) to over $300 where thorough lead paint inspections are desired or required.

When HOME or CDBG funds are involved, the homes must meet minimal federal Housing Quality Standards. Most local and state governments that pass through these funds allow the agencies or contract inspectors to inspect and certify compliance, but some require that a City inspector verify their work through a joint or separate inspection. The second alternative is obviously less efficient and tends to slow down the approval of subsidy financing.

We recommend the following as good policies and practices to streamline home inspections, but still ensure that buyers are getting decent homes:

▸ If the nonprofit is performing most prequalifying and lending functions for secondary financing, local government funding agencies should delegate inspections to the nonprofit. This requires the nonprofit to have a reliable system of inspections, and verification that deficiencies are corrected.

▸ Using contract home inspectors is more efficient than having an inspector on staff, unless the organization already has a staff member that is well trained in inspecting existing homes, as is the case in many organizations operating housing rehabilitation programs.

Special Problems with Inspecting for Lead Hazard Abatement

Buyers will want to know whether the home they are considering has lead-based paint or lead-based paint hazards. Under a federal regulation that went into effect in the fall of 1996, a sales contract on a home built before 1978 cannot be finalized until the seller or real estate agent gives the buyer a pamphlet discussing lead hazards in the home and tells the buyer about any lead-based paint or lead-based paint hazards that they are aware of. The sellers must allow a buyer 10 days (or other mutually agreed upon time period) during which time the buyer can hire a certified professional to conduct an inspection or risk assessment of lead paint hazards.

An inspection will tell the buyer what surfaces are coated with lead-based paint. A risk assessment will identify any immediate lead hazards--such as peeling paint and lead-contaminated dust or soil--and what steps are needed to correct them. The inspection or risk assessment should be carried out by a state-certified professional.

At a cost of $250 to $300, full inspections or risk assessments might be too expensive for many first-time buyers. If the buyers are using a home inspector to assess the condition of a home, they might ask if he or she has expertise in lead hazard evaluation. If not, the buyer should contact their local Health Department or call 1-800-FYI-LEAD for information on identifying lead hazards. Generally, one should be very concerned if there is peeling, flaking, or chalking paint inside or outside a home built before 1950.

Home buyers should be aware that attempting to correct lead hazards without the proper training can drastically increase the hazard. But they should also know that a thorough cleaning with a high-phosphate detergent (such as dishwashing detergent) can temporarily reduce lead dust contamination, the most frequent contributor to childhood lead poisoning.

A Primary Goal: Preparing Buyers to Get Financing

The fine points of counseling, training, and help with home selection should not obscure the fact that one of the primary purposes of the programs we studied is to help low-income buyers get home purchase financing. The next chapter explains in detail the kinds of financing products that programs offer directly, or refer clients to. It also addresses best practices in processing special financing, where the steps involved must mesh closely with counseling and training components of the programs.

4. Special Financing: Products and Practices

The special financing products used with low-income home buyers are numerous and complex in nature. Therefore, this chapter covers a number of topics, as follows:

Historical perspectives
Financial barriers for low-income home buyers
Lending risks associated with special loan products
Types of first mortgage products
Secondary markets
Revolving loan funds
Second mortgage products
Loan consortia
Resale restrictions
Lease-purchase arrangements
Processing issues with special financing
Loan collections and delinquencies
Post-purchase counseling

Historical Perspective

Financing of home purchases by low-income families is not a new phenomenon. Over 100 years ago, newly created savings and loans institutions practically created the nation's mass home building industry. The thrifts found that the growing ranks of blue collar workers could buy homes if installment loans were available. The loans were offered, and vast expanses of modest homes were built, sold, and financed in cities such as Philadelphia and Baltimore.

In the Great Depression of the 1930s, a 50 percent foreclosure rate on home loans and the total collapse of the nation's banking industry had a silver lining. Prior to the Depression, home loans were made for only three- to five-year terms but were renewable at the discretion of lenders. In bad times, many loans were made due and payable, with disastrous results for all but wealthy homeowners. With the invention of FHA mortgage insurance and other federal supports, the fixed-rate 30-year mortgage was born, and that problem was solved.

In many housing markets from the 1930s through the 1960s, new homes were relatively inexpensive to build, while interest rates were low by today's standards. As a result, low-income families bought homes in great numbers without any special assistance other than federal mortgage insurance, a program that supported itself on fees paid by borrowers.

From the late 1960s through the 1980s, inflation in housing prices and high interest rates changed everything. Even with FHA insurance, mortgage payments were no longer affordable for many low-income families. Through the Section 235 program, the federal government for a time subsidized interest rates for hundreds of thousands of homes each year, but by the early 1980s, the cost of these subsidies was deemed too high and the program was terminated.

During this same time, many inner-city neighborhoods became impoverished as industry moved elsewhere and jobs were lost. The urban riots of the 1960s--especially those after the assassination of Dr. Martin Luther King--left deep scars. Lenders pulled out of these declining markets and soon were accused of "red-lining" poor and minority areas as unsuitable for making loans.

New Financing Models in the 1980s and 1990s

The 1980s were a time of intense challenges and re-invention. Driven by inflation and Baby Boomer demand for homes, housing costs and interest rates reached 50-year highs. Nonetheless, a few nonprofit housing corporations started homeownership programs targeted to distressed, inner-city neighborhoods. In this book, the following program are examples of those pioneering efforts begun in the mid-1980s or earlier:

Chattanooga Neighborhood Enterprise
Famicos Foundation, Cleveland
Habitat for Humanity, Charlotte
Holy Name Housing Corporation,
   Omaha
NorthRiver Development Corporation,
   Toledo

All of these pioneering programs capitalized on one bright side of neighborhood decline and red-lining--at least the homes and land values were cheap. Liberation Community in Fort Worth and Jackson Metro Housing Partnership started similar neighborhood-targeted programs in the early 1990s.

Also in the 1980s, local and state governments began to significantly increase funding of these neighborhood-based programs through Community Development Block Grants (CDBG) and other HUD

programs passed through non-federal agencies. In Toledo and Omaha, for example, the local governments helped to write down costs of acquiring and renovating homes, either through direct grants or by subsidizing acquisition and infrastructure costs.

More recently, the write-down approach was also applied to infill new construction and tract home development, as illustrated in this book by the Chattanooga, Toledo, Omaha, and Santa Fe examples.

In the 1980s, city governments also began to offer home purchase subsidies in tandem with market rate financing from lenders, typically on a 20-80 ratio of public financing to private financing. As opposed to project write-downs--which go to the projects and reduce home prices--these purchase subsidies were grants or loans made directly to the home purchasers.

Initially, these grants or soft second mortgages, as they came to be called, were attached to certain home developments. But increasingly, they came to be used for purchases of existing homes in the open market. Thus, this new movement began to diverge somewhat from its early focus on neighborhood redevelopment.

Again, HUD funds were used for these tandem subsidies. Nine of the case studies in this book--featuring organizations in Chattanooga, Cleveland, Dallas, Garrett County, Fort Worth, Jackson, Omaha, Santa Fe, and Toledo--show examples of leveraged financing programs, in which second mortgage financing induces other investments. In all cases except Cleveland, first mortgage financing is leveraged. The Famicos lease-purchase program uses CDBG funds to leverage equity investments through syndications using federal Low-Income Housing Tax Credits.

Innovative Financing Sources

Other local programs began to tap innovative sources of low-cost financing, as illustrated by several case studies in this book:

▸ Habitat of Charlotte funds zero percent interest mortgages using charitable grants and loan repayments.

▸ Chattanooga Neighborhood Enterprise has used foundation funds and local government general funds to capitalize its loan pool.

▸ Liberation Community also used foundation grants to capitalize a revolving fund for first mortgages made at market rates, so the loans can be sold and the funds recycled.

▸ The Santa Fe Community Housing Trust uses cash contributions from high-end home developers to fund second mortgage loans that are due only when homes are resold.

▸ The City of Toledo earmarked repayments of an Urban Development Action Grant (UDAG) to capitalize NorthRiver Development Corporation's revolving loan fund, which is used for second mortgage financing.

Heightened Lender Involvement in the 1990s

During the 1970s and 1980s, active participation of lenders was the exception rather than the rule. The Community Reinvestment Act of 1977 placed only slight pressure on lenders. And by the end of the 1980s, the industry as a whole began to suffer. Housing inflation began to reverse itself, and in many markets foreclosures began to mount as homes were suddenly worth less than their first mortgage balances. Banks and thrift institutions went under, taxpayers bailed them out, and the stronger institutions began buying the smaller and weaker ones.

In the 1990s wave of bank consolidations, still occurring at this writing, CRA began to have real effects. Mergers could be held up and challenged by low-income advocacy organizations if the banks had weak ratings for their community reinvestment activities. Expanding banks began to offer aggressive new products for low-income home buyers. Down payment requirements were reduced, fees were sometimes waived, and underwriting standards such as debt-to-income ratios were liberalized.

Federal laws were also passed that encouraged more affordable housing lending by Fannie Mae and Freddie Mac--the two organizations that control most of the secondary market that purchases home mortgage loans. Both were government agencies, but were spun off as privately owned corporations. The federal government now sets targets for the percentage of both organizations' lending that benefits individual low-income families and areas with concentrations of low-income or minority populations. As a result, Fannie

Mae and Freddie Mac began to buy more loans from this segment of the market.

There are other reasons for the surge of interest in low-income home buyers. Until a few years ago, lenders and home builders expected home purchases to stagnate as the Baby Boom became the Baby Bust. But recent national studies have shown that home purchases by immigrants, minorities, and low-income people have created a new growth trend in this segment of the market. Many lenders are finding the business profitable. In the hyper-competitive lending industry, lenders that succeed with these market segments gain a competitive advantage.

Thus, as a result of federal regulations and market trends, national and regional banks and thrift institutions now actively promote their new community lending products through such marketing tools as special advertising and home fairs directed at the low end of the market. And while lenders are eager to work with local government- and nonprofit-sponsored programs, most of this business is coming to them directly. It is important to recognize that the industry makes hundreds of thousands of loans a year directly to low-income buyers--many times the number of loans made in conjunction with nonprofit groups and government agencies.

Financial Barriers for Low-Income Home Buyers

In the affordable housing industry, these are considered the major barriers for low-income families trying to obtain home purchase financing:

Lack of cash for funding the minimum down payments, closing costs, and minimum cash reserves required by lenders after purchase. Conventional loan-to-value ratios, limiting loans to 80 percent of appraised value, can also add to cash requirements.

Poor credit standing, due to poor credit, lack of a credit record, or a spotty employment record.

Underwriting ratios, which limit the amount that can be borrowed--both housing payment to income ratios (28 percent is conventional) and total installment debt to income (36 percent is conventional).

Unaffordably high monthly payments, which, ironically, can be a consequence of liberalized underwriting ratios. In other words, some families may not be able to afford 33 percent of income for housing payments.

How the Barriers are Overcome

Not surprisingly, each program studied addresses most, if not all of these barriers, in the following ways:

Reducing down payment requirements to five percent, or even three percent-- generally either through use of private mortgage insurance (PMI) or a second mortgage loan from a third party amounting to 15 percent to 20 percent of the amount financed. One program we studied requires no money down and finances all closing costs. Most require only three to five percent down payments and finance some or most of the closing costs.

Waiving cash reserve requirements. Generally lenders want to see that buyers have enough cash to cover closing costs and still have enough money in the bank to pay two monthly payments. We were not able to get good data on waivers of this requirement, but anecdotal evidence points to some waivers.

Waiving some loan-related fees by lenders or other parties to the sales transactions such as title companies or attorneys.

Improving borrower credit standing of program participants--usually through changes in spending habits encouraged by training and counseling.

Relaxing of credit and employment standards by first mortgage lenders.

Increasing underwriting ratios--most often from 28/36 to 33/38. The wisdom of this is not supported unanimously. In the study, most programs went as high as 33/38, but some preferred to use secondary financing to reduce the ratios closer to 28/36.

Increasing loan-to-value ratios used by first mortgage lenders--to as high as 95 or 97 percent--usually offset by the use of PMI.

Low-cost or no-cost financing--by offering a low-interest first or second mortgage loan or deferring all repayments until resale of the property. As described above, and below in more detail, this secondary financing can solve a number of problems.

Are Lending Risks Increased?

Liberalizing standards for financing helps families get home purchase loans, but it also increases risks of default.

A study by Mortgage Guarantee Insurance Corporation (MGIC) of loans it insured in the 1980s revealed that liberalized underwriting can increase the risks of default nearly seven-fold versus 90 percent loans made with normal underwriting ratios to clients with good credit. Absolute default rates were not given, but we estimate that the benchmark rate for "good" loans was about 1.5 percent then, so that the default rate on non-standard loans was about 10 percent.

We did not find those high levels of defaults in the programs we studied, as described earlier. Default rates ranged from slightly less than one percent to three percent in most programs.

MGIC did another study of loans insured in 1992 and 1993. This time, "clean" 95 percent loan-to-value loans were compared with others. These were the findings:

▸ Reduction of the down payment to three percent increased delinquencies 30 percent.

▸ Allowing cash reserves of less than two months increased late payments by 20 percent.

▸ Using housing payment-to-income and installment debt-to-income ratios of over 33/38 increased the delinquency rate by 20 percent.

▸ Two or more adverse credit items increased the rate by 20 percent, and no credit history increased it by a startling 70 percent.

The risks were looked at in isolation. In other words, no borrower had more than one risk factor. When they are layered together, the layered risk is unfortunately greater than the sum of its parts--as the earlier studied indicated.

In the industry, there is an assumption that training and counseling helps greatly in mitigating these risks, although, to our knowledge, no recent in-depth study has clearly proved this. Our data on delinquency and default rates give some support to the claim, but were self-reported and not compared to similar loans in the same markets where the borrowers received no training or counseling.

In a recent study by Freddie Mac, credit scores below 610 predicted a foreclosure rate of about eight percent [our estimate; they gave "relative rates"]--pointing to the overwhelming importance of having reasonably good credit. As described earlier, mortgage scoring promoted by both Freddie Mac and PMI Mortgage, combines credit data with other layered risk factors.

Since mortgage scoring appears to be a reliable predictor of loan delinquencies, we recommend that home purchase assistance programs experiment with using this tool in prequalifying and financial counseling. A high score can indicate that a prospective home buyer needs more credit counseling, or a second mortgage loan to make the monthly payments more affordable.

Like MGIC, Freddie Mac also found that foreclosure rates were barely increased by using higher underwriting ratios. But both MGIC's 1980 study and Freddie Mac's more recent study found that reducing down payments below 10 percent raised risks of default about two to two-and-one-half times.

Types of First Mortgage Products

Among the case studies, four types of first mortgage financing were found:

Portfolio: Loans made and held in portfolio by conventional lenders.

Tax-exempt: Loans originated under tax-exempt financing programs.

Secondary market: Loans made by conventional lenders and sold on the secondary markets.

Revolving loan fund: Loans made from a nonprofit organization's revolving loan fund. The loans are sometimes sold to secondary market institutions.

Each of these loan types has special characteristics that are explained in the following sections.

Portfolio Loans

Some portfolio loan products offer great advantages to home buyers and their nonprofit sponsors. Aggressive lenders can use these products to:

▶ Offer below-market rates.

▶ Waive some loan-related fees.

▶ Reduce down payment requirements.

▸ Liberalize underwriting criteria.

▸ Waive the normal requirements for mortgage insurance on low-down-payment, high-ratio loans.

In a majority of the cases studied, at least one lender offered most of these favorable terms. However, such generous terms were certainly not available everywhere and often were offered only temporarily. Policies such as these--particularly the discounting of rates--are likely to result in loans that are less profitable than the typical home loan.

Some lenders offered portfolio loans with liberalized underwriting, but required mortgage insurance--practices that have become common in the industry quite apart from community reinvestment programs. The Mortgage Guaranty Insurance Corporation (MGIC), a major provider of private mortgage insurance, reports that about half its business today is with loans amounting to over 90 percent of appraised value. That figure is up from 20 percent only five years ago.

A few portfolio lenders charged rates above the market, presumably reflecting the view that the loans carried higher risks.

Among the case studies, the most outstanding example of portfolio lending was the Jackson Metro Housing Partnership. The four largest banks in Mississippi helped to form the organization and fund some of its operating expenses. Nearly every client of the Partnership gets a loan from one of the lenders at a rate approximately one percentage point below market. Origination fees are capped at $500. All of the loans are currently held in portfolio, and none of the lenders intends to sell its loans in the near future.

When interest rate discounts are offered, or underwriting is liberalized without requiring mortgage insurance, loans generally cannot be sold right away to mainstream secondary market institutions such as Fannie Mae. The loans simply do not meet the underwriting standards of the secondary market. In these cases, many local lenders "season" the loans for a year or so and sell them when a timely payment record has been established. Others keep the loans in their own portfolios.

Tax-Exempt Financing

Throughout the U.S., local and state mortgage finance authorities issue tax-exempt mortgage revenue bonds that are used to finance home purchases by buyers with incomes as high as 115 percent of area median incomes. This mechanism results in mortgage interest rates that are up to a percentage point below market rates. Five percent down payments are a common feature of these programs.

Local lenders originate these loans with their own funds and then sell the loans to a mortgage finance authority that has agreed in advance to buy them. Lenders make a modest profit on the origination fees.

Among the programs surveyed, Chattanooga Neighborhood Enterprise (CNE) and the Santa Fe Community Housing Trust are intimately involved with tax-exempt financing. CNE is one of the few nonprofit originators of tax-exempt mortgages in the U.S., standing in the place of banks that typically originate the loans and selling them to the Tennessee Housing Development Authority. These low-rate loans accounted for about 70 of CNE's 281 loans last year.

Probably as a one-time event, the Community Housing Trust is the administrator of a special mortgage revenue bond issue of the City of Santa Fe. In this role, the Housing Trust coordinates the work of originating lenders, the bond underwriter, and the loan servicing agency. This occurred only because the executive director of the Housing Trust had experience in this field--but the happy coincidence enabled the City to raise low-cost mortgage financing for several key development projects, including one of the Housing Trust's. Ordinarily, the City does not issue mortgage revenue bonds, and local citizens must compete in a statewide market for these limited funds.

Along with those two programs, the New Orleans Neighborhood Development Foundation relies, in part, on tax-exempt financing for its clients. In this case, the City has a housing finance authority that repeatedly issues mortgage revenue bonds and creates a steady supply of below-market rate financing.

Many of the other programs studied do not use tax-exempt financing at all, while a few others use it with a small fraction of their clients. In the few cases where information was available about tax-exempt financing, there appeared to be two reasons for not using this seemingly ideal product more universally:

▶ Competition for these funds is stiff, and at times tax-exempt financing is simply not available because the federal government allocates only a limited amount of bonding authority to each state. Also, in each housing market, moderate-income home buyers (with incomes up to 115 percent of median income) compete with low-income buyers for these funds.

▶ In several instances, the underwriting for these loans was considered more conservative than for some other types of loans--driving borrowers with marginal credit or employment problems to other products with more liberal underwriting but higher interest rates.

It should be noted that each of these problems could, in theory, be addressed by the relevant mortgage finance agencies. In future bond issues, they could set aside portions of their allocations targeted to low-income borrowers--or low-income areas--or increase set-asides if they are already used. Also, underwriting could be liberalized for a small class of borrowers, if the risks could be spread over a large pool. Creative bond underwriters are willing to structure bond issues in this manner, if they are directed to do so by the bond issuer. But if this creativity is carried too far, it can hurt the bond rating and raise interest rates for the entire bond issue.

Secondary Market Loans

The case studies did not give a clear picture of how many loans are being sold to secondary markets. The nonprofits work with as many as 15 local lenders, some of which may offer multiple products. The nonprofits (our source of information) are not always aware of which loans are being kept in portfolio and which ones are being sold. Nor do they always know where the loans are being sold.

Several of the organizations noted that loans are being purchased by Fannie Mae. In the Dallas program, Fannie Mae is formally involved and buys over half of the loans. In Santa Fe, Fannie Mae buys about one-third of the loans. In the Fort Worth program, local lenders buy seasoned loans that were funded by Liberation Community's revolving loan fund. Then, they sell the loans to Fannie Mae.

There are other avenues to secondary markets. Some of the larger banks bundle their own loans together to back the issue of mortgage-backed securities. Sold in the general financial markets, these securities raise money for making new loans.

Without the availability of secondary market loans, some of the programs in this case study--particularly those in Dallas, Santa Fe, and Chattanooga that involve higher volumes of loans--would be seriously hampered in getting first mortgage financing for their clients.

Revolving Loan Funds

As already mentioned, several of the organizations studied operate revolving loan funds that are used to make either first or second mortgage loans, or both. These funds serve four purposes:

▶ Originating first mortgage loans that are immediately sold to secondary market institutions. Put another way, the nonprofit organization takes on a fairly conventional lending role.

▶ Making high-risk first mortgage loans to clients that are not bankable but considered acceptable risks by the nonprofit sponsor.

▶ Recycling repayments of second mortgage loans that were originally made with CDBG funds, HOME funds, or local funds. These revolving loan funds continue to leverage first mortgage loans from conventional lenders.

▶ In the case of Habitat for Humanity affiliates, making home purchase loans at zero percent interest. Not charging interest is one of Habitat's operating principles, so an internal revolving loan fund becomes a necessity.

In the 1980s, many nonprofit organizations used Community Development Block Grants from their local governments to fund second mortgage programs. Where these loans were not forgiven over time (as some were), repayments must be returned to revolving loan funds used for the same general purposes. These revolving loan funds provide a steady stream of funding for several of the programs studied.

However, in the 1990s, many local governments began to use HOME funds rather than CDBG for funding second mortgages. Ironically, in these times of scarce public funding, HOME funds are recycled less than CDBG funds. HUD regulations on this subject are somewhat murky, but many HOME-funded jurisdictions have ruled that repayments of HOME-funded loans must be returned to a trust fund of the original grantees. Because of this interpretation (and also in a spirit of generosity towards home buyers), some

HUD offices and local jurisdictions have advised nonprofits to forgive HOME-funded loans over periods of five to 15 years.

Among the groups studied, Chattanooga Neighborhood Enterprise (CNE) has by far the largest revolving loan fund. It funded nearly $6 million in first and second mortgage loans in fiscal year 1996. Most of that volume results from origination and immediate sale of loans to Tennessee's mortgage finance agency and secondary market institutions. This approach apparently arose from the unusual dearth of first mortgage lenders interested in lending on inner-city residential properties.

As an affiliate of the Neighborhood Reinvestment Corporation, CNE is able to sell loans to Neighborhood Housing Services of America, which (due to some grant funding) is able to buy loans originated at below-market rates. CNE also gets about $1 million a year in new CDBG funds and city general funds to continually add new capital to a revolving loan fund for second mortgage loans. Repayments of prior loans are also recycled through the fund.

Habitat for Humanity of Charlotte also has a large revolving loan fund. In 1996, it will fund about $1.5 million in first mortgage loans, which are repaid with no interest charge. About 25 percent of the loans are funded with repayments of prior loans. The remainder comes from charitable sources.

The revolving loan fund of NorthRiver Development Corporation in Toledo finances over $85,000 a year in second mortgage loans. About 60 percent are funded with repayments of prior loans, and 40 percent are funded from assigned repayments of a City loan made with UDAG funds in the early 1980s.

Liberation Community capitalized a revolving loan fund with a $100,000 foundation grant and uses it to finance home purchases for buyers who cannot meet conventional lenders' standards. While the fund has much higher than normal delinquency and default rates, it does allow Liberation to finance clients with very low incomes. Loans with good repayment track records are sold to local lenders, a technique that has multiplied the original capital fourfold.

Jackson Metro Housing Partnership operates a revolving loan fund used to make second mortgage loans. Last year, $232,000 in funding came from the HOME program, and $62,000 was generated in loan repayments.

The Famicos Foundation, in effect, operates a revolving loan fund, but not by that name. It uses its own surplus cash to finance home purchases by non bankable, very low-income clients. Loan repayments become part of the organization's cash reserves and are used to make new loans.

The Santa Fe Community Housing Trust and Dallas Affordable Housing Partnership also use revolving loan funds to fund deferred payment second mortgage loans that are due only upon resale of the homes that were financed. The Santa Fe organization, only four years old, has seen little repayment of its loans, which were originated with HOME funds, foundation grants, and capital from City and County housing trust funds. Likewise, the Dallas program has seen few repayments, since the bulk of its loans were made in recent years. But repayments will become an important source of funds in the future, since the typical home in the United States is sold every seven years.

Because of these eccentricities and the apparent success of RLFs in serving very low-income, non bankable borrowers, the mechanism deserves more careful evaluation by HUD and policymakers.

Second Mortgage Products and Other Tandem Subsidies

Among the case studies, three types of subsidy financing are used in tandem with first mortgage financing:

▶ Loans or grants for down payments and closing costs.

▶ Deferred payment second mortgage loans.

▶ Amortizing, low-interest second mortgage loans.

These financing mechanisms are explained in the next three sections.

Grants for Down Payments and Closing Costs

"Down payment and closing cost assistance" is a term used to describe a relatively small amount of soft funding for home purchases--in the range of $1,000 to $5,000.

The concept and terminology are confusing, since this funding is often accomplished through a deferred payment second mortgage, even though the assistance is typically called a grant. In most cases, these are loans made with a promissory note and often a lien on the property. Typically,

the indebtedness is forgiven over five years.

This mechanism first came into wide use during the 1980s, when HUD ruled that Community Development Block Grant (CDBG) funds could be used for this purpose. CDBG has explicit rules for this-- for example, no more than half of the down payment and closing costs can be funded. If the agency calls the CDBG assistance a "second mortgage loan," however, those limits do not apply.

Starting in 1990, the Federal Home Loan Bank (FHLB) system began funding down payment and closing cost assistance programs sponsored by nonprofits under the Affordable Housing Program. As with the CDBG-funded products, the amount of FHLB funding per client is relatively small and the assistance is given as grants or forgivable loans. At least up to this writing, FHLB did not want to monitor repayments, although this policy was being re-evaluated in 1996.

As a stand-alone subsidy, this mechanism appeared to be effective in lower-cost cities such as New Orleans, where larger second mortgage subsidies are not so widely available.

But in the programs we evaluated that provided more substantial second mortgage financing, down payment and closing cost assistance was often piggybacked as an extra subsidy. The use of this mechanism in combination with other subsidy financing appears effective, but begs the question of why the two forms of subsidies cannot be combined into one financial instrument. This would require cooperation among funding agencies and amendments to regulations, but it would make processing more efficient and perhaps reduce the number of families that are over-subsidized.

Deferred Payment Second Mortgage Loans

With several of the programs studied, a central feature is a deferred payment second mortgage loan amounting to 15 or 20 percent of the purchase price of a home. This mechanism erases a number of barriers to purchase, as follows:

Making up for lack of cash: Lenders have come to accept these loans as, in effect, part of the buyers' down payments. As a result, buyers need only provide as little as one percent of the purchase price as a down payment, and some portion of the closing costs.

Satisfying loan-to-value ratios: Providing 15 or 20 percent of the purchase price of the home adds to the security of the first mortgage loans. Lenders are more likely to get all their funds back in the event of a foreclosure. Thus, these second mortgage loans have encouraged lenders to participate in markets where loan security is more doubtful.

Reducing the need for mortgage insurance: If the second mortgage is large enough, mortgage insurance is either provided at a reduced cost or not needed. This saves buyers $30 to $60 a month.

Reducing monthly carrying costs and meeting underwriting ratios: All of the benefits just described can be accomplished with an amortizing second mortgage. The only unique benefit of a deferred payment loan is that is requires no monthly payment, and thus can help qualify home buyers who otherwise could not afford the monthly payments. In many cases, this type of loan helps clients stay under the maximum percentages of income that lenders allow for housing payments and installment debt.

As with down payment and closing cost assistance, there is some confusion in the industry about whether these loans should be repaid. As previously described, some HOME grantees and HUD offices encourage forgiveness of these debts. For example, among the case studies, the City of Dallas may make all future HOME-funded loans forgivable.

On the other hand, the Santa Fe Community Housing Trust has made over $1 million in HOME-funded second mortgage loans that must be repaid when the homes are resold. This is seen as a way to help the program become more self-sustaining and reduce the need for continual public subsidies.

At any rate, four of the local programs studied find these soft second mortgages essential: the Santa Fe Community Housing Trust, the Dallas Affordable Housing Partnership, Holy Name Affordable Housing in Omaha, and Liberation Community in Fort Worth. It is also used by NorthRiver Development Corporation in Toledo in conjunction with new homes, which otherwise would be priced out of the reach of low-income buyers.

In every case but Omaha, the loans are made directly by the nonprofit. In Omaha, the nonprofit organization prequalifies clients for a loan made by the City of Omaha. In every case, HOME is the predominant or exclusive source of funding.

Amortizing Second Mortgage Loans

Where market prices of homes are lower, amortizing second mortgage loans made from revolving loan funds seem to be highly effective and efficient in enabling low-income families to get first mortgage financing and buy homes. In comparison with deferred payment loans, amortizing loans have the benefit of recycling program dollars more quickly and reducing the need for continual infusions of grant money to nonprofit-sponsored programs. However, they do not substantially reduce the amount of the monthly housing payment, and thus are less effective (or ineffective) with some borrowers, particularly in high-cost markets.

Following are brief descriptions of the amortizing loan programs identified in this study:

Chattanooga Neighborhood Enterprise: CNE makes about 300 second mortgage loans a year. Very low-income families can borrow up to $7,500 for down payment and closing costs and repay the loan over 20 years at two percent interest. Low-income buyers can borrow up to $5,000, which is repaid over 10 years at four percent interest. Borrowers with incomes between 80 and 115 percent of median can get a $2,500 loan at six percent interest, repayable in five years. Average home prices are about $45,000.

Jackson Metro Housing Partnership: This organization makes second mortgage loans for 20 percent of purchase costs. The loans are repayable at two percent interest over 25 years. The average price of a home is about $40,000.

NorthRiver Development Corporation: The corporation provides a second mortgage loan for 25 percent of the purchase costs of homes, at rates of 3.9 to six percent, repayable over 30 years. Average prices of existing homes are about $25,000, while new homes sell for $35,000 to $53,000 (after write downs paid for by City grants).

Liberation Community: Using the revolving loan fund that was previously described, Liberation occasionally makes second mortgage loans for up to 40 percent of the purchase price of homes. The loans are made at market rates and are repayable over terms tailored to be affordable to each client. At this writing, the organization also receives about $150,000 in HOME funding from the City of Fort Worth, which is used for forgivable, deferred payment second mortgages. Liberation would like to convert that program to amortizing repayable loans in order to stretch scarce resources farther.

Use of Loan Consortia

Among the case studies, the use of loan consortia was identified in Dallas, Omaha, and Jackson. As mentioned, the **Jackson Metro Housing Partnership** consortium offers exceptional interest rates for its portfolio loans, about one percentage point below market. Members simply take turns funding home purchase loans with mutually agreed-upon terms and underwriting guidelines. The nonprofit partnership organization prequalifies, trains, and counsels buyers.

Omaha 100 is a consortium of 11 lenders in that city that counsels, trains, and finances low-income buyers. Omaha 100 works with local nonprofit housing developers, such as Holy Name Affordable Housing, which is the subject of one of the case studies. Itself an incorporated nonprofit, Omaha 100 originates some of the first mortgage loans and then sells participations to the member-lenders on its board of directors. In other cases, it simply refers clients to member-lenders. The consortia has received some grants that are used to provide modest down payment and closing cost assistance.

Dallas Affordable Housing Partnership (DAHP) started off in 1990 using a model similar to Omaha 100. It originated first mortgage loans and then sold them on a "round robin" basis to the original nine member-lenders. Unlike the Omaha program, DAHP also provides a deferred payment second mortgage loan amounting to 20 percent of the purchase price of homes. DAHP was separately incorporated as a nonprofit but is administered by staff of The Enterprise Foundation.

After DAHP's startup period, the program's managers and the member-lenders on its board determined that it would be more efficient to refer clients to member banks, which would market their individual loan products, prequalify clients, originate loans, and even do most of the paperwork for the second mortgage. Because of this decentralized approach, the program does not require uniformity of mortgage terms or underwriting criteria. Most of the lenders offer the going market rates with liberalized underwriting criteria.

Resale Restrictions and Long-Term Affordability Controls

In the programs examined, several mechanisms are used to assure that homes renovated, built, or financed by the nonprofits remain affordable over time. Primarily, these were associated with HOME funding, and consisted of requirements attached to second mortgage financing that homes be resold to low-income families during defined periods of time, no longer than 15 years.

Only one of the programs studied--**the Santa Fe Community Housing Trust**--placed stronger emphasis on long-term affordability controls. It is no coincidence that Santa Fe was the highest-cost market represented in the study, where both citizens and policy makers are greatly concerned about housing price increases over time.

In Santa Fe, wealthy retirees and owners of vacation homes have pushed up housing prices so much that low-income residents--many of them Hispanic families with roots going back eight or more generations--have been displaced from the city. Thus, keeping housing prices affordable over the long-term is a high-priority goal for the Community Housing Trust, the city, and other nonprofit housing providers.

In all the other case studies, long-term affordability was not even mentioned as an issue. Where HOME funds are used to finance second mortgages, that program's guidelines are followed. HOME-assisted buyers agree to restrict the resale of their homes to low-income buyers for between five and 15 years, depending on the amount of HOME funding involved. If the loan is paid off, the obligation goes away. In many cases, a certain amount of the loan is forgiven each year, so that the obligation is gradually canceled out during the time that resales are restricted (either five, 10, or 15 years).

In contrast, The Community Housing Trust takes a more aggressive, two-pronged approach with its deferred payment second mortgage and other project subsidies:

Recapture of the second mortgage: In more modest neighborhoods with less potential for appreciation, where subsidies are less than about 20 percent of the purchase price of homes, the Community Housing Trust simply requires that the principal amount of the second mortgage be repaid in full upon resale, with no interest charged. The program wants to recycle all these funds, and feels that forgiving the loans would allow buyers to reap unearned profits. Buyers still can benefit from every penny of appreciation on the homes.

A land trust and other shared appreciation mechanisms: In two situations, the Community Housing Trust exerts stronger controls over long-term affordability: 1) where deep subsidies are used to help very low-income home buyers; and 2) where homes are located in rapidly appreciating neighborhoods. In any of these instances, the organization uses a land lease, loan agreements, and/or a restrictive land use agreement to recover the original subsidy and, in some cases, also share in the home's appreciation. Even so, buyers earn appreciation pro rata with the amount of non-subsidized financing used to purchase the home and the value of their own sweat equity work and later improvements, if any.

Recommendations on Resale Restrictions

Looking at the eleven examples, we conclude the following:

▶ In markets without rapid home price appreciation--such as many inner-city markets and the rural county we looked at--minimal controls are needed. Requiring repayment of some or all of the subsidy at the time of resale is sufficient to avoid subsidized buyers reaping windfall profits through a quick resale.

▶ In markets that are flat or have less appreciation, forgiving some or all of the soft debt over time makes sense. Otherwise, families may not be able to build equity in their homes. This is particularly true where the amount of conventional and subsidy financing exceeds the appraised values of the homes at the time of the first sale--a necessity in many areas that have low property values, but where new construction or major rehabilitation of homes is needed to revitalize the neighborhoods.

▶ In appreciating markets such as Santa Fe, strong resale restrictions, repayments of subsidies, and even shared appreciation arrangements are called for. But as in Santa Fe, this should be done judiciously to ensure that buyers receive a fair proportion of any resale profits.

Lease-Purchase Arrangements

In four of the programs we studied, homes were leased with an option to buy. This approach is chosen when an organization wants to develop and sell homes, but clients are perceived as unbankable. In essence, the nonprofit gets the financing and uses rents to pay operating costs and debt service. Homes are leased until the clients become ready to get their own financing and assume the full responsibilities of homeownership.

These arrangements require a major commitment on the part of the sponsoring organization. In addition to being a housing developer, they are now landlords. It is a different business, requiring additional operating systems and staff skills to maintain properties over time and collect rent. New accounting systems and information management systems must be developed. The program must also provide financial counseling and home buyer training to clients.

The four examples suggest where lease-purchase arrangements can work, and where they may not be so effective.

Garrett County Community Action Committee (CAC) built five homes and leased them to five very low-income families in a self-sufficiency program. CAC staff reported that they probably will not continue the program. Our analysis is that the scale of their program was too small to be efficiently managed, and their new home purchase financing products combined with training and counseling can help very low-income families buy homes outright.

Jackson Metro Housing Partnership and **Liberation Community** successfully use ad hoc lease-purchase arrangements. Both are involved in revitalizing inner-city neighborhoods, and in that process end up acquiring large numbers of low-valued existing homes.

The Jackson Partnership finds it difficult to market these homes to home buyers, since revitalization of the neighborhoods is just beginning and the neighborhood are still perceived as less desirable. The Partnership owns and operates several dozen other rental units, so by leasing homes with a purchase option, it is not adding a new line of business. Thus, the organization decided to rent some of the homes to very low-income buyers who are happy to get a decent home, want to live in the neighborhood, and who stand a good chance of qualifying for conventional financing within a year or so.

Liberation Community in Fort Worth owns and operates only a handful of rental units, but finds the management tasks easy. It acquires and renovates about 30 homes a year, so it is relatively easy to rehabilitate and maintain the homes. It has its own first mortgage loan program, so that it already collects monthly payments from 30 to 40 families. And it is willing and able financially to take higher than normal risks with families that have very low incomes and other problems--accepting that some evictions and loan defaults will occur. As a result, it is not difficult for the organization to rent a few homes, some with lease-purchase arrangements, and others as conventional rentals.

In both the Jackson and Fort Worth examples, the primary motivation was the desire to provide housing right away to needy families that could not get bank financing.

Famicos and the **Cleveland Housing Network** (CHN), and other CHN affiliates, operate what are probably the largest and most successful lease-purchase programs in the country--collectively taking in over 300 new families a year. Many who examine the program for the first time are surprised to learn that most residents will not take title to the homes for at least 15 years. This, in the view of some outsiders, is an unnecessarily long period that probably reduces the residents' feeling of ownership.

Yet, a close examination of the program reveals that it works, in effect, more like a land installment contract than a lease-purchase program. CHN can get very favorable financing--grants of about $15,000 per home from CDBG funds, combined with the proceeds of tax credit syndications and a few other grant sources. Famicos, which originated the program, finances some of the homes itself but most of them through CHN. If CHN owns the homes, Famicos is paid fees to acquire, renovate, and manage the homes. Because of its skills and economies of scale, Famicos can buy and repair homes at very low costs.

Buyers could not find such low-cost financing or decent homes at such a low price. They lease the homes, and a portion of their rent payments amortizes the CDBG grant. The syndication proceeds do not have to be paid back. And title can be transferred when the limited partnership is dissolved, in about 15 years.

Processing Special Financing

Regardless of whether the assistance is a grant or loan, large or small, federally funded or not, directly providing special financing creates a number of challenges for program design and management.

The primary problem is that any secondary financing can slow down the home purchase process and create uncertainties. If these issues are not managed properly, they can frustrate real estate brokers, lenders, and prospective buyers. In the worst case, the program will be branded as bumbling and bureaucratic (whether this is fair or not), and have great difficulty in raising grants to cover operations.

So, most often, two underwriters have to look at the whole package to determine if the buyer qualifies for their part of the funding. In eight of the 11 programs, both the nonprofit agency and a private lender underwrite the buyers for financing. In these cases, the purchase is contingent upon primary and secondary financing coming through in the right amounts, at the right time, and at the right rates.

In several cases, a third underwriter comes into play--the local government providing the subsidy funds. The role of the government agency differs. It can be limited to property inspections, certifying incomes, or reviewing the entire package. Whatever the role, a third party complicates the process. A look at the Toledo case study illustrates this problem.

Even if there are only two organizations involved with underwriting, there is duplication. Typically, two credit reports are reviewed, two verifications of income are sent out, and there are two verifications of deposits.

Two credit reports can make sense if the nonprofit is reviewing a $15 on-line report at an early stage to help with prequalifying. Later, the bank will probably ask for a full credit report costing $40 to $60. Duplicate verifications make little sense if a lender and the nonprofit can work out a cooperative system of verifications, as with DAHP in Dallas. Other problems with dual underwriting have been raised elsewhere in this book.

A full discussion of streamlining loan processing is beyond the scope of this study, but here are some general recommendations:

- Government agencies should delegate underwriting and inspections to capable nonprofit partners wherever possible.

- Nonprofits should set up operating systems to assure that the incomes of buyers subsidized with federal funds are properly certified and the homes meet HQS standards.

- Nonprofits should have counselors and loan officers who understand underwriting, unless (as in Dallas) they totally delegate all underwriting to the conventional lender.

- If nonprofits are too small in scale or too inexperienced to meet these requirements, they should either delegate underwriting to lenders, think bigger, or not get into the business.

Subsidy Financing and Home Selection Problems

Sometimes, calculating the amount of subsidy can be a source of great friction between the nonprofit, a first mortgage lender, a real estate broker, and the client. A family's income can go up or down, changing what that family can qualify for. Sometimes, the program processes the financial assistance only after a first mortgage loan has been conditionally approved. Sometimes, the nonprofit group and the government agency that gave or allocated the subsidy must both underwrite the subsidy. And even worse, subsidy funds can run out by the time a qualified client finds a good home.

Probably no other part of the purchase assistance process creates more grief with brokers and lenders and necessitates more time spent on crisis management. This is an area where some programs have great opportunities for streamlining. To do so, we recommend the following:

- Funding agencies should give nonprofits firm forward commitments of subsidies.

- Programs should have clear funding formulas and caveats about how the funding level can change if income changes (with most federal and charitable sources of funds, this is an unchangeable reality).

- Programs should provide firm forward commitments to qualified clients, whenever possible.

- Programs should provide flexibility for clients who do not need a lot of training or counseling, or could get most of the benefits of training after purchase (e.g., a client with savings and excellent credit).

Loan Collections and Delinquencies

In six of the 11 programs studied, the program sponsors make significant numbers of first or second mortgage loans for which monthly payments are required. Three other programs (in Dallas, Santa Fe, and Garrett County) make soft second mortgages that are collected only on resale, or are forgiven over time. One program (in New Orleans) makes no loans and refers clients to conventional mortgage lenders. And one (in

Cleveland) does a little seller financing, but assists most of its clients in a lease-purchase program.

Thus, just over half of the organizations are involved in loan collections. But whether they make loans or not, all of the programs are concerned about timely repayments to lenders they work with. Most of the programs offer some level of post-purchase counseling when clients cannot make their payments.

The primary concern in this area is delinquency and default rates. The following chart compares national delinquency and default rates with mid-1996 statistics for the six programs with substantial loan collections. (Omaha 100 is the lender for Holy Name Affordable Housing, but the figures are for its entire citywide loan portfolio.)

The national figures were compiled by the Mortgage Bankers Association's National Delinquency Survey for the third quarter of 1995. The low-down-payment FHA loans are more comparable to loans in the programs we studied.

	Delinquency Rate	Default Rate
National:		
All US mortgage loans	4.25%	1%
All FHA loans	7%	1.5%
Case studies:		
CNE--Chattanooga	1.1%	<1%
Habitat--Charlotte	no data	1.6%
Liberation--Fort Worth	30%	6%
Jackson Metro	4-6%	0%
Omaha 100	15%	2%
North River--Toledo	10%	3%

Except for the low rates of the Chattanooga and Jackson programs, the number of problem loans raises some concerns. But the programs are very different in nature, and some intentionally take high risks.

Liberation Community has the highest rate of problem loans, but there are some mitigating factors. The numbers are given for loans made from its own revolving loan fund, which at any given time represents only a portion of the clients it helps. This pool is intentionally used for nonbankable clients who on the whole have a higher probability of default. But once a borrower has established a good payment record, loans are sold to conventional lenders. Thus, by selling good loans, Liberation is left with more problem loans.

While most of Liberation's clients are sent directly to banks and thrifts for their loans and the loan pool is a small part of its operation, the problem loans are still a little troubling to Liberation. It is hiring an experienced credit counselor to work one-on-one with the most delinquent clients to try to avoid foreclosure. However, in the event of foreclosure, Liberation has always quickly repossessed the homes--usually through expedited processes with deeds in lieu of foreclosure. Homes are then quickly resold to other clients.

Omaha 100 has just experienced a sudden rash of foreclosures and is assessing whether to upgrade its prepurchase counseling and training. The foreclosures all occurred with one group of new homes, which were among the highest-priced purchased in the program. But no certain reason for the problems has been determined.

Another factor to consider is that the average income of clients in all of these programs is considerably below the incomes of conventional borrowers and probably much lower than the incomes of borrowers using FHA insurance. Lower incomes often translate to less job security, more financial stress, and increased likelihood of missing a payment.

Loan Collection Techniques

Loan management experts say that quick reactions to any late payments are the key to reducing many delinquencies. They point to a few simple techniques that can help reduce delinquency and default rates.

10 days overdue: Most loans are written so they are due on the first of the month, but are subject to a late payment penalty only after the fifteenth of the month. For loans that have not been paid by the tenth of the month, Chattanooga Neighborhood Enterprise (CNE) sends out a friendly "almost late" notice reminding the borrower that they can still avoid the penalty.

15 days overdue: At this point, most lenders send out a late notice advising that a late payment penalty is now owed. This is certainly advisable if a 10-day notice has not been sent. At this point, or no later than the date when the loan is 30 days overdue, a loan collections person should make a phone call to determine what the problem is. Borrowers almost always promise to make the payment, and in fact, most make their payment after this call.

30 days overdue: At this point, a loan is considered delinquent. Another notice should be sent, and diligent organizations may want to make another call reminding the borrower of the serious financial implications of getting behind. In most cases, this will result in a pledge of payment by a certain date, which is logged in a tickler file so another call can be made if the payment is not received. If a genuine family emergency exists, the lender may consider entering into a **forbearance agreement** that lets the borrower reduce or suspend payments until they can be caught up later. This written agreement is signed by the lender and borrower. Most nonprofit organizations authorize their loan counselor or executive director to sign this agreement.

60 days overdue: If a payment is over 60 days overdue and repayment pledges are not working, a serious problem has developed and the probability of default has increased substantially. Phone calls continue, but a face to face meeting may be called for. The staff person should be authorized to enter into a forbearance agreement or negotiate **loan modifications** that change the original terms of the loan. Typically, the promissory note is modified to add the missing payments to loan principal and extend the due date of the last payment. Among nonprofit lenders, modifications such as these are usually approved by the executive director, loan committee, or board of directors.

90 days overdue: Loans in this category are at extremely high risk of default. Unless a genuine family emergency exists that justifies loan modifications, the lender must unfortunately prepare for a foreclosure. However, if the lender's collections procedures have not been rigorous up to this point, there is a relatively better chance of helping borrowers get caught up.

Instead of foreclosing on properties and putting the home up for auction, many organizations in this study negotiate a **deed in lieu of foreclosure**. This voluntary release of the property by the homeowner can greatly reduce the costs of foreclosure. Legal costs are minimal and an auction is avoided. The home can be resold immediately to another family, and is less likely to be vacant and suffer damage.

Better Collection Systems Are Needed

Of course, these techniques can best be used by the nonprofit organization if it is the primary lender, as was the case only with CNE, Liberation, Omaha 100, and Habitat of Charlotte. Two of these groups--CNE and Liberation--also make amortizing second mortgage loans, as do NorthRiver and Jackson Metro. With these second mortgage loan portfolios, the same techniques can work. But they are to no avail if the first mortgage loan is not being kept current. Thus, the nonprofit second mortgage lenders need to stay in close communication with the conventional first mortgage lenders for the respective loans.

Three of the groups--DAHP in Dallas, the Santa Fe Housing Trust, and Garrett County CAC--make soft second mortgage loans requiring no monthly payments. NDC in New Orleans makes no loans at all. In these situations the nonprofit can not be tipped off to problems by a late payment on its loan.

None of the organizations studied reported having a formal system by which first mortgage lenders reported delinquency problems back to the organizations that had counseled the clients. This appeared to occur only informally, by phone calls. We could not ascertain if the loan servicers for the first mortgage even had any way of knowing if a nonprofit was involved with prepurchase counseling. Thus, we suspect that lack of formal systems advising nonprofits of loan delinquencies is a widespread structural weakness in the first mortgage lending programs that has not yet been widely addressed by the banks.

While many conventional lenders rely on nonprofits to help with training, counseling, and special financing, almost none (to our knowledge) has an effective system for notifying their nonprofit partner when a payment is 15 days late. That is a critical time for intervention, since not long after that, the homeowner will need to double up his or her payments to get current.

Chase Community Development Corporation in New York City has worked out some of the best techniques for management of loan collections. We think they are worthy of emulation.

▶ An **early intervention officer** or officers should be appointed to deal with collections for special affordable housing products. If an officer reduces foreclosures by two or three a year, he or she adds to the profit line rather than creating an extra cost. Chase has one officer handling about 120 delinquencies a month.

▶ This specialist should have access to **real-time delinquency information** from the bank's data processing division.

▶ Systems should be developed for **constant communication with nonprofit partners,** who may agree to intervene and negotiate catch-up arrangements between the primary lender and the borrower. This, however, takes a major commitment by the nonprofit, including finding a source of funding for this extra work. The counselors who helped get the loan in the first place are ideally suited for this work, and the realities of working with collections can make them better skilled at prepurchase counseling.

▶ The nonprofit's **home buyer training should emphasize the pitfalls of getting behind** and encourage people to call the agency if they ever think they are going to miss a payment. Home buyers helped by the Santa Fe Community Housing Trust have heeded this advice and have been able to get early intervention help from the Housing Trust before the lender ever knew there was a problem.

▶ Nonprofits could operate modest **emergency loan funds** to tide over late payments in the event of a family emergency. While this technique has rarely been tried, the fund could be capitalized with a small grant and would avoid time-consuming negotiations between the nonprofit, the borrower, and the lenders.

Post-Purchase Counseling

Most of what is called post-purchase counseling is really loan collections work. Experts all agree that delinquencies must be nipped in the bud by diligent attention to late notices and personal contacts. If the family has a genuine financial crisis, the techniques described can be used to remedy it. If the borrower is simply sloppy about paying bills, the reactions must be speedy, friendly, and persistent. Nonprofits that do direct lending need to establish systems to

ensure that notices go out and calls are made.

In family emergencies, a post-purchase counselor (probably the same person as the prepurchase counselor) should be skilled in making referrals to agencies that might be able to help.

When borrowers are simply slow about paying their bills, the counselor will likely be addressing the same issues that came up at the prepurchase stage--too much debt and uncontrolled spending. If this is the case, either the agency counselor or a partner organization such as Consumer Credit Counseling might be able to help.

But some people are what they are-- impulsive · spenders and irresponsible borrowers who pay their bills late. Effective counselors and loan offices realize that these character issues are probably the most important factor in determining who should get a loan. Thus, effective programs identify the chronic late-payers and weed them out before they even look for a house. If they do manage to get financing, perhaps the shock of a pending foreclosure combined with good counseling will result in changing ingrained habits.

It is a mistake, however, for program managers and other staff to think they can cull out all the poor risks before they buy homes, or save them after they do. Loan defaults are painful, but if programs are so risk-averse that they aim for a zero default rate, they will probably end up helping mostly people who eventually could buy a home on their own.

Organizational Structures of Nonprofit Lenders

In describing the variety of special financing products used by the programs examined, this chapter has had to cover a number of topics--including the lending industry, barriers to financing low-income families, first and second mortgage lending, widely used financing sources, innovative sources of capital, revolving loan funds, lease-purchase arrangements, long-term affordability controls, loan processing, loan collections, and post-purchase counseling.

Except for affordable first mortgage loans offered by conventional lenders, the special financing products described are never offered by profit-motivated lenders. Their very existence is dependent upon a nonprofit or governmental agency. To undertake the complex business of lending along with providing other related services to low-income home buyers, nonprofits need highly developed organizational structures.

For example, lending affects who a nonprofit is affiliated with, what board members it recruits, how it staffs and manages its programs, where it gets money for administrative costs, and how it accounts for money. The next chapter addresses these organizational and funding issues.

5. Organizational and Funding Issues

What Kinds of Organizations Succeed?

In carefully examining 11 programs, our study gives some good indications of the organizational and funding systems that succeed in helping low-income families buy homes and begin to build assets. In the study, 10 of the 11 organizations have operated home purchase assistance programs for at least four years. All of the programs-- even one that had been operating for only a little over a year--have proven results.

From the standpoint of organizational structure, formal affiliations are significant. We found that eight of the organizations were affiliated with lenders, religious organizations, local government, or a national organization. By "affiliation" we mean strong board representation or operating agreements that influence how the program functions. Only three of the programs are independent, and one of those was an affiliated organization when it started.

Also, most of the programs were multi-purpose, focusing on other activities such as rental housing and social services. A few have effectively spun off other affiliated or subsidiary organizations.

Types of Organizations Represented

The organizations fall into one or more of these categories:

Lender-affiliations: Three organizations were strongly affiliated with lenders. These were the Dallas Affordable Housing Partnership (DAHP), the Jackson Metro Housing Partnership, and Omaha 100. Operated by The Enterprise Foundation's Dallas office, DAHP has an advisory board comprised only of lenders participating in the program. The Jackson Partnership was started with strong input and grant support from lenders, who comprise about a third of the board and provide below-market-rate financing to home buyers. Omaha 100 is a nonprofit organization controlled by lenders who provide first mortgage financing to low-income home buyers, including clients of the two Holy Name housing organizations in Omaha that we studied.

Religious affiliations: Four organizations studied have, or had, religious affiliations. One of the Holy Name organizations was started by the Redemptorist order, which still is represented on the board of directors and two of whose members, including the director, donate their time. Liberation Community was started by the Nazarene Compassionate Ministries but later became independent. Habitat of Charlotte is an ecumenical Christian ministry affiliated with Habitat for Humanity International (through a covenant, or formal operating agreement) and is also affiliated with local churches. Famicos was started over 25 years ago by the Sisters of Charity, a member of which still sits on the board.

Other affiliations: In addition to its lender affiliation, the Dallas Affordable Housing Partnership was designed and started by The Enterprise Foundation, working closely with the City of Dallas. Enterprise continues to staff the program under an operating agreement with the City of Dallas. The Garrett County Community Action Committee's board has strong representation from county officials.

Independent organizations: The Santa Fe Community Housing Trust, NorthRiver in Toledo, Chattanooga Neighborhood Enterprise, and Liberation Community are all independent in terms of their board structure and operations. This is not to say that they, like the other organizations, do not have important partners, including local governments, lenders, and national organizations such as The Enterprise Foundation, the Local Initiatives Support Corporation, and Neighborhood Reinvestment Corporation.

Multipurpose organizations: Every organization we studied does more than simply help low-income home buyers. Many are also involved in rental housing--either developing it, managing it, or providing rent subsidies. Some work with small business development and job training. In most cases, other housing and community development work seems to harmonize well with the home buyer assistance programs, and in some cases provides small to moderate contributions to overhead costs. One might worry about a possible loss of focus, especially among the organizations with smaller staffs. But most seem to thrive on diversity, and only one group is considering

cutting back some programs not directly related to homeownership.

Occasional spin-offs: One of the sponsors--Holy Name in Omaha--found a way to grow and diversify without adding staff and overhead. It helped start the citywide lender consortia already described, and it spun off a separate nonprofit corporation to work in a different kind of neighborhood on the other side of the city. Liberation Community in Fort Worth wants to spin off programs that it started in other neighborhoods, and a construction job training program that requires major fund-raising every year.

The Importance of Leadership

In a study such as this, it is difficult to address the issue of leadership. In the information we gathered about some organizations, it is clear that certain individuals or institutions played a key role in making the programs succeed. With other organizations, the role played by personal leadership is not so clear, but that is very likely due to a lack of complete information on our part or a desire on the part of the organizations not to single out individuals for praise.

It is clear that many of the organizations would not have been formed without the support of well-established government agencies and institutions, both local and national. But it was hard to discern in most cases what individual had the vision of a new program and persuaded colleagues or public officials to support the concept. Some of the programs have been around long enough that none of the original staff remains.

Several mayors played this role of catalyst, such as Mayor Gene Roberts in Chattanooga, and Mayor Kane Ditto in Jackson. Since the author met both of these individuals before the respective housing programs were established, he has some first-hand information. They along with other civic leaders in their communities had a vision that *something* should be done to revitalize their cities.

But neither had an exact blueprint. They called in outside experts--in both cases, from The Enterprise Foundation. They convened business leaders and community representatives to come up with a plan. In both cities, a plan was made that roughly outlined the expected products and services that would be provided for renters and home buyers. Chattanooga Neighborhood Enterprise and Jackson Metro Housing Partnership were the results.

At this point, the early civic leadership in these cities had to switch to more practical organizational leadership. As was true in every one of the 11 examples, a director or manager began the hard work of building an organization. The directors and some of their harder driving staff members were (and are) the real heros, who often have had to amend the original plan and improvise when expected funding did not arrive or a certain program simply did not work. We know the names of some exemplary staff people, but are reluctant to mention them for fear of slighting others we know less about.

Funding organizations have many unsung heros. Drawing on personal knowledge, the author can state that Liberation Community would not be where it is today without the quiet support of program officers and

directors in three Fort Worth-based foundations. Chattanooga Neighborhood Enterprise would not exist if the Lyndhurst Foundation had not believed in a dream of better inner-city neighborhoods. The Santa Fe Community Housing Trust and the other innovative housing initiatives in Santa Fe would not have been funded without the political support of Mayor Debbie Jaramillo, and the personal leadership of Joseph Montoya, the city's principal community development planner.

Robert Wolfe, a retired chemical engineer who was for many years the volunteer director of Famicos, summed up the value of personal leadership:

"Programs and paper don't do anything," said Dr. Wolfe. "People do everything."

Staff Sizes: Between 4 and 42 Positions

Staff sizes of the organizations studied ranged from a low of four to a high of 42. Larger staff size correlated with taking on labor-intensive functions such as in-house construction and origination of first mortgage loans.

CNE in Chattanooga, with the largest staff, originates about 160 first mortgage loans a year, sells loans on the secondary market, and also finances many home repairs for existing homeowners. Thus, much of its staff is involved in intense loan underwriting, loan processing, property inspections, and construction management.

Two other groups with staffs of 14 or 15 either had in-house construction companies or operated social service programs. Famicos in Cleveland, with 15 staff members, devotes six staff members to occupancy management and property maintenance in its lease-purchase program.

Management and Staffing: Thriving on Diverse Tasks

With regard to home buyer assistance, all of the organizations studied operate one or more distinct and separate "businesses:" training and counseling, direct mortgage financing, and sales of new or rehabilitated homes. Management and staffing approaches vary considerably depending upon the functions and scales of the programs.

By necessity, the programs that had smaller staffs and multipurpose programs had loose job descriptions. The Santa Fe program has six fulltime equivalent staff members and operates nine separate businesses: home buyer training and counseling, second mortgage financing, housing development, and six other housing programs unrelated to home buyer assistance. That program relies heavily on part-time staff and professionals working under temporary contracts.

The Housing Trust, along with several other organizations examined, defies the wisdom of most business management gurus, who advise small organizations to focus on one or two products and to "stick to their knitting." Instead, there seemed to be good synergy among the separate housing, neighborhood revitalization, and anti-poverty programs. Some cross-subsidized others. And handing a lot of programs seems to attract more funding. In only two cases, program managers reported difficulties in operating non-housing programs. The program manager in Fort Worth wants to spin off the organization's job training program. And NorthRiver in

Toledo has been struggling to get its economic development programs going.

A listing of the major job titles used gives a clear picture of the diversity of tasks involved in the home buyer assistance programs we studied.

Job Titles Used in Programs

President or executive director
Executive assistant
Director, lending
Director, housing development
Director, job training
Director, marketing and community relations
Fund raiser or grant writer
Construction manager
Rehabilitation or construction specialist
Construction supervisor
Construction crew member
Volunteer coordinator
Senior loan counselor
Loan counselor
Project manager (for real estate development)
Property manager (for lease-purchase properties)
Education counselor
Loan processor-underwriter
Loan closer
Loan originator
Loan originating assistant
Loan servicer
Chief financial officer (CFO)
Controller
Accounting manager
Accountant
Accounting assistant
Office manager
Administrative assistant
Receptionist

While many of these job titles may seem inappropriate for smaller organizations, they do indicate the wide range of staff functions that are possible. Since groups with smaller staffs do not seem to shy away from complex programs, in reality, their staffs may be wearing many of these hats. The terms "senior," "junior," "manager," and "assistant" indicate where levels of management and supervision are required. In the smallest-staffed organizations, the senior, manager, CFO, and project manager roles are often accepted by the executive director.

For seven organizations working with primarily minority populations, data was collected on the minority make-up of the staffs. Between 30 and 100 percent of staff members were members of minority groups. For those same organizations, between 80 and 99 percent of the clients are members of minority groups. In Dallas, Fort Worth, and Santa Fe, the clients are predominantly Hispanic; in Charlotte, Chattanooga, Jackson, and New Orleans, about 90 percent of the clients are African American. Two programs operated in non-minority areas, and for another two we did not collect data.

Some organizations use contractors rather than staff to carry out certain functions. Naturally, builders and renovation contractors are widely used. Aside from that, the most-used contractors were home inspectors, who in many states are certified professionals. Several groups used construction managers under contract, and one (Santa Fe) recently hired a certified public accountant (CPA) to act as chief comptroller--apart from the CPA firm used for audits.

Some organizations relied on other nonprofits and lenders--not under contract but as part of their normal course of business--to carry out critical functions. Holy Name's clients receive home buyer training from Omaha 100. DAHP in Dallas relies on other nonprofits for both training and counseling, and, as mentioned, has enlisted lenders' help with its second mortgage program. Many of the organizations count on referring some clients to consumer credit counseling bureaus.

Outputs In Relation to Staff Size

Because of the wide range of goals and functions of the various programs, rating their relative operating efficiency is difficult. Annual home purchases completed per staff member is a crude measure--this ranged from 80 home purchases per staff member in Dallas, down to three or four in several programs. The measure is imprecise, because in some cases we could only roughly estimate the number of staff members devoted solely to assisting with home purchases.

It is clear that renovating and building homes in distressed inner-city neighborhoods is very labor intensive work. Programs in which this work was prominent had the lowest number of home buyers per staff person. There are several explanations.

First of all, the organizations working in these areas operate a number of other programs involving rental housing and social services. Second, all of these programs build or renovate homes on scattered sites, making acquisition and construction harder to manage and execute.

In inner cities, even counseling and training is harder. Clients tend to have lower incomes and more problems qualifying, creating more staff work. And marketing the homes sometimes takes more work because the locations of home are perceived as less desirable.

As one might expect, new construction on large tracts, while challenging, is not as labor intensive per home produced. At the time of our study, in 1996, the Santa Fe Community Housing Trust, with only six staff members, had 165 homes in construction or financed and ready to start construction. All but five of the homes were being newly built. The two new construction projects included 35 and 120 homes, respectively, on two sites.

Nonetheless, that finding is not an endorsement for new construction in all cases. Santa Fe has a severe countywide shortage of affordable housing, and affordable new construction is indisputably needed. But in many inner-city neighborhoods, new homes cost roughly twice as much as existing or renovated homes, and require much deeper subsidies, particularly where property values and the incomes of prospective buyers were low.

The Highest-Output Programs

The high output of the DAHP program in Dallas has several explanations. First, the program is highly streamlined, with participating private lenders serving as the primary point of contact with clients. In addition, the program does not directly provide counseling or training, but refers clients to other organizations. This reliance on other organizations has come at a cost, though--most clients do not get personal counseling, and most use a take-home workbook.

Because of its new construction program and for other reasons that are alluded to in the case study, the Santa Fe Community Housing Trust creates the second highest number of home buyers--43--per staff person per year. If the staff working on non-home buyer programs were subtracted, the figure would be close to 60. Given that the program provides extensive counseling and training, and also builds and renovates homes for sale, we consider it the most productive citywide program among the case studies.

The Neighborhood Development Foundation in New Orleans had the third highest output per staff person--42. Considering the extensive counseling and training offered by the program, and its lack of any internal subsidy funds to attract and help buyers, this is a very productive program.

Because neighborhood-based programs face more challenging tasks and take on so many functions, they are not compared with the citywide programs. But among them, Liberation Community in Fort Worth had the highest number of home buyers--five--per staff member in the year we looked at.

Boards of Directors

The boards of directors of the organizations ranged in size from 12 to 24 members. As in most nonprofit organizations, the primary roles of the board members consist of policy setting, long-range planning, and help with fund-raising. In several of the organizations, board members volunteer to help with day-to-day operations. Board members and committee members of Habitat of Charlotte have the most hands-on roles--helping with family selection and construction in addition to more traditional board functions.

The composition of the boards varies considerably from organization to organization. Lenders make up as much as a third of board membership in organizations that have formal ties to banks and thrift institutions. On most of the boards, professionals account for a third to a half of the membership.

As one might expect, neighborhood-targeted organizations have more residents on their boards--between a third and half the membership. Three of the groups identified themselves as Community-Based Housing Development Organizations (CHDOs), a designation under the HOME program that requires one-third of the membership to be low-income or residents of low-income areas. But some organizations have few or no residents on their boards, and concentrate instead on fund-raising connections and professional skills.

Minority representation on boards appeared to be somewhat less than for the staffs. In organizations for which the information was gathered, about 25 to 50 percent of board members are members of minority groups.

Costs of Operations

We believe that the administrative costs of the sponsoring organizations are important analytical tools--for both the program managers and their funders. These are described in both budgets and financial reports. By "administrative costs" we mean all costs for staff and other overhead, but not funds invested in real estate projects or

loans made to home buyers. Those we characterize as "direct program expenditures."

Thus, we looked for information similar to that contained in a profit and loss statement for a for-profit business. Unfortunately, the standard accounting practices required for nonprofits typically do not present this information clearly.

Eight organizations provided financial information at a sufficient level of detail to draw some general conclusions. But one caveat: our characterizations of administrative costs and revenues are our interpretations, not the organizations'. Their accounting systems allocate staff costs to various programs, or may mingle program costs (such as loan-making) with overhead costs.

That said, what we characterized as administrative costs ranged from $190,000 a year for Jackson Metro Housing, with four employees, up to $2.34 million for CNE in Chattanooga. The other six ranged from $257,000 a year to $519,000.

Seven organizations reported detailed information on administrative expenses. They spent between 71 percent and 86 percent of their overhead on salaries, benefits, payroll costs, and professional services. Professional services included accountants, lawyers, home inspectors, and construction managers.

Thus, salaries and contract services are by far the major expense of these organizations--as they should be except in organizations that rely heavily on volunteers. The major "goods" of the programs are human energies that help clients and, in some cases, create new or renovated homes. The expense of producing the organizations' products--loans made and homes sold--do not and should not show up as administrative costs.

Other significant costs were office space, office supplies, travel, and insurance. Groups that spent more on salaries, and less on these expenses, typically paid less for office space (by owning the office building or getting discounted rent) and less for travel. Organizations that do property development and inspections, or travel out of town to conferences, incur more travel expense.

Where organizations provided detailed financial information on the sources and uses of administrative funds, we summarized it in the case studies. These are valuable templates for organizations wishing to start similar operations.

Primary Sources of Administrative Funds

Collectively, the programs we looked at rely heavily on grants to cover their administrative costs. Among the eight organizations reporting detailed information, the primary sources of revenue are:

Private grants and contributions: This ran neck and neck with government funding as the most important single source of support for operations. For two of the groups, it amounted to between 8 and 16 percent of revenues, but for the other six, contributions covered between a third and 90 percent of administrative costs. In Chattanooga, a major portion of this funding came from one local foundation. In Jackson and Omaha, where lender consortia are closely associated with the programs, banks underwrote between 37 and 67 percent of operating costs.

Government grants: This type of support amounts to between 25 percent and 65 percent of revenues that were applied to paying for overhead. Most of these funds were federal CDBG or HOME funds passed through the local government. Two organizations--Chattanooga Neighborhood Enterprise and the Santa Fe Community Housing Trust--received seven percent and 34 percent of their budgets respectively from City general revenue for the fiscal years we looked at. But nationwide, commitments by local governments to use their own funds for home buyer assistance programs is a rarity.

Fees and program income: These sources of revenue were important only to organizations that engage in real estate development, manage rental property, make and collect loans, and sell homes. CNE in Chattanooga received the highest percentage of program income--interest on loans and deposits totalled about a third of its budget. But for other organizations, this self-generated income covered less than 20 percent of the budgets.

Some revenues described as "fees" were actually performance-based grants. Famicos, for example, covers about half its budget from fees paid by the Cleveland Housing Network, a local nonprofit intermediary. But the sources of the funds to pay those fees are federal and private grants.

Developer fees were a minor source of income for a few organizations. Typically, these were construction projects using HOME or CDBG funds for write-down grants or soft second mortgages. Accountants characterized these "fees" as grants if the subsidies were given directly to the organization rather than the home buyers.

While several programs charge clients a fee for training and counseling on the order of $250, this was minor income on the order of $15,000 to $2,000 a year. While no organization broke out its counseling and training costs, these appear to range from $1,000 to $2,000 for every client that buys a home. This estimate includes the cost of training and counseling clients who fall out of the programs, a necessary cost of doing business.

More Specific Examples: The Case Studies

Up to this point, we have given a number of findings and recommendations concerning the best practices for assisting low-income home buyers. Drawing examples from the case studies, we have examined a number of approaches to counseling, training, financing, funding, and organizational management.

Now, we move from the general to the specific. The remainder of the book is devoted to case studies of individual programs.

Case Studies

6

Chattanooga Neighborhood Enterprise
(Chattanooga, Tennessee)

Program Highlights

Chattanooga Neighborhood Enterprise

Target Area:	City of Chattanooga (population 155,000) limited activity in surrounding Hamilton County
Program Goals:	Assist low- and moderate-income home buyers Revitalize inner-city neighborhoods
Major Elements:	Financial counseling and home buyer training First and second mortgage lending Acquisition and rehabilitation of homes for sale Construction of homes for sale
Average Client Income:	$24,000
Typical Home Price:	$45,000 (existing homes)
Year Started:	1986
Other Programs:	Rental housing development and management Special needs housing for the homeless Technical assistance to other nonprofit housing providers Technical aid to private landlords and/or City staff
Staffing:	42 fulltime staff members
Annual Output: (1994-1995)	382 clients received home buyer training 281 clients received first or second mortgage loans 29 houses renovated, 26 of these sold
Funding:	General revenue from city government Federal funds Lyndhurst Foundation and other private organizations Loan origination fees Developer fees

Overview

Chattanooga Neighborhood Enterprise, Inc. is a nonprofit community development corporation that operates one of the nation's largest locally-based homeownership programs targeted at low- and moderate-income clients.

In the 10 years since CNE was established, in December 1986, the growth of its home buyer programs has been exceptional. CNE provides individual homeownership financial counseling and training workshops, and assists low- and moderate-income buyers with their home financing. It is associated with local banks, which provide mortgage loans to first-time buyers. It acquires and refurbishes, as well as builds new homes.

As of June 1996, CNE had assisted with 1,486 home purchases involving nearly $70 million in financing. In the peak year of 1993-1994, it helped with 343 home purchases.

Among the organizations examined in this study, CNE has the largest and most sophisticated program for originating first mortgages. Almost half of its clients get CNE-originated first mortgage loans in addition to second mortgages. In this way, CNE is able to use tools that most of the local for-profit lenders have passed up--such as loan money for very low-income buyers from the state housing finance authority. This money is priced about two and one-half percentage points below market.

Thus, CNE is literally a nonprofit mortgage company. CNE's track record and financial capacity are strong enough that it can approve FHA-insured mortgages without any review by that agency. To our knowledge, it is the only nonprofit organization in the nation that has FHA direct endorsement authority. It is also an approved lender for Fannie Mae, Freddie Mac, and VA mortgages.

CNE got into the first mortgage lending business in the mid-1980s because local mortgage lenders had practically abandoned the inner-city residential market. The lack of interest was the result of years of economic decline, a trend that appears to have been reversed in recent years.

CNE is a partnership between the City of Chattanooga, private foundations, local banks and businesses, and state and federal governments. While its primary functions are lending and real estate development, CNE also conducts some activities geared at making low-income people more self sufficient. It sponsors job training programs, for example, and offering workshops on personal money management.

A Citywide Revitalization Agenda

A major factor in CNE's success has been the level of the commitment--in terms of time and money--of the CNE staff, City and State governments, and local businesses and individuals. CNE's founding and growth have been part and parcel of a two-decade-old, broad-based effort to reverse the economic and physical decline of Chattanooga's central city.

Chattanooga grew rapidly in the mid- and late 1800s as center of rail transportation and one of the South's major industrial centers. By the 1970s--as in many other eastern and southern cities--much of this industrial-era employment base had declined. Likewise, the city's population dropped.

However, during the 1970s and early 1980s, local business and civic leaders took a stand and slowly began to turn around the city's declining fortunes. Chattanooga Venture, a consortium of civic and business leaders that had the strong support of the locally-based Lyndhurst Foundation, began a long and ultimately successful program of revitalizing the city's downtown riverfront district.

As a keystone of this effort, the city government--with major funding from the Lyndhurst Foundation--built the Chattanooga Aquarium, now the city's premier tourist attraction.

CNE's Founding: A Big Vision

Helping with this transformation--and not simply providing housing assistance to the needy--was the primary reason CNE was established.

In 1985, with some downtown improvements already underway, Chattanooga Venture turned its attention to the blighted neighborhoods and housing stock that constituted much of the old central city. A local builder, Robert Corker, Jr. (now Tennessee's commissioner of finance), and the Lyndhurst Foundation provided seed money for Maryland-based Enterprise Foundation to create a new nonprofit entity that would make "all housing fit and livable in 10 years."

While this ambitious goal was not achieved in the intervening decade (and was, in fact, rejected by CNE's board shortly after its founding in favor of more "realistic" goals), this high vision in CNE's formative days nonetheless may have contributed to its scale of effort and ultimate success.

When CNE was being established, Mayor Gene Roberts (who is still mayor) saw CNE as an opportunity to privatize all the City-run housing programs, which then consisted entirely of federally-funded home repair programs for owner-occupants and investor-owners (leaving aside the programs run by an independent housing authority).

The City-run programs, along with their existing staff of about 10 housing inspectors and finance specialists, were immediately folded into CNE. A new director was recruited by Enterprise, which provided technical assistance during CNE's first five years and still maintains an affiliation with CNE.

CNE's first objectives were to:

▶ Increase the output and efficiency of the existing rehabilitation programs.

▶ Start a financing program for home buyers

▶ Undertake real estate developments that would help revitalize inner-city neighborhoods.

Since its founding, CNE has fulfilled its intended role in Chattanooga's revival by renovating many of the city's most dilapidated homes and building new housing developments on once empty city lots.

As CNE expanded its programs, it later became affiliated with the national Neighborhood Reinvestment Corporation, sponsor of the many Neighborhood Housing Service programs around the country.

Most of the neighborhoods CNE targets are in older parts of the inner city, the population of which is made up largely of the elderly, households headed by women, the disabled, and many homeless. These areas feature old and often architecturally significant homes, which have been split into apartments and allowed to deteriorate. CNE restores these houses or, in some cases, demolishes them and replaces them with new homes. However, the majority of homes financed by CNE are existing homes in the market.

With the financing provided by CNE, residents are able to purchase their own homes and bring pride and stability back into their neighborhoods.

Market Analysis

Chattanooga has many of the hallmarks of an aging industrial city--but one that is having some success in rebuilding itself. In the 1800s, it became one of the South's major industrial cities due to its position as a major railroad hub. It was known for its foundries, other heavy industry, wholesale businesses, and the famous Chattanooga Choo-Choo.

The industrial base began to decline noticeably after World War II. By the 1980s, the number of jobs in the city was still declining--by six percent in that decade alone. Per capita income grew only about two percent a year in the 1980s--significantly less than inflation. The city's population losses in that decade were among the largest of any city in this study.

A Turnaround in Negative Trends

Some of the negative trends have reversed themselves. The 1980s' population losses mask the fact that the number of households actually increased slightly during that period, marking a shift from larger to smaller families. And the current population estimate of 155,000 represents a turnaround from decades of population decline--a clear reflection of the overall revitalization of the city in which CNE has played an important role.

Hamilton County, which includes Chattanooga and had 285,536 residents in 1990, experienced no gain in population in the 1980s but had an overall job growth of nearly seven percent. While businesses migrated to the suburbs, more jobs became available to inner-city residents who could commute.

A relatively inexpensive housing stock provides ample opportunities for home purchases by low-income clients. The city's median home value in 1990 was almost one-third less than the national median for that year.

CNE serves a clientele with incomes that are predominantly below the local median. In a summary of all home-purchase assistance activity for five years ending December 31, 1994, 67 percent of clients had incomes below 80 percent of median income ($27,520 for a family of four in 1996), and 21 percent had incomes below 50 percent of median income ($17,200 for a family of four). The average household income of a CNE home buyer is about $24,000.

The table at the top of the following page provides key demographic data on Chattanooga.

	Chattanooga	USA
City population, 1990:	152,466	
Population growth, 1980s:	-9.8%	12.6%
Percent African American:	29%	12%
Percent Hispanic:	21%	9%
City median income, 1990s:	$22,197	$30,056
Metro median income, 1996:	$36,600	$41,600
Unemployment rate:	6.5%	6.7%
Poverty rate:	18.2%	13.1%
Median home value:	$54,100	$79,900
Home value increase, 1980s:	62.5%	67%
Median monthly rent:	$360	$447
Homeownership rate:	54.2%	64.2%

U.S. Census, 1990; 1996 median income from HUD.

Fifty-four percent of CNE's home purchase clients are minorities, who comprise about 35 percent of the total population. Forty-four percent of CNE's home buyers are female heads of household, who comprise only 17 percent of city householders.

CNE is a big player in the low end of the home sales market. During a recent period, it participated in 44 percent of the sales of homes priced $70,000 and below.

Operations and Financing

Marketing

Interested applicants find out about CNE in a variety of ways--by noticing signs in their neighborhoods, or through brochures, ads in local real estate publications, or word of mouth. Because of its great success, CNE has often been featured in--and commended by--not only Chattanooga's local newspapers, but newspapers in other cities and even in the *Congressional Record*.

CNE has a variety of well-publicized programs. The organization publishes brochures and fliers describing its programs and housing development activities. It has teamed up with other businesses and organizations in the city, such as Memorial Hospital, to get word of its home purchasing opportunities to a wider audience. CNE is featured significantly and repeatedly in the local media's news coverage.

CNE's lending department budgets about $4,500 a year for advertisements in real estate guides. CNE's staff sends brochures by direct mail to city renters and real estate agents and visits realtors to familiarize them with the advantages of working with CNE. The organization is working on obtaining a booth at the Homebuilders Association's next home show in the Chattanooga area.

CNE also publishes a newsletter, *Among*

Neighbors, which updates CNE customers and others on current projects and announces classes and programs being sponsored by the organization.

Financing of Homes

During fiscal year 1995, CNE was involved with a total volume of $13.3 million in lending to 283 low- to moderate-income home purchasers.

CNE performs three financing functions:

Origination of first mortgage loans: These loans are originated and then sold to Neighborhood Housing Services of America, the Tennessee Housing Development Authority and secondary market buyers of FHA-insured loans. In FY 1996, about 160 loans were projected, for a total value of nearly $5 million.

Brokering other first mortgage loans: For a majority of its home purchase clients, CNE provides help in obtaining home purchase loans from local banks. In FY 1996, about 160 of these loans are projected, for a total value of $7.7 million.

Making second mortgage loans: About 95 percent of CNE's home purchase clients also qualify for direct CNE second mortgage loans, intended to cover down payment and closing expenses. A total of $968,000 in funding for these loans was projected for FY 1996--$318,000 from CDBG funds and $650,000 from City general funds. Repayments of previous loans are also used to fund new loans.

About 300 loans were projected for FY 1996.

In many instances, CNE and its associated lenders provide financing for 100 percent of the sales prices of homes. In early 1996, second mortgage loans ranged in amounts from $739 to $7,500, and averaged about $3,500. The loans pay for closing costs, and where necessary, part of the down payment. Cash-to-close for most clients is kept in the neighborhood of $1,000.

Guidelines for second mortgage loans are as follows:

Incomes at or below 50 percent of median: Up to $7,500 can be borrowed, repayable over 20 years at two percent interest.

Incomes 50 to 80 percent of median: Up to $5,000 can be borrowed, repayable over 10 years at four percent interest. Borrowers must pay out-of-pocket two percent of the purchase price or $840, whichever is higher.

Incomes 80 to 115 percent of median: Up to $2,500 can be borrowed, repayable over five years at six percent interest.

Intake, Screening and Counseling

Applicants to the program are screened according to their employment record, level of debt, and credit standing. Although poor credit is not an obstacle to being accepted into the program, those who need help with their financial situation are not approved for the prepurchase program. Instead they are directed into long-term budget counseling or

Life Skills Training, recently developed by CNE.

The Life Skills Training program consists of five workshops aimed at developing a more thrifty lifestyle. The curriculum covers such topics as effectively managing household finances, becoming a savvy consumer, maintaining good relationships with family and neighbors, and maintaining a house and car, among other things. After successfully completing this classroom training or individual budget counseling, a customer is considered ready for FasTrak pre-purchase training.

Counselors and trainers are drawn from the CNE staff and from volunteers--local home economics teachers, hardware store personnel, professionals, YMCA staff, and others volunteer as trainers.

To date, over 2,500 prospective home buyers have received individual counseling from CNE, and 24 have completed Life Skills Training.

Qualification for Assistance

CNE can help buyers with household incomes up to 115 percent of the area median income with down payment and closing cost assistance, but most of its clients have incomes below 80 percent of median income, and some of its loan products are available only to those with incomes below 50 percent of median income.

Following are the income limits for a family of four, for CNE's three types of home purchase clients:

50% of median income	$18,300
80% of median income	$29,280
115% of median income	$42,090

For most financing assistance offered by CNE, buyers must purchase homes within Chattanooga. CNE has a limited amount of funding for down payment and closing cost assistance in the surrounding sections of Hamilton County.

Loan-to-value ratios for the combined first and second mortgage sometimes slightly exceed 100 percent of appraised value. CNE will lend up to the purchase price or appraised value (whichever is lower) plus the amount of closing costs. But in every case, borrowers must at least pay out-of-pocket two percent of the purchase price or $840, whichever is higher.

The CNE second mortgage program is the only nonprofit-sponsored loan program to use credit scoring as an underwriting criteria. Credit reporting agencies provide the score, and if it is under 600, the applicant is either denied or must be approved by two separate underwriters.

Those receiving second mortgage commitments may get their first mortgages anywhere. But the loan must be at a fixed rate and may not be priced more than two percent over current Fannie Mae market rates. Since low-cost, fixed-rate products are available, this prevents buyers from being charged too high a rate or exposing themselves to possible increases in their monthly payment.

Some of CNE's first mortgage products also have special qualifying rules. For example, CNE originates purchase loans under the Start-Plus program of the Tennessee Housing Development Authority (THDA). This program is targeted to households with incomes below 50 percent of median income and homes priced at $44,000 or less, although in very low-income areas, households with incomes up to 115 percent of median can qualify. In mid-1996, Start-Plus offered a first mortgage loan with a subsidized interest rate of 5.5 percent. Also, THDA provides a second mortgage loan of up to $2,500 for down payment and closing cost assistance.

Homeownership Training

FasTrak to Homeownership, CNE's prepurchase training program, covers the home purchase process from initial prequalification through closing, as well as ongoing budget, credit, and maintenance issues. Clients attend either two sessions of four hours each, or one eight-hour session.

The sessions cover topics such as what to expect from homeownership, how to find an affordable home, terms and definitions found in mortgage loans, explanations of the closing and settlement processes, budgeting, and the responsibilities and benefits of homeownership.

There is a $100 per person fee, which helps finance the program. A total of over 1,400 couples and single buyers had graduated from CNE's FasTrak program as of mid-1996. Fannie Mae has approved CNE's own home buyer manual and training program, as have the Tennessee Housing Development Agency and the Neighborhood Reinvestment Corporation.

CNE's FasTrak training program has become a national model--one that is presented by CNE staff at training institutes sponsored by the national Neighborhood Reinvestment Corporation.

Home Selection

The sale prices of homes financed in the first half of 1996 ranged from a low of $30,000 to a high of about $75,000. The average price is in the mid-$40,000s. CNE staff helps with prepurchase inspections and negotiations of sales contracts.

CNE publishes fliers announcing the sale of new homes in projects it has developed.

Housing Development Activities

CNE, through a specialized development division, is involved in housing development projects throughout Chattanooga. Its Orchard Village development, constructed in 1994, won the Urban Land Institute Award for Excellence in that year. The division is also developing other communities, including Fairview Park, Lincoln Park and Mountain View Park.

Following are thumbnail profiles of each of these developments.

Fairview Park: This is a mixed-use, mixed-income, inner city community that includes 18 newly built homes and 20 renovated rental units. The project cost $2 million and the homes cost between $32,000 to $70,000.

Orchard Village: CNE built 58 new single-family homes on 7.3 acres. The project cost $3.2 million and the homes cost between $46,000 to $60,000.

Lincoln Park: Targeted to a very small neighborhood, this project involved the construction and renovation of 31 homes over a six-year period. The total project cost was approximately $1 million, and the per-home cost was about $32,000.

Mountain View Court: In this project, 23 homes were acquired and renovated for sale to home buyers. The project cost $647,000 and individual homes cost $28,000.

At this writing, CNE's most ambitious development plan involves the comprehensive revitalization of a near-downtown area containing pockets of boarded-up homes and overgrown lots--to be called the Bi-Centennial Neighborhood. A three-year plan calls for $33 million in financing, primarily for housing but also for small business loans and neighborhood improvements.

In this project, CNE has set a goal of assisting 480 renter and owner households through repair loans, home purchase assistance, and development of income-limited and market-rate housing. Of the total, 120 households will be assisted with home purchases, 60 with repairs of existing homes, and 300 with rental housing. The plan includes community improvements such as parks, greenways, and community policing.

Employer-Assisted Housing

In 1994, CNE launched a pilot program in association with Memorial Hospital to test the idea of employer-assisted affordable housing. The hospital invested $100,000 in a fund to provide second mortgage loans for down payment assistance. CNE administers the loan program, which follows the guidelines of the second mortgage program described earlier. The hospital's loan fund had leveraged over $600,000 in market-rate loans by the end of 1995.

In addition to funding second mortgage loans, the hospital provides a $400 grant for each employee buying a home. Purchasers go through a counseling and training process that follows CNE normal procedures for home purchase assistance.

Eighteen hospital employees purchased homes in 1995, and 16 more loans were being processed in mid-1996. CNE hopes to expand this program in coming years to include more employers in Chattanooga. Two staff members will work on this effort.

Long-Term Affordability Controls

The CNE program has no special requirements for maintaining the long-term affordability of the homes financed. Because the homes are relatively low-priced and the market is appreciating only modestly, there appears to be little need for special resale requirements. Even if controls were desired, the modest amounts of the second mortgage loans, and the requirement for repayment, give the program little leverage to control resale prices or restrict resales to low-income buyers.

Federal HOME funds are not used to fund second mortgages, so the resale requirements of that program are not a factor.

Assistance to Neighborhood Associations

In many neighborhoods in which CNE works, neighborhood organizations have existed for some time. Elsewhere, CNE has, on occasion, helped to organize new neighborhood associations and has provided ongoing technical assistance with organizational and maintenance issues when warranted.

Loan Collections and Post-Purchase Counseling

CNE has a portfolio of approximately $16 million in loans that it services. The portfolio is divided about 50-50 into home repair loans and CNE second mortgage loans for home purchases. The portfolio also includes a small volume of first mortgage loans that CNE originated but has not yet sold.

The over-30-day delinquency rate for CNE's home purchase loans is a remarkably low 1.1 percent, far below the national average of about 2.5 percent. CNE attributes its clients' on-time payment record to the effectiveness of its counseling and homeownership training assistance.

Of the 2,100 loans that have been serviced over 10 years, only 14 have been foreclosed on, and not for the usual reasons of simple nonpayment. Many rehab loans were made to elderly people. Eleven of these clients have died and left no heirs, requiring a foreclosure to clear title on the homes. Two borrowers moved and left the homes abandoned. And one paid off the first mortgage but refused to pay off the second.

CNE provides one-on-one post-purchase financial and technical counseling to its home buyers.

Partnerships

CNE's key partners are the City of Chattanooga, the Lyndhurst Foundation, local banks and lending institutions, and with other nonprofit housing groups in the city. Many of its construction and community programs are carried out in association with Habitat for Humanity in Chattanooga.

CNE also has strong alliances with YouthBuild, Construction Corps, and YouthCorps and other programs that target city teens and get them involved with construction projects. The teens gain experience building homes and working on landscaping at housing projects throughout Chattanooga.

Administration

Management and Staffing

Aside from HUD-funded public housing authorities, CNE is one of the nation's largest nonprofit organizations focusing almost exclusively on housing assistance. It has 42 fulltime, permanent staff members. There are four departments in the organization: home purchase, home improvement, rental/real estate, and development. The staff includes the following positions:

President and CEO
Assistant to the President
Vice-President and CFO
Controller
Vice-President, home improvement
Senior home improvement specialist
Home improvement specialist
Home improvement manager
Senior home improvement loan counselor
Home improvement loan counselor
Home improvement counselors (2)
Home improvement assistant
Vice-President, development
Development construction manager
Development project manager

Development assistant
Vice-President, real estate
Real estate assistant
Rental housing managers (2)
Education counselor
Vice-President, lending
Director, lending operations
Senior loan processor/underwriter
Loan closer
Loan processor/underwriter
Loan counselors/originators (2)
Loan servicer
Lending assistant
Director, marketing and community
  relations
Accounting manager
Accountant
Accounting assistant
Assistant, origination
Loan collection counselor
Administration secretary
Switchboard/Receptionist

Thirteen staff members are minorities.

In 1995, CNE also employed three interns, two sponsored by Community Corps and one sponsored by HUD.

Board of Directors

CNE, as of mid-1996, had a 28-person board of directors. Five of the members were business people, six were local elected or appointed government officials, and the balance were professionals or community representatives. Ten of the board members were members of minority groups.

The board, at that time, had a nine-person executive committee, which included the Mayor, one other local government official, CNE's CEO, three representatives of

financial institutions, and three community representatives.

Administrative Funding

For fiscal year 1995 (ended June 30 1995), CNE's general and administrative expenses were nearly $2.35 million with payroll costs amounting to almost half of that total. Costs allocated to CNE's single-family programs are about $700,000 a year, including both rehab and home purchase programs. The overhead for single-family lending is roughly $450,000 a year, while the overhead for single-family real estate development is about $250,000 a year.

For fiscal year 1996, the following sources of funds were projected as available to pay for administrative expenses:

Lyndhurst Foundation	$1,000,000
Program income	744,000
CDBG	272,000
City general funds	270,000
Hope 3 program	26,000
Hamilton County	24,000
Total	$2,336,000

Program income consisted of loan origination fees, home buyer training fees, interest incomes, and fees from real estate development projects.

Each participant in the FasTrak to Homeownership program pays a $100 fee, which contributes to the expenses of running the training program. Training fees are expected to net about $37,000 in 1996.

Another significant source of revenue is an average $1,045 in fees earned by CNE for each loan it originates. For FY 1996, these fees were projected to generate about $120,000 in revenues.

Financial Management

The scale and scope of CNE's financial activities require sophisticated management and accounting systems, which appear to be well established.

A significant part of CNE's staff is devoted to client financing and internal financial management. One of the five vice-presidents is the chief financial officer, who supervises a staff that includes a controller, an accounting manager, and two accounting assistants. A 12-person lending staff reports to the vice-president for lending.

CNE's financial health is highly dependent upon government funding and its volume of fee-generating business. While volumes of business and fees were below projections for FY 1995, its financial position remained strong, with over $484,000 net revenues versus $317,000 for the previous year.

CNE's fund balance (net worth) as of June 30, 1995 was $4.7 million, attributable mostly to equity in real estate properties and cash reserves. Its cash assets were nearly $1.2 million, generating over $76,000 in interest for the year. Its property was valued at over $4.4 million.

None of the below-market rate second mortgages originated by CNE is carried on its balance sheets. Since the loans were made with grant sources and are repaid at below-market rates, the organization has chosen not to show them as assets.

CNE's monthly management reports and annual report are forthcoming about potential management and financial weaknesses, and include continually updated action plans for achieving objectives and dealing with problems.

Information Management

Chattanooga Neighborhood Enterprise uses a custom-designed computer program to track each case from beginning to end. Its database provides access to current accounts, archives old accounts, and lists the number and types of cases worked since the program's inception, as well as billing and financial information. The system can easily retrieve information on individual cases, or create custom-designed summary reports for any time period in CNE's history.

Cash flow reports and projections are produced on a monthly basis.

Lessons Learned

Strengths of the Program

There is little question that CNE is achieving its overall mission to "develop, finance, renovate, and manage affordable housing for Chattanooga's and Hamilton County's low-to-moderate income citizens."

On an annual basis, CNE's single-family program helps more home purchase clients than almost any other single program in the country. The Neighborworks campaign sponsored by Neighborhood Reinvestment Corporation--of which CNE is an affiliate--tracked 83 participating programs for a 30-month period ending June 31, 1995. Having assisted 738 new homeowners, CNE was the clear leader. Its nearest competitors, Northside Minneapolis NHS and New York

City NHS, helped 367 and 264 clients respectively.

In this study, only the Dallas Affordable Housing Partnership (DAHP) exceeded CNE's annual number of home buyers. CNE sets tougher goals for its program in terms of home buyer training, counseling, and housing development. And its amortizing second mortgage loans, while effective and efficient in terms of fund usage, are less attractive to buyers than DAHP's loans, which are about three times larger and for which payments are completely deferred until resale of the property.

One can only speculate about the factors that contributed to the success of CNE's home purchase program. One, no doubt, is the big vision of the civic leadership that started CNE. Another factor, related to the first, is the major financial support CNE has received from the Lyndhurst Foundation and the City of Chattanooga. It is rare to find any city in the U.S. willing to invest the level of general fund monies that Chattanooga provides through CNE for housing assistance.

Achievement of Goals

CNE sets annual goals for production and financial performance in its various programs and development projects. The current FY 1996 business plan calls for assisting 320 home purchase clients with $13.7 million in financing.

As described earlier, CNE's management reports and annual report clearly indicate progress versus goals in both output and financial performance. Furthermore, rather than ignoring or glossing over problems,

CNE management acknowledges them and reacts.

For example, in FY 1995, the number of assisted home purchases was 23 percent lower than projected--attributed to an overall 32 percent dip in home sales in the local market during that period. The response was pragmatic--CNE trimmed personnel costs, increased client services through efficiency measures, and decreased the following year's production goals by 13 percent.

A Shallow-Subsidy Model

CNE uses what can be described as a shallow subsidy model. No assisted home purchaser gets a loan for more than $7,500, and all of the loans are repaid with interest over five to 20 years. This is in contrast to other programs that offer soft second mortgages of $15,000, $30,000 or more (with all repayments deferred until resale) to help make the home purchases more affordable.

This system appears to have worked in Chattanooga for three reasons.

▸ Homes are relatively inexpensive in Chattanooga, so second mortgage subsidies are less needed to keep monthly payments affordable.

▸ CNE has invested heavily in outreach, training, and counseling buyers so first mortgage lenders (including CNE itself) are more comfortable in exceeding the maximum 80 percent coverage of the purchase price that is common in many programs.

▶ The program works with a broader band of household incomes than many programs. Clients near the high end of CNE's range--115 percent of median income--obviously need less subsidy.

Future Prospects

CNE has experienced a slight three-year decline in its annual number of assisted home buyers. But the overall volume of housing assistance has not slowed. New real estate development projects on the drawing board are weighted more heavily toward building or renovating rental housing and including more market-rate housing with subsidized homes and apartments.

The home purchase program, at least for now, is increasing its focus on rehabilitating homes. It is beginning to offer market-rate rehabilitation loans to existing homeowners and is promoting HUD 203(k) insured loans for purchase of homes needing renovation.

CNE management is also planning for a future with less federal funding by exploring new sources of low-cost capital. One source is employer-financed second mortgages, described earlier.

In 1994, CNE branched out in another area by forming a subsidiary, Affordable Housing Services, Inc., to provide training, technical assistance and other services nationwide. This group provides formal training on CNE's techniques and contracted with GE Mortgage Insurance Corporation to provide post-purchase counseling via telephone to delinquent borrowers.

As the operator of one of the largest home purchase assistance programs in the nation, CNE has many lessons to offer other cities and housing finance organizations.

Among its most important contributions to the industry are its well-honed operating systems--represented by such things as its training manual, counseling procedures, and sophisticated computer software. These are the kinds of tools needed by other organizations that want to "think big."

Information Source

For more information, contact:

Leigh M. Ferguson
President & CEO
Chattanooga Neighborhood Enterprise, Inc.
535 Chestnut Street
Chattanooga, TN 37402
Phone: (423) 756-6201
Fax: (423) 756-6206

7

Dallas Affordable Housing Partnership
(The Enterprise Foundation, Dallas, Texas)

Program Highlights

Dallas Affordable Housing Partnership

Target Area:	City of Dallas (population 1,036,309)
Program Goal:	Assist low-income home buyers
Major Elements:	Deferred payment second mortgage loans First mortgage loans from lender consortium Referral to home buyer counseling and training
Average Client Incomes	$24,000
Typical Home Price:	$63,000 (existing); $75,000 (new) before subsidies
Year Started:	1991
Other Programs:	Capacity-building with nonprofit housing providers Hope 3 program Loans to multifamily housing projects
Staffing:	5 fulltime equivalent staff members
Annual Output: (1995-1996)	400 clients buying homes
Funding:	HOME funds from City of Dallas State housing trust fund CDBG program income Fees from participating banks Lender consortium (first mortgages) Federal Home Loan Bank

Overview

The Dallas Affordable Housing Partnership (DAHP) began in 1991 as an initiative of The Enterprise Foundation, the City of Dallas, and a consortium of private lenders. The intent was to bring more private financing into affordable housing programs in Dallas.

Five years later, DAHP is among the nation's highest-volume nonprofit-sponsored programs that assist low-income home buyers. In fiscal year 1995-1996, 400 home buyers received financial help. From the program's beginning in 1991 through September 1996, 1,021 deferred payment second mortgage loans have been made with over $7.5 million in funds provided by the City of Dallas, leveraging over $40 million in private financing.

As initially designed, DAHP was a separate legal entity that originated first mortgage loans for a consortium of local lenders. It was staffed by The Enterprise Foundation. Initially, DAHP originated single-family first mortgage loans using a line of credit from one of the participating lenders. DAHP also made soft second mortgage loans using HUD subsidy funds provided by the City.

As the program evolved, DAHP's managers learned that it was more efficient for the participating lenders to originate the first mortgage loans. Today, the program focuses exclusively on providing second mortgage financing for low-income home buyers in tandem with first mortgage lending from DAHP member-lenders.

The program is very streamlined. DAHP markets the program to banks and real estate brokers, who in turn help DAHP market the program to clients. Loan officers of the lending institutions take the applications for the program. Outside agencies provide counseling and training to prospective homeowners. Property inspections are performed by certified home inspectors, while an Enterprise inspector audits and reviews inspections.

As with most second mortgage programs, DAHP's helps to overcome the inability of clients to make conventional down payments. The borrower needs to contribute only three percent of the purchase price, while the DAHP second mortgage loan makes up another 20 percent. And because the first mortgage principal is reduced and no payments are due on the second mortgage loan until resale of the homes, the buyers' monthly housing payments are made more affordable.

In 1995, the maximum home price was increased from $65,000 to $80,000 and the maximum second mortgage loan amount from 10 percent to 20 percent. The maximum borrower income has been raised from 50 percent of median income to 80 percent.

The program is staffed and administered by The Enterprise Foundation's Dallas office, with the City, lenders, foundations, and Enterprise covering the operating costs. The Dallas Enterprise office also provides technical assistance and financing to local nonprofit housing developers with funding from HUD's HOME program, the National Community Development Initiative, and other sources. For every new home built for sale by nonprofits (these are currently small in number) DAHP generally provides first and second mortgages to the buyer.

Prior to the creation of the DAHP program, the City and lenders were frustrated in their efforts to increase homeownership among low-income families in Dallas. The City has a remarkably low rate of homeownership (44 percent versus 64 percent nationally), and the prevalence of homeowners tends to be even lower in low-income, inner-city neighborhoods.

In the early 1980s, the City had little involvement in housing development, even though it directly operated home repair programs financed with HUD funds and helped finance moderate-priced housing by issuing mortgage revenue bonds.

During much of the 1980s, the City searched for an effective strategy to expand its housing efforts and help revitalize declining areas. By the late 1980s, some growth in affordable housing production began to occur, particularly by nonprofits working with Enterprise. Even then, the production was mostly focused on multifamily housing. Because so much of the housing stock in low-income areas is investor-owned, many apartment buildings were distressed and crying out for attention, and the apartment buildings were easier to package and finance than scattered site single-family homes.

Pioneering in a Challenging Environment

In the mid- to late 1980s, the City had several contracts with nonprofit organizations and private lenders to help assist more low-income home buyers. But output was meager, and the City searched for other solutions. One of the obvious problems at that time (as in many cities) was the lack of any organized system for marketing first mortgage loans to low-income buyers and tying in special second mortgage financing. Community investment loan products were virtually unknown in Texas in the 1980s, and lenders were very shy about making loans to families with marginal incomes.

So in 1990, Enterprise proposed a new system to the City and a group of interested lenders. It was modeled after other successful homeownership assistance programs operated by Enterprise-affiliated organizations, in these ways.

▶ The soft second mortgages resembled those used in Baltimore and a number of other cities that had achieved success with inner-city housing development programs.

▶ The DAHP group of lenders was similar to lending consortia being launched in a number of cities at that time.

▶ A small but growing stream of single-family loans from community reinvestment programs was being sold to the secondary market, a nationwide trend that promised nearly limitless sources of capital for these programs.

Fannie Mae was closely involved in the design of the program, and as a result promised to buy its loans. Even so, the soft seconds and low down payments, which were approved by Fannie Mae, were thorny issues for local lenders. Some were concerned that foreclosures would be higher than average because buyers would have very small financial stakes in their new homes.

During the program's startup in the early 1990s, there were other complications. In Texas, overbuilding in the 1980s led to a decline in the real estate and banking industries. This regional real estate recession was more severe than the national one. As a result, some banks failed, and many others were bought out by larger banking firms. The turmoil in the industry made it appealing for Enterprise to originate the first and second mortgage loans and sell the first mortgage loans to Fannie Mae.

But by 1993, the participating lenders had all developed "affordable" lending products. Enterprise then could convince lenders to take on more program functions. Enterprise stopped originating first mortgage loans. Instead, clients were referred directly to lenders. Now, the lenders also process much of the paperwork for the second mortgage loans.

Enterprise coordinates the overall effort, certifies client incomes, ensures that the homes are properly inspected, approves the second mortgage, and manages the portfolio of second mortgages.

Market Analysis

The City

Dallas, with just over one million residents, has grown steadily over the years to become the nation's seventh largest city. Along with Fort Worth and Arlington, it is situated in one of the country's major metropolitan areas, which has a population of over four million.

The following table lists key demographic and economic data for the city:

	Dallas	USA
City population	1,006,877	
Population growth, 1980s:	13%	12%
Percent African American:	29%	12%
Percent Hispanic:	21%	9%
City median income, 1990s:	$27,489	$30,056
Metro median income, 1996:	$48,300	$41,600
Unemployment rate:	6.9%	6.7%
Poverty rate:	18%	13.1%
Median home value:	$78,800	$79,900
Home value increase, 1980s:	78.3%	67%
Median monthly rent:	$426	$447
Homeownership rate:	44.1%	64.2%

U.S. Census, 1990; 1996 median income from HUD.

In the 1900s, Dallas grew and thrived on the prosperity of the oil, land development, and cattle-raising businesses. But as with many cities in Texas and the West, much of its growth occurred during and after the wartime 1940s.

During the 1980s, despite a decline in the oil industry that led to a severe regional recession, Dallas' population still grew by about 1.3 percent a year--about the same rate as the nation as a whole.

As the statistics indicate, Dallas is a multicultural city. Like many of the larger midwestern and Texas cities in this study, Dallas has been a mecca for African Americans emigrating from the agricultural areas of East Texas and the deep south--largely as a result of the mechanization of cotton-growing and other agricultural businesses after World War II. Spanish-speaking people from rural Texas and Mexico have followed similar paths, leaving subsistence farms for the lure of jobs in the city.

The DAHP program almost exclusively serves minority home buyers. In September, 1996, 88 percent of clients approved for loans were Hispanic, and 11 percent were African American.

Boom and Bust Cycles

Historically, housing affordability in Dallas has been subject to wide swings as the city has experienced the notorious Texas boom and bust cycles. Economic prosperity (as in the oil boom of the early 1980s) quickly attracts new residents in search of jobs and tightens up the housing market. The real estate industry then over-builds, leading to sometimes dramatic drops in rents and home values. For example, during the 1980s, the number of households grew by 13 percent, but the number of housing units grew six percent faster.

These ups and downs have had major effects on low-income families and neighborhoods. For example, in 1984, over 2,000 families had federal Section 8 rental subsidy certificates in hand but could rarely find apartments that would accept them--and then almost never in the suburbs. In contrast, by 1990, suburban apartment owners experienced high vacancy rates and were advertising for Section 8 tenants.

Home values increased by 78 percent from 1980 to 1990, the second highest increase of any city in this study (only neighboring Fort Worth had a bigger increase). A much larger increase occurred before 1987, only to be reduced by a deflation in housing values during the late 1980s.

While the over-building of the late 1980s brought a little relief to low-income families, it had some negative effects on inner-city neighborhoods. Some stable, long-time residents found less expensive housing elsewhere and moved out. This created a negative winnowing effect that left the inner city with a higher percentage of families in poverty and resulting social problems. Some pockets of West Dallas and South Dallas experienced serious abandonment of housing. Today, most of that abandoned housing has been rehabbed, torn down, or reoccupied, although much of it is still in substandard condition.

Many housing developers and their lenders were also hurt by the housing recession in the late 1980s. Until recently, the Dallas-Fort Worth housing market had one of the largest inventories of foreclosed homes, apartment properties, and residential land in the country.

The housing market has since stabilized with the lower interest rates and steady economic growth of the 1990s. But despite a better environment for homeownership, Dallas is still a city of renters. As of the 1990 census, its homeownership rate was the second lowest of any city in this study.

But a low percentage of homeowners is more an opportunity than a problem in an entrepreneurial city that knows how to build and sell homes in large numbers.

Operations and Financing

Marketing

Since DAHP has always aimed to be a high-volume program, marketing is a high priority. When the program was originating both first and second mortgages, the enormous task of marketing a new program to the entire city was one of the factors that held back the program's growth. Also, because the program was trying to "do everything," it got a reputation with real estate brokers as being slow and cumbersome.

These marketing problems have lessened since the program was approved by Fannie Mae, lenders began originating the first mortgage loans, and the second mortgage loan processing was streamlined.

The 15 participating lenders market the program through all their branch offices. Enterprise staff members train the staff of participating lenders. And on a monthly basis, the lenders and Enterprise conduct seminars for real estate brokers, who bring most of the clients to the program. The seminars are used to explain the income criteria, the formula for funding second mortgages, and other aspects of the program.

Enterprise staff also attend housing fairs sponsored by various organizations in Dallas and pass out fliers at public celebrations and neighborhood events, often on a weekly basis.

Financing of Homes

The lender-members of DAHP are as follows (those marked with asterisks were founding members):

Bank of America, Texas*
Bank One, Texas*
Bank United of Texas*
Comerica Bank*
Compass Bank*
Fannie Mae
GMAC Mortgage Corporation
Guaranty Federal Bank*
Jefferson Mortgage
NationsBanc Mortgage Corporation*
Norwest Mortgage
Savings of America
Summit Mortgage
Sunbelt National Mortgage Corporation
Texas Commerce Bank*
Wells Fargo Bank (formerly First
    Interstate* in Texas)

The majority of DAHP first mortgage loans have low market interest rates. In addition, some members offer portfolio products (held in their own portfolios and not sold right away) with rates as much as a percentage point below market. Many of the members waive some fees. About 90 percent of the loans are sold to Fannie Mae.

All of the participating lenders offer very low-down-payment products, requiring only three to five percent of the purchase price. Fannie Mae requires only a three percent down payment.

For qualified low-income clients, DAHP makes a second mortgage loan for up to 20 percent of the sale price of the home, or appraised value (whichever is lower). Since home purchase prices are capped at $80,000, the maximum loan amount is $16,000. The average second mortgage loan is about $11,500. The loans are made at zero percent interest, with all repayments deferred until the property is resold, leased, or the title is transferred. The loans are funded with federal HOME funds passed through the City of Dallas to the program.

Currently, these loans must be repaid when homes are resold, but the City is considering a change that would make the loans forgivable over time.

Typically, a minimum three percent down payment is required by lenders. On a $60,000 home, closing costs (including prepaid interest, homeowner's insurance, and property taxes) average about $2,800. Down payments average about $1,800, for a total average cash requirement of about $4,600. About 90 percent of DAHP clients get $2,000 in closing cost assistance from the City, bringing the cash-to-close down to about $2,600.

The City has asked Enterprise to consider merging DAHP second mortgages and closing cost assistance into a one-stop program.

Most of DAHP's second mortgage loans are funded with the City's HOME entitlement grant. DAHP is a component of a broader HOME-funded and Enterprise-managed program called the Revolving Loan Fund. Also, Enterprise uses program income from repayments of multifamily project loans that were made with Community Development Block Grant (CDBG) funds.

Qualification for Assistance; Underwriting Criteria

To qualify for assistance, a client's household income must be below 80 percent of median income. This translated to $38,650 for a family of four in 1996.

To qualify for the DAHP second mortgage loan, the home purchased must be a one- to four-family structure located within Dallas. The home must appraise for at least 100 percent of the combined first and second mortgage amounts.

The standard Fannie Mae product offered by many of the lenders has flexible underwriting ratios--a maximum 33 percent of income for housing payments and 38 percent for all installment debt.

Other eligibility requirements for the second mortgage loan are as follows.

▶ Borrowers must successfully complete either a home buyer training course provided by a DAHP-approved organization or a take-home workbook.

▶ Borrowers must provide at least $500 out of pocket toward the purchase or meet the member-lender's minimum requirement. This requirement applies to clients who are using special portfolio first mortgage loan products that require very low cash-to-close amounts.

Intake and Screening

Most prospective DAHP clients have a home under contract when they apply for the program. Real estate brokers refer their lower-income clients to DAHP and perform a limited amount of prescreening. Most clients could not buy the homes without DAHP assistance, so brokers must be able to plug in the correct second mortgage amount and roughly screen for income eligibility.

Formal intake and screening functions for DAHP are performed by the lender in tandem with the application for a first mortgage loan. Funds for a DAHP second mortgage can be reserved for clients by a faxed application from the lender. The bank then forwards an abbreviated loan package to The Enterprise Foundation office, which is responsible for certifying that clients' incomes are at or below the maximums allowed by the HOME program and approves the second mortgage. In some cases, the lender's information is considered sufficient for qualification. If there are any inconsistencies, Enterprise staff asks the bank to perform further verifications.

When purchase contracts are being negotiated and loan applications made, Enterprise staff fields a high volume of phone calls from real estate agents and lenders to explain the fine points of the program.

Homeownership Training and Counseling

DAHP does not directly offer financial counseling or homeownership training. Instead, clients are referred to DAHP-approved training programs or they complete a take-home workbook published by Fannie Mae. The majority of clients complete the workbook rather than attend training. About 30 percent complete training and counseling offered by the Dallas County Home Loan Counseling Center. Smaller numbers of clients attend training offered by other nonprofit groups.

The County program consists of two to four hours of classroom training, plus referral to individual counselors in some cases.

Home Selection and Inspections

To date, DAHP has almost exclusively financed older, existing homes in the $50,000 to $80,000 price range. In late 1996, the average price of existing homes was about $60,000. More recently, builders have begun producing homes in new subdivisions and on infill lots that meet the program's cost guidelines. A total of about 30 new homes have been financed, with prices ranging from $65,000 to $79,000.

The 1,021 homes financed by DAHP up to September 1996, are located throughout Dallas, with no obvious concentrations in any one neighborhood.

Before any client can close on a home purchase, the property must be certified as meeting HUD's Housing Quality Standards (HQS). An approved inspector must conduct the home survey, which costs about $150 and is paid as a closing cost expense. In addition, a termite inspection company, paid by the seller, must certify that an existing home is termite-free. For new homes, the builder must provide evidence of soil treatments and other measures taken to prevent termite infestations.

In the early days of the program, Enterprise staff performed all the home inspections. As the volume of loans increased, a decision was made to use certified inspectors rather than add new inspectors to the staff. To control quality, the Enterprise inspector accompanies outside inspectors on the first five houses they inspect and audits 20 percent of their visits thereafter. Also, to be approved for the program, inspectors must successfully complete a training session with the Enterprise construction manager. In this way, inspectors new to the program receive on-site training in HQS compliance.

If HQS-related repairs are needed, sellers are required to complete them before closing (often as a condition of the sales contract). In this event, a certified and Enterprise-trained and approved inspector must certify HQS compliance before closing can take place.

Loan Collections and Post-Purchase Counseling

No formal study has been done to determine delinquency and default rates among DAHP clients. Staff members say that lenders are reporting these problems at normal rates.

Long-Term Affordability Controls

Each home purchased with a DAHP second mortgage is subject to a 15-year resale restriction (20 years for new construction) that tracks the requirements of the federal HOME program. If the home is sold during that period, it must be sold to a purchaser earning 80 percent or less of the Dallas area median income. However, if the second lien is repaid in full before resale, the income restriction is lifted.

Administration

Management and Staffing

The Enterprise Dallas office has a staff of 10, of which five fulltime equivalent positions are assigned to work on the DAHP program, as follows:

Dallas office director (half-time)
Single-family program manager
Loan administrators (2)
Single-family construction manager
Administrative assistant (half-time)

Two of the staff members are African American and one is Hispanic.

Board of Directors

In the early days of the DAHP program, its board of directors oversaw a separate legal entity. While administered by Enterprise staff, all funds passed though this separate corporation. But when the program stopped originating first mortgage loans, this separate legal and financial entity was no longer needed.

Nonetheless, the 15-member DAHP board has continued meeting and remains active in advising the program. The board makes decisions on admitting new lender-members. Out of concern for the long-term quality of the program, a group of board members is currently evaluating the homeownership training and counseling component. There is a consensus that this could become more effective.

Administrative Costs and Funding

The annual administrrative cost of the program is about $300,000. Salaries and other personnel-related costs total about $220,000.

Most of the administrative costs of the program are funded with HOME dollars from the City of Dallas. The administrative costs of the program were not made available.

Lessons Learned

Strengths of the Program

Among all local nonprofit-sponsored programs that offer special financing to low-income home buyers, DAHP may well have the highest annual output, having helped 400 families in its most recently completed fiscal year.

Several factors contributed to this success:

▶ Turning over origination of first mortgage loans to individual lenders in the DAHP program, rather than trying to centralize this function.

▶ The strong support of Fannie Mae, which buys about 90 percent of the first mortgage loans.

▶ Substantial funding for the second mortgages from the City of Dallas. In the last fiscal year, over $4 million in HOME funds were made available and used.

▶ Raising the maximum loan amounts, maximum allowed home prices, and maximum income limits for the program.

▶ Streamlining the processing of the second mortgage loan--primarily by using a portion of the first mortgage loan application package as the application for the second mortgage.

The program has also been resourceful in adapting to changing conditions. When the program began, the local lending industry was in the throes of consolidation and had very few special lending products to offer low-income home buyers. Thus, the program directly originated loans for a period of time and sold the loans to Fannie Mae.

As lenders added more flexible loan products, DAHP stopped originating first mortgage loans and began its move toward streamlining. More than any program in this study, DAHP relies on the energy of private, for-profit businesses to propel the program forward.

Achievement of Goals

DAHP sets annual goals as part of its contract with the City of Dallas. While in the past these goals were sometimes not achieved, 1996 saw the full effects of the streamlined approach. The program promised to close 375 loans in the past program year and exceeded that goal by 25 loans.

Hopes and Fears for the Future

Looking toward the future, the program's managers and the lenders on its advisory board will try to move in two directions: 1) further streamlining, and 2) increases in quality.

With regard to streamlining, the City of Dallas in mid-1996 asked Enterprise to develop a proposal for a one-stop program that would incorporate closing cost assistance, a deferred-payment second mortgage, and home buyer education. A plan is being worked on and will be presented to the City.

Regarding quality, DAHP wants to improve the training and counseling offered to clients. There is some concern that the take-home workbook is not sufficient to prepare all the clients. Also, DAHP wants to comply with any new lead hazard inspection and abatement procedures that may be required by federal laws and regulations.

Success has created some other challenges. Because of the high volume of loans being made, additional funding sources will be needed for the second mortgage loans.

As it confronts these opportunities and challenges, DAHP will continue to be a useful model for assisting large numbers of clients with very low internal overhead costs.

Information Sources

For more information, contact:

Julie Gunter, Director, Dallas Office
Sue Carlisle, Manager, Single-Family
  Program
The Enterprise Foundation
100 N. Central Expressway, Suite 1299
Dallas, TX 75201
Phone: (214) 651-7789
Fax: (214) 651-7231

8

Famicos Foundation
(Cleveland, Ohio)

Program Highlights

Famicos Foundation

Target Area:	Low-income Cleveland neighborhoods: Fairfax, Glenville, and Hough (combined population: 54,533)
Program Goals:	Assist low-income home buyers Revitalize inner-city neighborhoods Help families become self-sufficient
Major Elements:	Financial counseling and home buyer training Single-family housing development Lease/purchase program Other home sales
Average Client Income:	$18,000
Typical Home Price:	$35,000 before subsidies
Year Started:	1970
Other Programs:	Rental housing development and management Single-room-occupancy development Development assistance to other organizations Rental assistance program Emergency home repairs
Staffing:	6 fulltime and 4 part-time employees
Annual Output: (1993-1995)	25 homes developed and leased through the Cleveland Housing Network (average per year) 24 homes deeded to owners (average per year)
Funding:	Community Development Block Grants Equity raised from Low-Income Housing Tax Credits Net rental income and proceeds of home sales Developer and property management fees Foundation grants and individual contributions Fee-for-service contracts

Overview

The Famicos Foundation is a nonprofit community housing development organization founded in 1970 by the late Sister Henrietta Gorris, a member of the Sisters of Charity.

Committed to serving the neediest members of the population, the mission of the Famicos Foundation is to provide affordable housing to very low-income families in the Cleveland area. It specifically targets families that earn less than 30 percent of the median area income. Famicos began operating out of the Our Lady of Fatima Mission Center, distributing furniture, clothing, and food to the needy.

The Famicos Foundation operates in Hough, Glenville, and Fairfax, three contiguous low-income neighborhoods east of downtown Cleveland. Hough, in particular, was the epicenter of riots in the 1960s that scarred the neighborhood and led to widespread abandonment of its housing. In this difficult environment, Famicos began its housing program in 1970 by building eight new houses and helping existing homeowners with home repairs.

In an effort to achieve two goals--increased homeownership and rehabilitation of the neighborhood's housing stock--Famicos developed the lease-purchase model in 1976. Famicos was among the first, if not *the* first, nonprofit organization in the United States to use this model in an ongoing program.

Today, working in partnership with the Cleveland Housing Network, Famicos acquires substandard but structurally sound one- and two-family homes, usually through purchase but sometimes through donations from private individuals. Some of the properties have been repossessed by the FHA or a bank. Famicos thoroughly renovates the buildings and leases them at rents averaging under $300 a month to low-income people. A portion of the monthly rent pays off the debt incurred by Famicos in purchasing and rehabilitating the property. When the debt is repaid or almost repaid (15 years on average), the occupants of the house have the option to take ownership of the property at a nominal cost, generally less than $5,000.

As of 1995, over 450 homes had been renovated and leased in this way by Famicos, first working alone and later in conjunction with the Cleveland Housing Network. To date, 250 of the leased homes have been purchased by the occupants, who are now graduating from their lease arrangements at the rate of about 24 families a year.

Over the years, with a lean staff, Famicos has become a sophisticated housing provider and has branched into other areas of housing assistance. The organization now administers a tenant-based rental assistance program for Cuyahoga County, offers construction management services to other nonprofit groups, and administers a City-funded home repair grant program. It also has developed conventional but low-cost rental housing, having acquired and rehabilitated several multifamily buildings.

In 1996, Famicos began a large-scale construction program that is intended to revitalize the Rockefeller West area adjacent to Glendale. The first phase includes 50 new homes and 10 rehabilitated homes. Also, in an effort to improve the diversity of its target neighborhoods, Famicos is planning a new program to build market-rate homes and sell them outright.

The Lease-Purchase Program and the Cleveland Housing Network

The lease-purchase program was developed under the leadership of Dr. Robert Wolf, a retired chemical engineer who was recruited as a volunteer by Sr. Henrietta. Dr. Wolf served as volunteer director of the organization for over 20 years. In the early 1980s, he in turn recruited the current director, James Williams, to become one of the rehabilitation contractors for the lease-purchase program.

People who enter the lease-purchase program pay rent of between $175 and $370 a month. To remain in the program, they must remain tenants in good standing, increase their income and be off welfare by the lease's seventh year, take part in training sessions, perform certain maintenance duties, and maintain their rent payments to amortize the outstanding debt on the house.

All homes in the program are existing homes that require rehabilitation. Famicos acquires and renovates the homes for a total cost that averages about $35,000. All problems with the structure and mechanical systems are addressed. Clients are expected to provide some "sweat equity," which usually consists of painting and low skilled or semi-skilled work.

In 1980, Famicos began to replicate its lease-purchase model in other Cleveland neighborhoods by helping to found the Cleveland Housing Network. Today, the Cleveland Housing Network includes 14 member groups and produces about 300 units of affordable housing per year, about half of this using the lease-purchase model.

Self-Sufficiency Program

The Cleveland Housing Network is governed by a board comprised of representatives of the member housing organizations. Together, the Network and these organizations have renovated nearly 1,100 homes, of which half are simply rented to very low-income families, and half are subject to lease-purchase agreements. Citywide, just over 50 percent of the lease-purchase participants receive public assistance. Of these, about one-third (including many Famicos clients) are enrolled in a self-sufficiency effort called the Family Development Program. Through this program, which relies on government and private grants, families get help finding job training, day care, and employment.

For its part, Famicos helps families in the self-sufficiency program by granting temporary rent reductions while the head of household (typically a woman) completes job training. In one example, the rent was reduced from $208 a month to $24 a month for a 35-year-old tenant with four children.

Famicos has always stressed a minimalist, least-cost approach to rehabilitation, an approach that has kept homes affordable and easier to finance.

Initially, rehabilitation jobs focused on must-do repairs, structural work, and upgrades or replacements of mechanical systems. Painting and cosmetic work was often left to the families to complete after move-in. In the 1980s, the total development cost target was $15,000 per home, a figure that has crept up to $35,000 due to inflation and an expansion of typical scopes of renovation work. This penny-pinching strategy has been subject to some controversy. A recent audit of the citywide lease-purchase program found extensive deferred maintenance, but it was unclear whether this was the result of incomplete rehabilitation, lack of ongoing maintenance, or both.

Famicos--being one of the better-staffed, more financially solvent, and higher-producing lease-purchase organizations in Cleveland--has experienced less deferred maintenance than other developers.

Both Famicos and the Cleveland Housing Network have received extensive technical assistance and financing from The Enterprise Foundation. An Enterprise subsidiary, the Enterprise Social Investment Corporation, helped structure the first syndications of lease-purchase homes using the Low-Income Housing Tax Credit. Enterprise also provides low-interest loans, advice on project development, and more recently, expert help with upgrading Famicos' financial management systems.

Famicos and the Cleveland Housing Network (CHN) have also received major support for operations from the National Community Development Initiative (NCDI). NCDI has made grants to CHN that were used to increase staff funding and staff capacity of CHN-affiliates such as Famicos.

The NCDI grants were performance-based--that is, passed through as fees earned for completing certain development and management tasks. NCDI is funded by a consortium of major national foundations, corporations, and HUD. The program is administered in Cleveland by Enterprise, the Local Initiatives Support Corporation, and Neighborhood Progress, Inc.

Market Analysis

The City

Cleveland is a textbook example of a once booming city that in the late 1950s became part of the "rustbelt" as its heavy industries became outdated and challenged by global competition. With the demise of labor-intensive agriculture and mining in the south and Appalachia from the 1920s through the 1960s, Cleveland became a mecca for migrating rural families. Many of them were African American, and nearly all of them were very poor. The decline of the city's economy led to frustrated expectations among the new arrivals and ultimately to serious racial tensions and civil disorder.

The Target Areas: Glenville, Fairfax, and Hough

The Glenville, Fairfax, and Hough neighborhoods in East Cleveland, once home to middle-class and wealthy citizens, suffered a considerable decline that began in the 1950s and was accelerated by riots in the city in 1966. According to the 1990 census, the population of these areas can be broken up as follows: Fairfax, 8,973; Glenville, 25,845; and Hough (pronounced "Huff"), 19,715. The population of these areas is approximately 98 percent African American. An average of 55 percent of adults in these neighborhoods never finished high school. The median income for the combined area is $9,141 (Fairfax: $8,260; Glenville: $12,455; Hough: $6,719).

The following table lists key population, income, and housing statistics:

	Cleveland	USA
City population:	505,616	
Population growth, 1980s:	12.4%	12.6%
Percent African American:	46.5%	13%
Percent Hispanic:	4.6%	9%
City median income:	$17,822	$30,056
Metro median income, 1996:	$44,600	$41,600
Unemployment rate:	8.5%	6.7%
Poverty rate:	28.7%	13.1%
Median home value:	$40,900	$79,900
Home value increase, 1980s:	4.5%	67%
Median monthly rent:	$322	$447
Homeownership rate:	48%	64.2%

U.S. Census, 1990; 1996 median income from HUD

Approximately 29 percent of the homes in Fairfax are owner-occupied, while 17 percent are vacant and 54 percent are renter-occupied. In Glenville, 39 percent are owner-occupied and 48 percent are rental properties, while 13 percent are vacant. In Hough, only 20 percent of the homes are owner-occupied, 65 percent are renter-occupied, and 15 percent are vacant.

The median sales prices of homes in the neighborhoods are among the lowest in the country: $7,000 for Fairfax, $12,445 for Glendale, and $14,000 for Hough, according to the 1990 Census. The prices reflect the deteriorated state of existing housing, the lack of new construction, extremely low incomes of those with roots in the neighborhood, and lingering negative perceptions about the neighborhoods. However, because of the gradual revival of Cleveland's economy and the revitalization of the nearby downtown, property values are expected to creep up.

Famicos acquires and rehabilitates single family homes, many of them the old Victorian houses that line these once affluent streets. Including them in the lease-purchase program accomplishes two goals: making homeownership a possibility for low-income families and revitalizing declining areas of the city.

Operations and Financing

Marketing

Much of the marketing to new clients occurs through word-of-mouth referrals. Staff members at neighborhood churches, day-care facilities, and day camps are well aware of the program and make referrals. Famicos continually networks with other organizations and receives frequent media coverage.

Financing of Homes

Since the early days of the lease-purchase program, virtually every home has been financed by Community Development Block Grant (CDBG) dollars from the City of Cleveland--initially in the form of loans at zero percent interest that had to be repaid over 15 years. Each home receives $10,000 in CDBG financing. Rent payments are calculated to amortize the acquisition and rehab financing for each individual home and pay for each home's share of the management and operations of the rental properties as a group.

Over the years, the amount of rent calculated for payment of debt service has increased somewhat to yield an interest rate of five percent. The City allows Famicos or the Cleveland Housing Network to retain all repayments in revolving loans funds to be used for future development and financing activities.

But as the program expanded citywide, production increased, costs went up, and additional sources of funding had to be found.

In 1986, with assistance from The Enterprise Foundation and The Enterprise Social Investment Corporation, the Cleveland Housing Network (including Famicos) developed equity syndications, a unique approach to financing lease-purchase homes. Beginning in 1986, homes were financed in part by equity investments attracted by the newly created Low-Income Housing Tax Credit. This new approach created, in effect, a cash subsidy of about $15,000 per home. As an inevitable result of this complicated financing technique, it also increased soft costs by about $4,000.

For the syndicated homes, legal title is held by a limited partnership in which the Cleveland Housing Network is general partner. With non-syndicated homes financed by CDBG dollars, bank loans, and Famicos' cash flow, Famicos holds title. But with both types of homes, Famicos is the developer, construction manager, and property manager.

While federal tax credits have been used to finance multifamily, cooperative housing, the Cleveland lease-purchase program is one of the few examples of using these tax provisions to promote ownership of single-family homes.

In other ways, the lease-purchase program has stretched the envelope of federal programs. During the 1980s, Famicos and other members of the Cleveland Housing Network helped tenants get Section 8 rent subsidies so rent payments could be increased to market rates, which are about $100 higher than the discounted rents that are otherwise charged. In many cases, the subsidy reduces the tenant-paid portion of the rents, since tenants pay only 30 percent of income for rent and utilities, and HUD pays the difference between that payment and market rent. The higher cash flow allowed lease-purchase sponsors such as Famicos to borrow and repay conventional loans on the properties. Famicos hopes to recruit Section 8 recipients for its new Rockefeller West project.

Intake, Screening, and Counseling

Prospective participants in the lease-purchase program go through a rigorous screening before they can be accepted. To apply for the program, individuals must fill out an application and bring in copies of their birth certificate, a photo I.D., and current pay stubs. Their current landlord and employer are called for references. A police report and credit check are run. Then, if these hurdles are passed, a Famicos staff member conducts a home visit and a face-to-face interview.

During this process, some financial counseling occurs. But most of that takes place later, in formal homeownership training classes.

Qualification for Assistance

In order to qualify for the lease-purchase program, clients must have incomes at or below 40 percent of the area median income. Their landlord and employment references must check out. They must have minimally acceptable credit and no serious criminal record. They must accept the goals of the program. And they must show a willingness to attend training. There are no minimum requirements for income or employment. Applicants may be totally reliant on public assistance for cash income.

However, the program does look for positive attitudes and aspirations, and reviews past employment history. Applicants with poor employment histories and no career goals may not be accepted.

Homeownership Training

Until late in 1995, Famicos never offered formalized homeownership training workshops. Referrals were made to other agencies, and Famicos staff trained families one-on-one in home maintenance and the responsibilities of homeownership.

The new training program, developed in 1995, focusses on teaching two fundamentals: home maintenance and homeownership management. The training is required both for new clients and those who are about to take title to their homes. New clients do not necessarily attend the training before they move in. Some are allowed to attend later.

The training stresses maintenance and the responsibilities of homeownership. Since the acquisition and rehabilitation of homes is financed by Famicos or the Cleveland Housing Network, and participants will not take title to homes for 15 years, mortgage financing is not covered in the workshops, as it is in most home buyer training courses. (Even when homes are sold, Famicos self-finances about half the purchases.)

Home maintenance training combines on-site classes with hands-on practice of skills needed to properly maintain a home. The classes teach a basic understanding of a house's structure and systems, safety, conservation and energy efficiency, and specific maintenance and repair techniques.

The homeownership management segment of the training emphasizes the legal and financial aspects of ownership and covers such matters as deeds, liens, mortgages, and taxes. It also stresses the homeowners' responsibilities in managing their properties in ways that are supportive of the communities in which they live.

The training program is one of the most extensive of any examined in this study. It consists of 40 hours in 10 separate sessions.

Home Selection

Except on rare occasions, participants in the lease-purchase program have no role in selecting properties for purchase by Famicos. This is accomplished by Famicos' staff and volunteers, who choose homes to be acquired and rehabilitated based on their location, potential contribution to neighborhood revitalization, and--most importantly--the estimated total development cost. Famicos tries to keep this cost at $35,000 or less. Generally, acquisition costs are $5,000 to $10,000, reflecting the poor condition of the homes and low property values. Rehabilitation costs are $25,000 to $30,000.

Once homes are acquired by Famicos, families at the top of a waiting list can sometimes choose from among the homes under development. But on other occasions, they must take the only home that is available and of suitable size for the family.

Housing Development Activities

After about 10 years of acquiring and rehabilitating lease-purchase homes, Famicos branched out into other types of housing development.

Multifamily acquisition and rehabilitation of small multifamily properties--Between 1993 and 1996, Famicos purchased and renovated--and now manages--six buildings containing 71 rental apartments.

Lexington Village development--In 1984, Famicos completed an ambitious project in Hough that was a joint venture with a major national real estate development firm, McCormack-Baron & Associates. The 300-unit, mixed-income apartment and condominium project was the largest redevelopment project ever undertaken in Hough. In addition to conventional financing, the project received low-cost loans and grants from the City of Cleveland, the Cleveland Foundation, Ameritrust, the Ford Foundation, and the Gund Foundation.

Single-room-occupancy development-- In 1994, Famicos bought a 46-unit apartment building near downtown that was acquired through a court-ordered receivership. As of this writing, a $1.4 million renovation project is nearly completed. The units are a mix of efficiencies and small apartments.

Historic apartment building rehabilitation--A 19-unit apartment is being renovated with Low-Income Housing and Historic tax credits, as part of a larger revitalization effort in Hough.

Famicos is also starting two new projects intended to make a major impact on the Rockefeller West area, which overlaps the Glendale and St. Clair-Superior neighborhoods.

Scattered-site homes project--In this program, for the first time, Famicos will build new homes on a large scale. Fifty new houses are planned to fill in vacant lots that blight the neighborhood, and 10 existing homes are currently being renovated. All of the homes will be subject to lease-purchase arrangements.

A second historic apartment building rehab--An abandoned but prominent five-story building--the former Notre Dame Academy--will be converted to apartments for the elderly and a community center.

Long-Term Affordability Controls

Neither Famicos nor the Cleveland Housing Network places any special controls on resale prices of homes that are eventually sold under the lease-purchase program.

Assistance to Homeowners' Associations

Famicos has no formal ties to neighborhood associations but sometimes works with them informally when planning real estate developments, as with the Rockefeller West development.

Collections and Post-Purchase Counseling

Like any landlord, Famicos must be firm about tenants staying current with rent payments. For those lease-purchase participants who ultimately are unable to catch up on their rent, Famicos or the Cleveland Housing Network (whichever is the owner of record) must respond with eviction proceedings. Over the years about one in 20 participants in Famicos' lease-purchase program have been evicted.

Partners

As with many long-time survivors in the nonprofit housing world, Famicos has increased its abilities, respect, and influence over the years. This has led to a number of partnerships in addition to those already described (with the City of Cleveland, local and national foundations, NCDI, the Cleveland Housing Network, and 13 other Network member organizations). As a capable, well-staffed organization with 25 years of housing experience, Famicos is increasingly asked to advise and help other housing groups.

As examples of these partnerships, Famicos has recently worked with these organizations and projects:

► Mount Pleasant Now, Inc.: An 18-unit SRO development outside Famicos' target neighborhoods.

► AIDS Housing Council: A 12-unit supportive housing project.

► Cleveland Health Care for the Homeless: A day shelter and permanent housing for 20 homeless individuals.

► Family Transitional Housing: Rehabilitation of four townhouses and placement of 40 housing graduates in permanent housing operated by this special needs housing organization.

► Women Together, Inc.: Rehabilitation of a building to be used for transitional housing and an emergency shelter for single women and their families.

If there is a binding theme to these partnerships, it is Famicos' long-standing tradition of helping the very poor and most needy members of its community, the core of its mission since its founding days.

Administration

Management and Staffing

The Famicos homeownership program has 15 fulltime staff members and two part-time staff members. There is also a group of volunteers who assist with the various programs.

Executive director
Associate director
Development manager
Project managers
Special projects coordinators
(1 fulltime, 1 part-time)
Property managers
Assistant property manager (part-time)
Construction manager
Maintenance manager
Accountant
Receptionist
Interns

In 1996, a new construction company was being spun off. When fully operational, it should have 25 employees and should be self-supporting from revenues.

Board of Directors

Famicos' present board of directors has nine members, with the bylaws allowing a board with six to 12 members. Members include Dr. Wolf (the former volunteer executive director), the current Executive Director, James G. Williams, one other staff member who is a member of the Sisters of Charity, professionals, and neighborhood residents.

Administrative Funding

Famicos' financial statements for the fiscal year that ended in December 1995, showed income of $847,000, expenses of $765,000, and net revenues of $82,000 (all numbers are rounded to the nearest thousand). The statements included all of Famicos' activities except real estate purchases. Salaries were $269,000 for the year, with an additional $69,000 in benefits and payroll taxes. Other core overhead expenses (excluding direct program expenditures) were $67,000, for a total administrative cost of about $405,000.

The major sources of funding that paid the overhead and contributed to the revenue surplus were:

Proceeds of home sales	$83,000
Net rental income	$44,000
Development fees	$59,000
Grants	$9,000
Property management fees	$60,000
Construction management fees	$124,000
Donations	$18,000
Cleveland Housing Network pass-through funding	$15,000
Administrative fees for rental assistance program	$9,000

Many of the fees are the result of Famicos' relationship with the Cleveland Housing Network in operating the lease-purchase program. All of the construction management fees, $52,000 in property management fees, and $30,000 in developer fees were attributable to Famicos' relationship with the Network. In order to simplify syndications, the Network keeps title to the properties and pays member organizations, such as Famicos, on a fee-for-service basis out of the financing, cash flow from the program, and the NCDI grants previously described.

Financial Management

Given Famicos' involvement in real estate development and management activities, net revenues are subject to some swings. For example, in the fiscal year that ended in December 1994, Famicos experienced a $250,000 loss, as compared to an $82,000 gain in the following year. The loss was mostly a paper one--attributable to a write-off of $175,000 for the value of homes that were donated to tenants when they took title. The balance of the loss was attributable to startup costs of development projects in anticipation of future fees and other revenues--in effect, an investment in the future.

However, the organization has the resources to weather down years. In the 1994 financial statements, Famicos showed current assets of $815,000 versus current liabilities of only $191,000, real estate valued at about $560,000 after taking into account accumulated depreciation of $614,000. Long-term debt was only $270,000. Net worth at the end of 1995 was over $975,000. In addition, Famicos has available to it a $400,000 trust fund established by the O'Neil family. The fund can be used as flexible working capital for as long as Famicos is in business.

Information Management

Famicos has reached a scale of operation at which it can benefit from automation of its information and financial transactions. Personal computers are used for spreadsheets, word processing, accounting, and specification writing. Currently, property management software is being installed.

Lessons Learned

Strengths of Program

Famicos holds two special distinctions among nonprofit housing organizations in the United States. First, having been founded in 1970, it was one of the grandparents of the neighborhood-based housing development movement that only began to have a national impact in the 1980s. And second, it was the first nonprofit organization in the country to start a formalized, ongoing lease-purchase program.

The "Cleveland model" of lease-purchase--now operating throughout 14 neighborhoods in Cleveland--is not without flaws. Its low rate of renters graduating to homeownership is troubling to its sponsors and others (although Famicos has done better than average). Some outsiders may question whether a 15-year lease term really constitutes a homeownership program--particularly in light of the fact that lease-purchase programs in other cities allow lease periods of only a few months to a year.

But these concerns must be held up against the daunting market and social conditions faced by Famicos and other sponsors of the lease-purchase program in Cleveland. When they started, Cleveland was seen as a "has-been" city. Distressed neighborhoods such as Hough had lost as much as half of their population due to white flight, the loss of well-paying jobs, the aftermath of riots, and a resulting vicious cycle of poverty. Famicos' neighborhoods contain some of the poorest census tracts in the United States.

In this context, the long lease term appears to be a response to the very low average incomes and fragile economic circumstances of clients in the program. Few, if any, can go from renters to bankable home buyers in a year or two. In addition, the use of syndicated financing now dictates a 15- to 20-year lease term.

Overcoming Formidable Obstacles

The obstacles to running a home ownership program in this environment are difficult to fathom. But driven by a mission to serve the very poor, Famicos accomplished what was said to be impossible--bringing homeownership to a population whose primary incomes consisted of public assistance, and in neighborhoods full of boarded-up houses, vacant lots, and a predominance of renters. Even today, few professional planners would consider a conventional homeownership program feasible in Famicos' neighborhoods, even though Cleveland as a whole has received nationwide recognition for its recent renaissance.

Since very few of the prospective homeowners were bankable, Famicos had to go to the bank for them. Since the rents had to be very low--in fact, not far above the bare operating costs of the housing and the program--conventional debt was not

possible, and the "bank" had to be the City of Cleveland and generous foundations. Even though banks have been involved in subsequent projects, the low market values in the target neighborhoods are still a major impediment to conventional investment. And since subsidy money was scarce and the needs for decent housing seemingly endless, Famicos has always been an advocate for pinching pennies and containing costs.

Given these realities, the fact that Famicos and its partnership with the Cleveland Housing Network have created 250 homeowners is more remarkable than its having 200 families still to graduate. The recent effort to provide intensive homeownership training may increase the graduation rate. Even so, if some families remain renters for the foreseeable future a basic goal of providing decent, affordable housing has still been served, and neighborhoods are gradually being revitalized house by house.

Service-Enriched Housing

Famicos also helped to pioneer another approach to community development that is now rapidly gaining favor--so-called "service enriched" housing. This approach is attributable to Famicos' origins in a religious order dedicated to serving the poor. Early in the lease-purchase program, Famicos appointed a family advocate to work with families on immediate crises and long-range goals, such as job training and employment.

It could even be said that Famicos' primary business is people development, not housing development. This focus on putting needs of clients first is evidenced in its branching out from the lease-purchase program and expanded participation in developing homeless shelters, transitional housing, housing for the elderly, rent subsidy programs, and self-sufficiency programs for those at the bottom of Cleveland's economic ladder.

The wide range of Famicos' activities could easily overwhelm a less experienced organization. But Famicos appears to be building on strengths--namely, its financial capability and its skills in project and construction management. And it always keeps a businesslike eye on the bottom line, earning fees and program income wherever it can.

Hopes and Fears for the Future

Looking toward the future, Famicos has a number of ambitious goals besides the continuation of its lease-purchase program. They include:

► Developing more housing for populations with special needs;

► Expanding new construction of homes;

► Beginning to make outright sales of both new and rehabilitated homes;

► Expanding its in-house construction management group to allow hiring of more people from the neighborhoods, homeless people, minorities, and women.

Continuing cutbacks in federal funds and the impending sunset of the Low- Income Housing Tax Credit could hamper future production. But Famicos will fare as well as any nonprofit housing organization in an uncertain future. It has a number of assets: experience; internal financial resources; and strong alliances with city government, the Cleveland Housing Network, and other nonprofits.

Information Source

For more information, contact:

James G. Williams, Director
Famicos Foundation, Inc.
7049 Superior Avenue
Cleveland, OH 44103
Phone: (216) 431-3461
Fax: (216) 431-9962

9

Garrett County Community Action Committee
(Oakland, Maryland)

Program Highlights

Garrett County Community Action Committee, Inc.

Target Area:	Garrett County, Maryland (population 29,024)
Program Goals:	Assist low-income home buyers Eliminate substandard housing Increase family self-sufficiency
Major Elements:	Financial counseling and home buyer training Assistance with first mortgages; second mortgage subsidies Single-family housing development
Average Client Income:	$21,000
Typical Home Price:	$70,000 before subsidies
Year Started:	1995
Other Programs:	Rental subsidy assistance for existing housing Home weatherization grants and home repair loans Energy assistance Revolving loan fund for private rental housing development Shelter grants and loans for homeless persons Housing, nutrition, and other services for the elderly Head Start; economic development assistance Surplus food and co-op food buying programs
Staffing:	115 fulltime and 4 part-time employees for all programs 2 fulltime equivalent positions assigned to homeownership
Annual Output: (1995)	131 prospective home buyers trained 17 second mortgage loans made to buyers 5 homes newly constructed and leased with purchase option
Funding:	Private mortgage financing HOME funds (for second mortgages) Rural Housing Service Section 502 loans Federal Home Loan Bank Community Improvement Program Counseling and training fees paid by home buyers State, federal, and local grants for administration

Overview

The Garrett County Community Action Committee (CAC) began a new homeownership assistance program in 1995 as an outgrowth of nearly 30 years of experience helping low-income people with a variety of services and other kinds of housing programs.

The Community Action Committee was founded in 1966, one of many local nonprofit agencies that were organized at that time in response to newly available federal funding for anti-poverty programs. Its mission is to address the needs of the low-income, elderly, and handicapped residents of Garrett County. Through a number of housing and human services programs, CAC is helping about 2,300 low-income households at any given time.

CAC's other housing programs include home weatherization grants, home repair loans, rent subsidies, and housing development.

Over the years, the agency has helped to rehabilitate 325 housing units and has built 185 new housing units, most of them rental apartments.

Its experience with helping new homeowners goes back to 1987, when it developed a 19-lot subdivision. At that time, the agency began to provide information and referrals for the State of Maryland's mortgage assistance program. In 1989, CAC also began acquiring scattered-site house lots for resale to low-income families.

The organization's newest homeownership program provides home buyer training, counseling, and soft second mortgages for up to 20 percent of the purchase of a home in tandem with first mortgages from a local lender.

The financial assistance program started in 1995 using federal HOME funds passed through the state Department of Housing and Community Development, and this was augmented in 1996 by low-interest loan money and loan guarantees from the federal Rural Housing Service (formerly called the Farmer's Home Administration).

In the first stage of CAC's history, it was primarily a community organizer. It identified six target communities in the county with pockets of poverty and helped them provide such essential services as fire protection and community centers. At that time, it also helped to establish countywide service programs for the elderly, pre-school children, the developmentally disabled, and substance abusers.

In the early 1980s, CAC began to expand into more social service programs and housing development. Developing self-sufficiency from revenue-producing activities rather than relying almost solely on government grants became a priority. CAC established revolving loan funds for housing, directly developed some elderly housing using a variety of state and federal funds, and entered into partnerships with private housing developers. The agency administers State- and HUD-funded Section 8 rental subsidies that assist 274 low-income households in private rental housing. It also provides emergency loans and grants to help house the homeless.

In the late 1980s and early 1990s, CAC began to place much more emphasis on family self-sufficiency as a unifying theme for all of its programs. Instead of operating isolated projects and programs, CAC aims to provide a seamless service system, whose success is measured by positive changes in families, rather than the amount of services that have been provided. As part of this philosophy, CAC aims to provide a continuum of housing services that leads from emergency shelter to rental assistance to home ownership.

Market Analysis

Garrett County is a rural county in westernmost Maryland. It is situated entirely in the Allegheny plateau of the Appalachian Mountain range about 120 miles south of Pittsburgh and 180 miles west of Baltimore.

The population is widely dispersed. The Oakland/Mt. Lake Park area is the most highly populated with over 6,000 people. But less than 22 percent of the estimated 1992 population of 29,024 lives within any one of the county's eight incorporated towns. Historically, the economy was based on farming, mining, and timber-related industries. But since the 1970s, the primary employers have been government, retail trade, and tourism. Deep Creek Lake and skiing resorts are major tourist destinations. Twenty-five percent of the land is owned by the state.

The relatively low poverty rate masks the fact that an unusually large number of county residents have extremely low incomes. Nearly a third of all households had incomes under $15,000, according to the 1990 census--more than any other city or county in this study, but fairly typical of rural counties that are far removed from urban areas.

Employment in Garrett County has increased steadily over the past two decades. Despite this, the unemployment rate, at 11.6 percent in 1995, was still twice as high as in the state of Maryland as a whole. Over three-quarters of the county's poor are employed, which indicates that much of the employment is seasonal and pays low wages.

In the table below are key statistics for population, income, and housing:

	Garrett County	USA
County population:	28,138	
Population growth, 1980s:	9.6%	12.6%
Percent African American:	<1%	13%
Percent Hispanic:	<1%	9%
City median income:	$22,773	$30,056
County median income, 1996:	$32,500	$41,600
Unemployment rate:	10.7%	6.7%
Poverty rate:	14.7%	13.1%
Median home values:	$60,000	$79,900
Home value increase, 1980s:	68.6%	67%
Median monthly rent:	$310	$447
Homeownership rate:	79%	64.2%

U.S. Census, 1990; 1996 median income from HUD.

Seventeen percent of housing units are mobile homes. The homeownership rate, at 79 percent, is the highest of any city or county in this study, and high even for a predominantly rural area. But the low-wage economy still results in serious housing affordability problems. HUD data from 1994 shows that 78 percent of the county's households with incomes below 30 percent of the median have housing problems--in terms of excessive cost burdens, substandard conditions, or both.

Operations and Financing

Marketing

Clients for CAC's current home buyer assistance program are recruited from among its 274 clients who receive rental assistance payments and through referrals by local lending institutions.

CAC publishes brochures advertising its program. The brochures and leaflets spell out income requirements for prospective participants, as well as the features and benefits of the program. The program puts out press releases and has received good media coverage.

Other marketing techniques have included speeches at civic clubs, contacts with churches, and fliers put in the pay envelopes of county employees.

Financing of Homes

Until recently, CAC only offered second mortgage financing of up to 20 percent of

acquisition costs plus closing costs in tandem with a first mortgage loan from a conventional lender. The second mortgages are actually originated by the Maryland Department of Housing and Community Development's Home Loan Program, but CAC does the marketing and most of the processing and has the authority to approve loans. The state agency allocated $250,000 in federal HOME funds for the first year of the program, which is unique to Garrett County.

To date, cooperating private lenders have included American Trust Bank, First United Bank, and First Federal Bank, which originates loans for the Keystone Financial Mortgage Company.

The deferred payment second mortgages are made at zero percent interest, with all payments deferred until sale of the property. The loan principal is forgiven over the following number of years:

Less than $15,000	5 years
$15,000 to $40,000	10 years
Over $40,000	15 years

Innovative Tandem Loans

In 1996, Garrett County became one of nine communities in the U.S. selected to participate in a national homeownership project intended to field test a partnership between the CAC, the Federal Home Loan Bank System (FHLB), the Rural Housing Service (part of the Department of Agriculture), and the Local Initiatives Support Corporation.

The program results in better interest rates, so most CAC home buyer clients are expected to use this new product. By late

1996, eight families had already bought homes through this pilot program. Over the next two years, the program is expected to provide about 100 low-cost mortgages for low- and moderate-income families.

Under this program, families will qualify for a 33-year fixed-rate mortgage at below-market rates. Initially, the loans were originated by the American Trust Bank, which used a matched funding arrangement with FHLB to reduce mortgage rates. The bank borrows long-term capital at wholesale market interest rates from FHLB's Community Improvement Program to compensate for making low-interest loans. This matched funding approach acts as a hedge against future increases in interest rates, which could otherwise make the loans unprofitable in future years.

RHS uses its Section 502 program to guarantee mortgages for buyers with incomes up to 115 percent of median income. That brings the interest rates down even more, since the secondary market will price these very secure loans at below-market rates.

In addition, income-qualified borrowers can get an interest-subsidized Section 502 loan from RHS that is secured by a second mortgage. Called the Leveraged Loan Program by RHS, this approach is normally used with market-rate first mortgage loans. In this case, it is being used creatively with below-market first mortgage loans, creating a very low blended rate. For RHS to participate, the bank must lend at least 50 percent of appraised value.

If the interest rates in this program are still too high for some very low-income clients, CAC can piggyback its HOME funds as a deferred payment third mortgage.

While this pilot program is complex in terms of sources and types of financing, it meets the needs of a broad band of low- and moderate-income buyers.

Qualification for Assistance; Underwriting Criteria

In order to qualify for CAC's special home purchase financing, applicants must live in Garrett County, have an income below 80 percent of the area median income ($33,600 for a family of four), demonstrate a stable income or employment history, and indicate an ability to assume the financial responsibilities of homeownership.

Applicants must be first-time home buyers, and the homes purchased must be located within Garrett County. When HOME funding is used, the appraised value of the home must not exceed the HUD-established limit for Garrett County, which was $85,500 in early 1996. An applicant must be able to secure a loan from a conventional lending institution or otherwise finance with non-CAC funds at least 80 percent of the purchase costs of the home. In addition, the total of the liens on a home may not exceed its appraised value.

A fee of $1,150 is collected at closing to cover costs of training and counseling.

Those who are participants in Section 8 rental housing programs are particularly targeted as potential home buyers. If interested, these clients receive extra counseling to improve their employment and credit standing.

A typical lender, Keystone Financial Mortgage Company, uses conventional underwriting criteria with most of its CAC clients: a 28 percent ratio for housing payments, a 36 percent ratio for all installment debt, and an 80 percent loan-to-value ratio. But cash required from the borrower has been reduced to only three percent, and application fees have been waived. If mortgage insurance is used, the debt ratios are liberalized to 33/40, and the loan-to-value ratio is increased to 95 percent.

Interest rates of the participating lenders were within the typical range of market rates as of August 1996.

Intake, Screening, and Counseling

When applicants sign up for the program, they are automatically enrolled in a counseling and training program that prepares them for buying a home. No preapplication or screening is required before the training takes place. The real screening for the program comes when applicants apply for loans from participating lenders. If they can obtain a first mortgage loan and meet the program's income criteria, approval of the second mortgage loans is nearly automatic. Counseling on finances and the home purchase process is provided as needed by CAC personnel.

Homeownership Training

The Community Action Committee's six-hour training workshops concentrate on budgeting, understanding mortgages and mortgage guidelines, the process of home selection and purchase, and home maintenance. The workshops feature loan officers, financial planners, and other guest speakers from the local business community.

Home Selection

Prospective purchasers can buy homes, or lots for homes, anywhere in Garrett County, as long as the home or building plan falls within their income limits. Working with Habitat for Humanity, CAC is able to help people prepare for the building of new homes on sites they have chosen.

Conventional homes range in price from $60,000 to $80,000, while the cost of Habitat homes is considerably less. CAC is planning to provide some of its low-cost financing to Habitat clients, but had not done so as of late 1996.

Lease-Purchase Program

Recently, CAC built five homes for clients in its self-sufficiency program. All of them are renters but are expected to buy the homes when they can qualify for a first mortgage. The first buyers were expected to close in the fall of 1996.

Currently, CAC has no plans to sell additional homes under lease-purchase agreements.

Housing Development Activities

CAC has become increasingly involved with real estate development. Since 1984, nearly $10 million has been invested in successfully completed projects, and another $7 million in projects are in development. These include rental projects, land development, public facilities, and new offices for the agency. CAC also provides direct assistance to other private, nonprofit, and public developers in the form of financing and technical assistance.

To date, CAC has sponsored several real estate developments designed to encourage homeownership, as follows.

Woodridge Park subdivision (1987): This 19-lot subdivision was created in cooperation with Habitat for Humanity. CAC purchased and improved the raw land (streets, water and sewer) and helped families qualify for mortgages from FmHA, Habitat for Humanity, and the State of Maryland. Total development costs were $315,000. The average price of homes was $54,122. The average household income of home buyers was $14,871. All of the homes have either been bought or have a buyer.

Scattered-site homeownership program (1989): In this program, 14 lots were acquired at various locations around the county and were sold to low-income families. CAC also helped the families obtain mortgage financing. The lots ranged in price from $5,000 to $17,000, and the total costs of lots and homes ranged from $28,000 to $66,000.

CAC has also been involved in developing the following rental properties.

Moderate Rehabilitation Program (1984-85): This program used HUD's Section 8 Moderate Rehabilitation rent subsidies to help support mortgage financing for rental properties needing rehabilitation. CAC converted several properties into 14 units of low-income family rental housing, at a total project cost of $455,575. It also assisted 11 private developers, who produced 50 more units. A revolving loan fund helped finance the projects.

Truesdell Assisted Elderly Home (1985): CAC converted a single-family home into a group home for six frail, low-income elderly residents who require 24-hour assistance but do not need nursing care. Development costs were $110,000 and were financed with CDBG funds, financing from local banks, and equity funds. CAC owns and manages the home.

Parkwood Village (1993): This is a 32-unit low-income family rental property. Total development costs were $2 million. The Community Action Committee is the general partner and contracts with a private firm for property management.

Oakwood Village (1994): This 32-unit rental project for elderly and disabled residents was funded by FmHA, ARC, HOME, and tax credits. Total development cost was $1.9 million. The Community Action Committee is the general partner and contracts out management.

HOME-funded rental units (1995): CAC acquired and rehabbed five units for low-income family housing. CAC is the owner and manager of the units. Total development costs were $224,000. Financing came from local banks, HOME, and ARC.

Loan Collections and Post-Purchase Counseling

CAC officials say they are not aware of any delinquencies or defaults in the second mortgage assistance program. But because the program started in 1995, it is unlikely that these problems would be experienced as of this writing, less than a year later.

Long-Term Affordability Controls

Buyers who purchase homes with CAC's second mortgage financing are not subject to any special resale controls, except for those who receive HOME funding. Then, the minimal HOME requirements apply--these encourage resales to low-income buyers.

Assistance to Neighborhood Associations

CAC has no formal ties to neighborhood associations, but it is willing to assist "where needed and when requested."

Partners

CAC works with American Trust Bank and Keystone Financial Mortgage Corporation of Oakland, Maryland, to finance the purchase of homes. The agency also works closely with Habitat for Humanity to both obtain financing and build homes. Habitat offers no-interest mortgages with no down payment.

Most of CAC's funding comes from federal and state sources. The state Department of Housing and Community Development is an indispensable partner for the second mortgage financing program. The home buyer assistance program also benefits from close cooperation with builders and

realtors and the broad support of the community.

Likewise, CAC's relationships with the Rural Housing Service, and the Federal Home Loan Bank's Affordable Housing Program have also gotten good results.

Administration

Management and Staffing

The staff of Garrett County Community Action Committee consists of 115 fulltime and four part-time staff members. The administration is broken down into: executive office, finance general services, family development, community services, community development programs, and economic community development.

Two staff positions are dedicated to the homeownership program--a loan director and a loan officer, who does the counseling work.

Board of Directors

As of December 1995, CAC's board of directors had 15 members. These included five private organization representatives--a banker, a District Court judge, a health department official, a realtor, and a social worker. The membership also included five low-income/community representatives, and five county commissioners. The county commissioners appoint the other members.

Administrative Costs and Funding

For the fiscal year ending September 30, 1994, CAC showed the following core overhead expenses on its tax return (all figures are rounded to the nearest thousand dollars).

Salaries and wages	$1,279,000
Employee benefits	546,000
Telephone	35,000
Office space and utilities	160,000
Equipment	37,000
Travel	289,000
Insurance	53,000
Staff training	28,000

The balance of the organization's total $5.2 million in expenses were related to direct program costs. For example, $1,144,000 was spent on rental assistance and fuel assistance. Administrative costs of the homeownership programs were not separately identified in the financial statements.

On the same tax return, total revenues were over $5.9 million and came from the following sources (rounded to the nearest thousand dollars).

Government grants	$4,648,000
Public support	551,000
Program revenues (including government contracts)	698,000
Investment income	32,000

Financial Management

As of late 1994, CAC was very healthy financially. It had $4,151,000 in fund balances (net worth) and net revenues in that fiscal year of $705,000. A five-person finance department tracks and manages the organization's complex finances.

Information Management

In 1994 and 1995, CAC upgraded its automation of information management for tracking and managing client services and financial transactions. It installed Fund Ware software that fully integrated its accounting system and automated its accounting for rent subsidy payments. In addition, it installed an automated client referral and tracking system that, in part, was an outgrowth of the organization's focus on client results rather than client services.

Lessons Learned

Strengths of the Program

In many rural areas, starting a home buyer assistance program involves difficulties not experienced in urban settings. First, the scale of rural markets is typically very small--there are fewer ready buyers and fewer suitable and affordable properties on the market. In Garrett County, fewer than 2,200 households are not already owner-occupants. Many of these--because of age, infirmity, incomes that are over the program limits, or other reasons--are simply not candidates for the program.

Second, in Garrett County, as in many rural counties, home prices appear affordable at first glance, but are out of reach for many buyers because their incomes are exceptionally low. Also, there are fewer opportunities for stable employment, making it harder for prospective home buyers to get loans even if their incomes (for the moment) are sufficient to make repayments.

On the other hand, potential home buyers in rural areas are more likely to have savvy and skills related to building and renovating homes. Thus, it is fitting that the Community Action Committee's program would start by developing lots rather than homes, and that it has worked with Habitat for Humanity, which taps the great potential for sweat equity and volunteer work to make housing more affordable.

With the HOME-funded second mortgage program, the level of subsidy--20 percent of the acquisition costs as a deferred payment loan--seems appropriate for this kind of market. It is large enough to reduce the risks for private lenders and to get them involved with providing first mortgages to marginally eligible buyers.

The newer product, using Federal Home Loan Bank advances and Rural Housing Service loan guarantees and second mortgages can be combined with HOME to serve very low-income clients. The combined financing mechanisms are innovative and replicable in many rural markets.

Hopes and Fears for the Future

While CAC is happy with its new program, it faces a number of challenges. Educating clients proved to be harder than expected. It was especially difficult to impress upon them the importance of monitoring their credit and purchasing habits. The lack of decent, affordable homes in the market is another problem, especially when weighed against the fragile job market in Garrett County. At this writing, the local Habitat for Humanity is helping provide some new low-cost homes, but there is a limit to what sweat equity and volunteer programs can produce.

If all goes well, CAC's new and creative financing programs could create a new market for homebuilders who want to concentrate on the low end of the market.

In order to encourage more home purchases, the agency hopes to further streamline its application and qualifying processes and improve its marketing. And over the long term, it hopes to use its substantial experience and resources to construct entry-level homes.

Information Sources

For more information, contact:

Duane Yoder, Executive Director, or
Pam Nelson, Director of Community
  Services and Family Development
Garrett County Community Action
  Committee, Inc.
104 East Center Street
Oakland, MD 21550
Phone: (301) 334-9431

10

Habitat for Humanity
(Charlotte, North Carolina)

Program Highlights

Habitat for Humanity of Charlotte

Target Area:	Low-income census tracts in the City of Charlotte (combined population, about 12,000)
Program Goals:	Assist low-income home buyers Revitalize inner-city neighborhoods Encourage family self-sufficiency Encourage bonds between affluent and low-income people
Major Elements:	Financial counseling and home buyer training New home construction with sweat equity and volunteers Provision of mortgages
Average Client Income:	$14,000
Typical Home Price:	$47,000 (all new homes)
Year Started:	1983
Other Programs:	Support of Habitat program in El Salvador
Staffing:	14 fulltime staff members
Annual Output:	31 new homes built and sold (1996 estimate)
Funding:	Private contributions Corporate grants In-kind donations Repayments to loan fund Government funds (for land and infrastructure only)

Overview

Habitat for Humanity of Charlotte, founded in 1984, is one of the leading local Habitat affiliates in the country.

Among Habitat affiliates, the organization was the first to build 200 homes with volunteers, to build a home in 24 hours, and to build 22 homes in one week. It was also the first to build a home with all women volunteers, and another home with all youth volunteers. It was the first to see existing Habitat homeowners raise funds and build a home for another homeowner.

The parent organization, Habitat for Humanity International, was organized in 1976 in Americus, Georgia, as an ecumenical Christian housing ministry. Its founder and director is Millard Fuller, a successful businessman who renounced his wealth to start an organization that has become famous worldwide for its efforts in bringing homeownership to poor families. To date, the organization has been involved in over 1,200 home building projects in the United States and 100 others in 30 foreign countries.

Habitat affiliates get the most publicity for their House Raising Week. During this week, the Jimmy Carter Work Camps conduct a home-building blitz, choosing a different U.S. city each year. When Jimmy Carter helped Habitat in 1987, it set its record of building 22 homes in one week.

In years past, Habitat for Humanity International sponsored and managed some local projects in the United States, and it continues to do so overseas. But in the United States today, all new Habitat projects are carried out by over 600 affiliated local organizations. The affiliates are all incorporated as separate legal entities.

In Charlotte, as elsewhere, the local affiliate has its own board of directors and is responsible for raising its own funds, recruiting staff and volunteers, and managing its own programs. Habitat International provides technical assistance and moral support to the affiliates, as well as national publicity for the Habitat movement. New affiliates follow a how-to operations manual published by Habitat International. A small staff of technical advisors covers different regions of the country.

In addition, local affiliates are asked to abide by some general operating principles. Affiliates must commit to rely on volunteers and sweat equity, to accept only limited government funding, and to charge no interest on their loans. While contractors and paid staff are used for technical tasks and program management, most Habitat homes are built with volunteer labor and tax-deductible contributions of money and materials.

Typically, Habitat affiliates provide 100 percent financing of the cash costs of the homes. Repayments are returned to revolving loan funds to finance future housing construction.

Besides providing decent, affordable housing, one of the core goals of the Habitat movement is to have affluent and needy people work together in order to build new relationships and a sense of community. Likewise, sweat equity by future homeowners is valued not just as a cost-cutting measure, but as a tool to build pride of ownership and to develop relationships among home buyers and community volunteers.

With community volunteers, Habitat works with homeowners and purchasers in building or renovating a home. Houses are sold at no profit to low-income families, and no-interest mortgages are issued over a fixed period. Currently, a typical Habitat house in the United States costs an average of $35,000.

Habitat of Charlotte also helps with the overseas housing program. In 1995, it provided $65,000 in contributions and 25 workers to its sister affiliate in El Salvador for its home building program.

Habitat is essentially a grassroots organization. Neighborhood and community volunteers get together and plan ways to raise funds. Those interested in starting new affiliates may contact the International Headquarters in Americus, Georgia. The address is listed at the end of this case study.

For the Future: Foundation 2000

Habitat of Charlotte has set an ambitious goal for the year 2000. Under its Foundation 2000 Program, the organization plans to build 250 more homes by the end of that year. This will bring the total number of Habitat homes built to 500 by the end of the year 2000. This project will require a great deal of volunteer labor, so an extra staff person was added in 1996 to coordinate volunteers. To achieve these goals, Habitat of Charlotte will have to nearly double its production, from 32 homes a year to 60.

Market Analysis

The City

Founded in 1768 as a trading center for tobacco- and cotton-growing plantations, and later a major textile center, Charlotte is now one of the leading cities of the "New South." It is also one of the nation's fastest growing cities. Annexing outlying areas, its land area grew by about 20 percent in the first half of the 1990s. Its population was estimated at 455,000 in 1995, up 44 percent from 1980.

Historically a major textile center, Charlotte is now home to various manufacturing businesses and is a commercial center for the southern Piedmont region. While it is only the 32nd largest city in the country, Charlotte is the nation's third largest banking center. This is a result of major acquisitions and expansions of NationsBank and First Union Corporation, both of which are headquartered in the city. Other major employers are BellSouth, IBM, US Air, Duke Power Company, and the state government.

The city's economic vitality has led to high population growth and high employment levels. Population increased in the 1980s at two and one-half times the national rate of increase. Economic and population growth have led to some pressure on the housing market. While the surrounding region has below average housing prices and an abundance of mobile homes, Charlotte has a mixed housing affordability picture. While 1990 rents were 13 percent below the national average, the median value of a single-family home in 1990 was a little higher than the national

	Charlotte	USA
City population, 1995:	455,000 (estimate)	
Population growth, 1980s:	32%	12.6%
Percent African American:	31.8%	12%
Percent Hispanic:	1.4%	9%
City median income, 1990s:	$31,873	$30,056
Metro median income, 1996:	$45,400	$41,600
Unemployment rate:	5%	6.7%
Poverty rate:	10.8%	13.1%
Median home value:	$81,300	$79,900
Home value increase, 1980s:	76.7%	67%
Median monthly rent:	$389	$447
Homeownership rate:	55%	64.2%

U.S. Census, 1990 (except city population); 1996 median income from HUD.

average, and among the highest of any city in this study. In the 1980s, home values increased about 7.7 percent a year, compared to 6.7 percent nationally.

The table above lists key demographic and market statistics.

There is no overall housing shortage. Construction of homes and apartments has consistently out-paced the growth in the number of households. But this has not helped poor families. As elsewhere, because their incomes are so low, conventional builders cannot supply new housing that this group can afford.

The minimum cost of new homes in Charlotte is about $75,000. Habitat's average sale price is $47,000. With Habitat's zero percent financing, this is affordable to families with take-home incomes that are considerably below the poverty level--as low as $11,000 a year.

Target Areas

Habitat of Charlotte targets its home construction program to nine low-income neighborhoods that have a combined population of approximately 12,000 persons. The neighborhoods are predominantly African American and have poverty rates that average about 30 percent, over twice the national rate. The homeownership rate-- averaging about 33 percent--is far below the percentage of homeowners in the city as a whole and about half the national rate. The average vacancy rate is 14 percent for the combined stock of rental and for-sale housing.

The table at the top of the next page cites key demographic statistics for each neighborhood, as compiled from the 1990 Census by City and County planners.

	Population	Percent African American	Poverty Rate	Ownership Rate	Vacant Units
Villa Heights	2,321	82%	20%	46%	8%
Optimist Park	864	75%	23%	41%	29%
Lincoln Hts	2,673	99%	30%	47%	5%
Todd Park	439	43%	43%	58%	9%
Seversville	774	99%	16%	21%	11%
Oakview Terr.	1,039	92%	26%	16%	13%
Lakewood	749	85%	22%	34%	17%
Genesis Park	322	100%	33%	23%	26%
Belmont	2,884	96%	61%	15%	11%

U.S. Census, 1990

Habitat's clientele mirrors the neighborhood demographics. The median income in 1990 for all the neighborhoods was approximately $15,000, closely in line with the average income of the families assisted. About 90 percent of its home buyers are African American. The remaining 10 percent are Asian and Hispanic.

Most families served by the programs have incomes of around 40 percent of the area median income, currently about $18,000 for a family of four before taxes and $15,000 after taxes.

Operations and Financing

Marketing

As noted earlier, Habitat for Humanity enjoys wide recognition, associations with celebrities, and strong connections with church organizations. The international organization has been featured many times on television programs, in newspapers, and in popular magazines. Habitat programs, such as House Raising Week Worldwide, are very well publicized. Affiliates have to do their own fund-raising, of course, but this heightened public awareness and interest helps every Habitat program nationwide.

In marketing to prospective home buyers, Habitat uses several approaches. Staff members or volunteers make contact with businesses and churches, which then refer needy families. Advertisements for the program appear on city buses, and brochures are periodically mailed to all addresses in a targeted census tract where homes are being built. A clear set of brochures and forms explains to clients the organization's home building and buying processes.

Financing of Homes

Habitat of Charlotte is both the seller and the mortgage lender for the homes it builds. In 1996, the organization expects to provide about $1,457,000 in seller-financed mortgages for 31 homes. Habitat always provides 100 percent financing. Home prices (and therefore mortgage amounts) are not based on market value. The loan amount is derived from the amount of labor and materials put into each house, plus an allocation of certain overhead costs.

The organization does not fund mortgages with borrowed and deposited funds as a bank does. It uses its own cash to finance home construction and then takes back a seller mortgage. It has sufficient working capital to finance up to a dozen homes in various stages of completion.

Only two kinds of funds are used to finance homes:

▶ Loan repayments, which cover about 19 percent of total construction and operating costs.

▶ Charitable contributions, which cover the other 81 percent.

In addition to these cash sources, in-kind donations of materials and services average about $2,000 to $3,000 per home. The value of sweat equity and volunteer labor is estimated at $10,000 per home. The cost of a three-bedroom, one-bath house is $46,400, and a four-bedroom, two-bath home is $49,600.

Habitat of Charlotte's no-interest loans are written for 15- or 20-year terms. Previously, increasing-term mortgages were used, but Habitat now offers straight-line mortgages as the norm. As no interest is charged, the mortgage payment is comprised of principal and escrows for taxes and insurance. Examples of typical monthly mortgage payments on both the 15- and 20-year mortgages are as follows.

	15-year mortgage	20-year mortgage
3-bedroom home		
loan payment:	$258	$193
escrow:	67	67
	$325	$260
4-bedroom home		
loan payment:	$276	$207
escrow:	70	70
	$346	$277

Closing costs for home purchases average about $700.

There is very limited government involvement in the financing of homes. In this regard, Habitat of Charlotte follows the principles of its charter (called an affiliate covenant) with Habitat for Humanity International. The covenant limits the use of government funding to paying for land costs, purchasing existing homes, and infrastructure. Habitat's philosophy is that using government funding for construction and overhead would undermine its ability to raise private funds--and that private giving is the heart and soul of the program.

While the City supports the Habitat program, it does not provide free land or on-site infrastructure. It has helped to reduce water and sewer connection fees by paying for them with CDBG funds, and allowing Habitat to pay the City back over a number of years at zero percent interest. The City also funds the total cost of some off-site infrastructure such as sidewalk reconstruction.

Qualification for Assistance; Underwriting Criteria

There are three criteria for acceptance into all Habitat for Humanity programs:

▶ A need for housing.

▶ An ability to pay for a home.

▶ A willingness to be a partner with Habitat. (Habitat of Charlotte has added a fourth criteria: a minimum one year of residence in Charlotte.)

A need for housing is deemed to exist if people are living in overcrowded (more than two children per room, adults sharing a room with children, children of different sexes in one room) or substandard housing, or if they currently reside in public housing or an unsafe neighborhood, and if they have been unable to secure adequate housing through the private market.

An ability to pay is defined, in part, by the following program income guidelines:

Household size	Minimum income
2 persons	$900
3 persons	$1,000
4 persons	$1,200
5 persons	$1,300
6 persons	$1,450

In addition, home buyers must have a demonstrated ability to save, a history of regular rental payments, and no large amounts of outstanding debt.

While the program does not use formal housing cost-to-income ratios, the program's minimum income requirements mean that most families pay about 30 percent of after-tax income (or about 25 percent of gross income) for a home.

Willingness to partner is evidenced by a history of responsible behavior--timely payments, stable work history, lack of any criminal arrests that indicate a likely future risk, a desire to perform sweat equity, and a commitment to living in a safe, drug-free community.

Habitat of Charlotte checks with credit bureaus, employers, and landlords, and looks at police records to help evaluate prospective buyers.

A credit check is performed on the day of application. Although perfect credit is not a requirement at the time of sale, all delinquent bills must be paid up by that time. Occasionally, exceptions are made--for example, for families with large unpaid medical bills.

To fulfill the partnering requirements, home buyers must agree to put at least 125 hours of sweat equity into their own homes and donate 175 hours of work on other people's homes. Applicants must also commit to live in a drug-free environment.

If clients can qualify for the higher monthly payments of the 15-year mortgage, they are required to do so. This recycles funds for new houses more quickly. To fall into the 15-year mortgage category, applicants must have stable employment and the potential for pay increases, a high school diploma or higher, earn at least 40 percent (and preferably over 45 percent) of the HUD median income for the area, demonstrate a history of rental payments of $250 and higher, and have a budget that allows for operating expenses and savings.

If an applicant does not meet all these criteria he or she may be considered for a 20-year mortgage. Because longer mortgage terms result in less money flowing back into the revolving loan fund, Habitat stretches the payment term only when necessary. Only about 10 percent of clients are given 20-year mortgages.

While the program is Christian in philosophy and Bibles are given to all new homeowners, no applicant is required to meet religious requirements. Very few of the program's Asian home buyers are Christian.

Intake, Screening, and Counseling

As with most Habitat affiliates, Habitat of Charlotte's application process is lengthy. The process begins with monthly orientations--group meetings that include Habitat staff members, board members, and prospective home buyers.

After the orientation, volunteers conduct interviews with applicants, and an application is filled out. References are checked by volunteers. A family selection committee, also made up of volunteers, meets frequently to determine which applicants will be selected. The committee's decision must be ratified by the full board of directors.

After being accepted into the program, a family is assigned a volunteer family partner who stays with them throughout the entire home-building process. Because of the program's goal of increasing ties between the well-to-do and less fortunate families, partners (usually middle-class people) are encouraged to stay in touch on a permanent basis.

During this preliminary stage, participants begin to fulfill their required 175 hours of volunteer work on other families' homes. They begin to attend homeowner-in-process training sessions. And they attend at least two meetings with a financial counselor, usually a volunteer lender or other professional familiar with the home purchase process.

Both the family partner and the financial counselor help clients develop a monthly spending plan and a total indebtedness statement and go over the client's credit report. Families are encouraged to save for their closing costs, moving expenses, and decorating of the new home. Two individual financial counseling sessions are held about four to five weeks apart. Home buyers and counselors can schedule extra sessions if they feel they are necessary. A neutral site, such as the library or a fast food restaurant, is recommended for these meetings.

If more in-depth financial counseling is required, clients are referred to the local Consumer Credit Counseling agency.

Most clients who fail to be accepted into the program have high outstanding debts and are offered transition counseling. Transition counseling is done mainly on the telephone and consists of motivating applicants and informing them of the financial steps that need to be taken in order for them to qualify.

Homeownership Training

Currently, 11 group workshops are being offered. Their topics are as follows:

"10 Steps to Success"
Stress management
Job hunting skills
Owning versus renting, and family budgets
Family health issues
Avoiding substance abuse
Home maintenance
Family values
Creative problem solving
Personal awareness
Nutrition

The workshops consist of 15 sessions, totalling 25 hours.

Home Selection

Once these preliminary steps and homeowner training sessions are completed--a three- to four-month process--the family is allowed to pick a house lot from a list of available sites. Home construction begins in about three to four weeks. Actual construction takes about 12 weeks.

While some Habitat affiliates renovate existing homes, Habitat of Charlotte focuses exclusively on building new homes. Clients choose from seven stock house designs. In the interest of controlling costs, these blueprints are never customized.

The cost of a house in the Habitat program includes a range, central air conditioning and heating, and the choice of refrigerator, washer/dryer, or $500 towards the purchase of a fence.

Housing Development Activities

Sites for home construction are generally acquired one at a time through donations by private individuals or purchase from the City.

The city government has an active code enforcement program in inner-city neighborhoods, which focuses on the many single-family "rent houses" owned by investors. When a landlord refuses to comply with City housing codes, the home is condemned and torn down. Habitat is then able to acquire the land for a price equal to the back taxes plus the cost to the City of demolishing the home. The average cost to Habitat is about $2,500 to $3,000.

Typical development costs per home are as follows.

Site acquisition	$ 1,000
Materials and subcontractors	33,000
Construction supervision by staff	7,000
Other overhead	6,000
Total	$47,000

These figures do not include in-kind donated materials--which are worth about $2,000 to $3,000 per home--nor the value of volunteer labor and sweat equity, valued at about $10,000 per home.

To date, all Habitat homes have been located in Charlotte's inner-city neighborhoods, described in an earlier section. This strategy has had several advantages: the neighborhoods needed revitalization; the lots were low-cost or free; and most infrastructure was already in place. But the organization is concerned about continuing this approach. The strategy has the downside of adding to the concentration of mostly low-income and African American families in certain areas. And Habitat's board is worried that at some time in the near future, low-cost inner-city lots will be harder to come by.

While construction will continue in inner-city areas, the organization's five-year plan for 1996 to 2000 calls for building more homes in economically and racially diverse neighborhoods. This, in turn, means acquiring suburban land with much higher costs of infrastructure development. The added cost is estimated at about $10,000 per home.

Management of Volunteers and Sweat Equity

Habitat affiliates use many methods of managing volunteers and sweat equity, from informal work days on evenings and weekends to highly formalized systems. With its high production levels, Habitat of Charlotte must rely on well developed and predictable management systems, namely:

Adopt-A-Home: In this well-advertised program, a church congregation, business, or other organization agrees to take responsibility for building a home. In the ideal case, the group builds a series of homes. This increases efficiency over time as volunteer crews become experienced in both construction management and building tasks. Often, they bring their own tools (and donate funds to cover the cash costs of a home).

Volunteer crews: Individual volunteers and small groups are recruited to build homes. From time to time, these include groups of volunteers (students or church members) from the metropolitan area. These crews, being less experienced on average, require somewhat more management by staff members.

"Blitz" projects: Six times in the past nine years, Habitat of Charlotte has sponsored building blitzes, where between five and 22 homes have been built in a week or two.

Volunteers are scheduled by the organization's volunteer coordinator. For the most part, volunteers are part of groups that keep coming back to build more houses. Most groups come from a specific business, sorority, fraternity, or high school class. Many are so experienced (or become so experienced) that they require little or no supervision. For these volunteers, materials are simply dropped off, and a staff construction supervisor drops in a few times a day.

Each of the four construction staff members supervises three or four jobs at a time--meaning that none of them is able to act as an on-site supervisor. One person in each volunteer crew usually takes the responsibility for managing the job. However, the supervisors do spend more time on-site with less experienced crews.

Individual volunteers and families performing their sweat equity work are simply scheduled to work with one of these crews by the family selection committee and one of the construction supervisors. But apart from the participation of future homeowners and a few individual volunteers, almost every crew is made up of affiliated individuals who have worked together before building Habitat houses. A few crews specialize in certain aspects of construction--such as drywall and roofing--but all-purpose crews are easier to schedule and manage.

Unlike some Habitat programs, Charlotte uses very few out-of-town volunteers.

Therefore, it does not have to coordinate temporary lodging for its volunteers.

Habitat of Charlotte credits much of the success of its program to the broad range of volunteers who have been willing to build homes. Never forgetting this contribution, the organization takes the time to thank and recognize its volunteers.

Loan Collections and Post-Purchase Counseling

Starting in 1996, First Citizens Bank took over loan servicing responsibilities. As its contribution to the program, the bank agreed to service 250 loans at no cost.

In the 13 years in which the program has been operating, it has experienced only 10 defaults on loans--a default rate of about four percent. All defaults have resulted in the property being deeded back to Habitat of Charlotte. New families are found to buy the homes, and since little or no construction is needed, the families perform their required sweat equity on other homes.

Habitat of Charlotte offers post-purchase counseling to clients who get behind in their payments. Counselors seek to discover if there is wasteful spending in the family's budget or if current income simply is not sufficient to cover their home payments. The counselor and the homeowner then work out a budget and a payment plan to help the clients get back on track.

Long-Term Affordability Controls

Habitat of Charlotte does not impose any special controls over resales of homes--such as limitations on profits received from resales. To date, this has not been needed, since the market value of homes in the target neighborhoods rarely exceeds the $47,000 average sale price. Therefore, there is little or no chance of a family receiving windfall profits from reselling a home.

Because of problems with crime and the image of its target areas, middle-class families are rarely attracted to relocate in these areas. Because of this, property values are generally depressed.

In the future, increasing property values and the potential for windfall profits may become an issue. In a few of the target neighborhoods, private builders are beginning to build and sell homes priced somewhat higher than Habitat's.

Assistance to Neighborhood/Homeowners' Associations

Habitat of Charlotte encourages all of its homeowners to join and support pre-existing associations in their neighborhoods. Because of this, no special effort is made to organize residents in new associations.

Partnerships

On a day-to-day basis, Habitat of Charlotte's most important partners are its volunteers, donors, and homeowners. And as described, the City helps the program by selling lots and funding off-site infrastructure.

In recent years, community-based organizations have also become partners. One community development corporation provided lots for Habitat to build on, and in a neighborhood where Habitat was already building homes, it teamed up with a church to build a preschool.

Administration

Management and Staffing

Habitat of Charlotte supports a fulltime staff of 14 people. They fill the following positions.

Executive director
Director of operations
Development director
Administrative coordinator
Volunteer coordinator
Family services coordinators (2)
Construction superintendent
Construction staff members (4)
Construction staff assistant
Receptionist

Four staff people are members of minority groups.

As with most Habitat affiliates, Habitat of Charlotte is at least as much volunteer driven as staff driven. The large volunteer board of directors not only sets policies but is intensely involved in day-to-day operations. The staff forms liaisons with board members who serve as volunteer managers or workers in assigned areas of operations--for example, family selection, fund-raising, or construction.

Other volunteers also perform an extraordinary amount of work that would otherwise be done by staff or contractors. Over 10,000 volunteers have helped with the program to date.

Board of Directors

Because of its deep involvement with program operations, the board of directors of Habitat of Charlotte is large (it had 24 members in late 1996) and has many active committees, as follows:

Executive committee
Construction
Development (fund-raising)
Family resources
Family selection
Finance
Personnel
Policy (internal policy)
Safety
Site acquisition
Volunteers

Board members include lenders, business people, other professionals, and church representatives. One nonvoting member is the owner of a Habitat-built home. Six members are African American, and one is Asian.

Administrative Costs and Funding

Even though Habitat of Charlotte does not allocate all of its costs to home building, contributions are needed to cover both housing development costs and such indirect expenses as fund-raising and support of the Habitat program overseas. Taking these costs into account, the organization needed about $2,266,000 in income during 1996. It was expected to come from the following sources.

Private contributions	$1,827,000
Loan repayments	440,000

In 1995, budgeted administrative costs broke out functionally as follows (numbers are rounded to the nearest thousand):

Construction management	$231,000
Family services	63,000
Administration	108,000
Fundraising and PR	104,000
Salary increases	13,000
Total	$519,000

Habitat for Humanity International requests that its local affiliates give regular tithes (or donations) to its worldwide program. For its part, Habitat of Charlotte gave $64,000 in 1995. Also in 1995, Habitat of Charlotte made payments on borrowed capital of $77,000. Capital expenses were $20,000 and direct construction costs amounted to $1,046,000--making up a total budget of over $1.7 million.

In 1996, the total budget was projected at $2,266,000, reflecting a higher target for home construction and the desire to add $215,000 to reserve funds. Projected sources were $440,000 in loan repayments and $1,826,000 in charitable donations.

Charlotte uses two specific programs to raise funds. These are the Samaritan program and the Adopt-A-Home program. Both give members of the community the opportunity to fund the building of specific Habitat homes.

A majority of funds are raised under the Samaritan program. Individuals or groups sponsor the cost of building one home. Donors pay $40,000 in a one-time payment, or pay slightly more (to account for inflation) over a two- to five-year period. This covers the cash costs of materials, mechanical subcontractors, and overhead. During 1995, Habitat of Charlotte determined that, in general, corporations were more likely to give to tangible items (that is, a house) than intangible administrative work.

Under the Adopt-A-Home program, congregations, businesses, and other organizations not only pledge the funds for one home but provide regular volunteer crews to help build it. Many such sponsors end up funding and helping to build a series of homes.

Special events are also used to help raise funds. In 1996, Habitat of Charlotte scheduled a three-on-three basketball tournament, an imported art sale, a haunted house event, and an auction of unique birdhouses.

Apart from all these methods, corporations and individuals also make major contributions to the program, and individuals are solicited to make small gifts through the organization's newsletter and personal contacts.

Financial Management

Habitat of Charlotte's treasurer is a retired certified public accountant who volunteers to help the administrative staff design and generate financial reports. The organization also receives a donated audit from the accounting firm Arthur Anderson.

Lessons Learned

Strengths of the Program

The conventional wisdom among nonprofit housing providers is that construction volunteers and sweat equity from future homeowners simply do not save money. They may be good in small doses for community building, but emphasizing this approach will lead to low production and extraordinarily high overhead that often wipes out any savings on labor.

While this is certainly the case with many low-volume programs and startups, Habitat for Humanity of Charlotte and many other productive Habitat affiliates have disproved the doubters. The Charlotte group is a particularly good model, not just for other Habitat affiliates but for any housing organization that wants to emphasize volunteers or sweat equity.

These appear to be the keys to its success.

A "think-big" mentality: The founders, current board members, and managers have over the years consistently developed workable plans for increasing production.

A giving community: Charlotte is known nationwide for its civic spirit and the generosity of its businesses, churches, and individuals.

A supportive local government: The City of Charlotte has given strong support to community development and affordable housing in general and to Habitat in particular.

Religious and social motivations: Even Habitat affiliates vary considerably in the strength of their religious and social convictions. This is the "fuel" that runs most volunteer efforts, and Habitat of Charlotte appears to have more of it than average. The major commitments in El Salvador are a telling example of this.

Effective operating systems: Habitat affiliates from around the country learn from Habitat of Charlotte some of the most effective systems in the U.S. for fund-raising, volunteer management, and management of sweat equity work. However, it should be noted that these are tailored to Habitat of Charlotte's relatively large scale of operations. While elements of the program might work "in miniature," it is hard to image a low-output nonprofit replicating all the features and operating systems of the Charlotte program.

Successful integration of board members in operations: Many Habitat affiliates and other groups that rely on "involved" board members struggle with conflicts between staff and board members, and ambiguous lines of authority. Charlotte has a very well thought out and apparently effective organization chart that integrates decision-making and work by board members and staff.

A revolving loan fund--at this point, it can fund the construction of about nine homes a year without the need for fund-raising.

Achievement of Goals

Habitat of Charlotte has set annual goals for home construction that are a little higher than its annual production. In 1995, 28 homes were built versus a goal of 32 homes. In 1996, 31 homes are scheduled to be built versus a goal of 36 homes.

A major part of "thinking big" is long-range planning. Habitat of Charlotte is currently implementing the first year of a set of five-year goals. The goals are described in a document called *Foundation 2000*. It is essentially a strategic plan that describes in general terms how the goals will be achieved, some challenges to be overcome, and the likely financial requirements of the increased production.

Hopes and Fears for the Future

As described earlier, Habitat of Charlotte is concerned about the concentration of homes in very low-income and minority neighborhoods, and the decline in the number of suitable house lots available in these areas. The response--an attempt to include some suburban development--will be a major challenge for the organization. Land development tasks will add another layer of complexity and cost.

At the same time as it wants to move into more expensive locations, Habitat of Charlotte also sees a need to help families with incomes below the minimum currently required in the program. The organization is considering a number of approaches to solving this problem. It might modify its mortgage terms to make monthly payments lower for some families by stretching out repayments to 25 or more years. It is also considering a preapplicant program, which includes intensive family services and transitional housing for certain applicants.

Over time, of course, the net effect of changing mortgage terms would be to reduce revenues to the revolving loan fund. This factor, together with greatly increased production and possible increases in infrastructure costs, will greatly accelerate demands for fund-raising. Revenue requirements are expected to more than double, from just over $1 million in 1996 to over $3.7 million in the year 2000.

Fortunately, Habitat of Charlotte is better positioned than most nonprofit housing organizations to raise the $3.7 million in a year. It has built a strong reputation and an unparalleled network of volunteers and donors. Over the years it has capitalized a revolving loan fund, and repayments meet about one fifth of total revenue needs. Because its funding base is mostly private, it will likely feel few effects from cutbacks in federal housing funds.

Based on the organization's past success, Habitat for Humanity of Charlotte will very likely achieve its goals and maintain its reputation as one of the premier nonprofit home builders in the United States that relies on volunteers, sweat equity, and private donations.

Information Sources

For more information, contact:

Bert Green
Executive Director
Habitat for Humanity of Charlotte
P.O. Box 34397
1320 N. Caldwell St.
Charlotte, NC 28234
(704) 376-2054

Habitat for Humanity International
121 Habitat St.
Americus, GA 31709-3498
(912) 924-6935

11

Holy Name Housing Corporation and Holy Name Affordable Housing
(Omaha, Nebraska)

Program Highlights

Holy Name Housing Corporation and Holy Name Affordable Housing

Target Areas:	North Omaha and South Omaha neighborhoods
Program Goals:	Assist low- and moderate-income home buyers Revitalize inner-city neighborhoods
Major Elements:	Financial counseling and home buyer training Prequalifying buyers for 1st and 2nd mortgages Single family housing development
Average Client Income:	$15,000 in North Omaha; $30,000 in South Omaha
Typical Home Prices:	$35,000-$50,000 (rehabilitated); $80,000-$110,000 (new)
Year Started:	1982; subsidiary formed in 1991 to expand to South Omaha
Other Programs:	Rental housing development and management Housing maintenance program Assistance to other nonprofits in Omaha
Staffing:	Holy Name Housing Corporation--12 fulltime staff persons Holy Name Affordable Housing--shared director plus 2 other staff members
Annual Output: (1995-1996)	Both organizations combined: 50 clients received mortgage loans 15 homes newly constructed; 13 sold 37 homes acquired, renovated, and sold
Funding:	First mortgage loans from consortium of private lenders CDBG and HOME funds from the City of Omaha Performance-based grants from lender consortium Other corporate grants HUD Hope 3 grant Net proceeds of home sales Private contributors Net rental income

Overview

Holy Name Housing Corporation was established in 1982 as a nonprofit community development corporation devoted to addressing the problems of deteriorating housing and unemployment in the North Omaha neighborhood comprising the Holy Name parish. The organization was created by members of the Catholic Redemptorist order, who staff the parish and who continue to support the organization with funds and personnel.

Initially, the program trained unemployed residents of the neighborhood who went to work rehabilitating run-down homes that were then sold at affordable rates to low-income families. Over time, Holy Name Housing Corporation expanded its rehabilitation efforts to include all of North Omaha and became involved in the construction of new homes.

The three main goals of the Holy Name Housing Corporation are: 1) to build and renovate affordable homes in North Omaha; 2) to make these homes available for sale to low- and moderate-income families; and 3) to hire unemployed neighborhood residents and train them in construction skills. In this way, decent, affordable homes are made available to low-income purchasers, neighborhoods are built up and revitalized, and residents gain employment, experience, and increased income.

Holy Name Housing Corporation works with home buyers to help them meet basic underwriting criteria--good credit, steady employment, and sufficient income. Through counseling and training workshops, Holy Name Housing Corporation educates its clients about the process of obtaining a mortgage, which they can then secure from a local lending consortium at reduced interest rates. The City of Omaha provides low-income clients with substantial soft second mortgages. The Federal Home Loan Bank also funds modest closing-cost assistance for low-income clients, in the form of a deferred payment loan due only upon resale of the property.

Since it began in 1982, Holy Name Housing Corporation has renovated over 150 homes in its original target neighborhood and has built another 50 homes on vacant lots in other North Omaha neighborhoods.

The City helps with acquisition of land for new construction, either by buying lots and donating them or subsidizing infrastructure such as water lines, sewer lines, or new streets. Lots are very low-valued--worth $500 to $3,000 each.

When acquiring homes to repair and resell, Holy Name simply approaches sellers. As a nonprofit housing organization, Holy Name has a priority to buy HUD- and VA-repossessed homes. In North Omaha, existing homes bought for resale cost from $10,000 to $20,000, while the renovations average $22,000. The average total cost of a renovated home is about $35,000 including limited soft costs but not including the organization's overhead associated with this development work. In South Omaha, prices of rehabilitated homes range from $35,000 to $70,000. New homes cost between $75,000 and $110,000.

Holy Name has always carried out its renovation work using an in-house crew and subcontractors. But initially, new home construction was entirely contracted out. In 1994, faced with a general contractor who walked away from an 18-home new construction project, the organization began acting as its own general contractor for all construction work--a strategy intended to increase quality and control over the process. However, the in-house crew--currently six people--is used only on renovation projects.

As it has grown, Holy Name Housing Corporation has evolved from selling homes at an actual loss to showing modest profits since 1993.

Holy Name Housing Corporation also owns and operates rental housing. One property has 37 apartments for the elderly, renting from $285 to $400 a month. In addition, 11 single-family homes were renovated and are rented to low-income families. While rental housing development is not the primary goal of the organization, these rental properties do generate cash for the organization's other programs and provide decent housing for households with incomes below the levels needed to achieve homeownership.

Creation of Lending Consortium

This respected, neighborhood-based organization is remarkable for having established a citywide lending consortium--Omaha 100--that provides: 1) construction financing; 2) operating support and technical assistance to nonprofit housing groups throughout Omaha; 3) a dependable pool of mortgage financing for low- and moderate-income home purchasers; and 4) counseling and training for home buyers not receiving these services from other nonprofits.

Eleven local financial institutions participate in Omaha 100, which was formed in 1991 and named for its goal of helping to finance 100 affordable homes a year. With a staff and board of its own, Omaha 100 operates independently from Holy Name Housing Corporation.

From its inception in early 1992 through August 1996, Omaha 100 had made or facilitated 243 loans amounting to over $9.4 million--to clients of the two Holy Name organizations and other nonprofit housing organizations. In addition, about 20 percent of its clientele are low-income borrowers unaffiliated with any neighborhood-based nonprofit organization. Typically, loans are made to higher risk borrowers, those who could not qualify for conventional mortgages.

Spin-Off: A South Omaha Program

In 1991, Holy Name Housing Corporation and residents of South Omaha formed a subsidiary, Holy Name Affordable Housing, to begin a new housing program in South Omaha. North Omaha and South Omaha residents identify their areas as separate and different, so it was felt that a new housing organization operating in South Omaha would be more effective than an expanded effort by Holy Name Housing Corporation.

Holy Name Affordable Housing operates in much the same way as the parent Housing Corporation. The major difference is the South Omaha organization's ongoing partnership with a for-profit property developer, NuStyle Development. Through this joint venture, Holy Name Affordable Housing has avoided the need for a large staff.

NuStyle Development, owned by Todd Heistand and his sister Tammy Barrett, is committed to renovating and constructing housing for low- and middle-income families. This firm has provided personnel for both real estate development and office support, as well as office space. The partnership has worked well. Holy Name Affordable Housing educates prospective home buyers in the process of obtaining loans and the responsibilities of homeownership, while NuStyle builds and renovates affordable homes. As with the North Omaha program, financing for the homes is provided by Omaha 100 and the City of Omaha.

Along with NuStyle Development and the Nebraska Equity Fund, Holy Name Affordable Housing has been able to renovate 22 condemned houses and 41 rental units in South Omaha, which have been sold and rented to new residents. Holy Name Affordable Housing manages all of its rental units.

Market Analysis

The City: Prosperous, With Relatively Low-Cost Housing

Omaha, bounded on the east by the Missouri River, has evolved from a frontier town and livestock shipping center to a thriving and diversified center of commerce with nationwide markets. The home to billionaire investor Warren Buffett and other financial success stories, Omaha's economic base includes insurance companies, railroads, heavy construction, and credit card processing. A revitalized downtown offers a new pedestrian park, restaurants, theaters, and shops.

Prosperity has helped even low-income Omaha residents. The city's poverty rate is among the three lowest of all the cities in this study, and the unemployment rate in 1990 was the lowest. Nonetheless, as in most U.S. urban areas, city residents are much less prosperous than suburbanites.

Unlike most other cities with high employment and low housing vacancy rates, Omaha has experienced very modest housing cost inflation. During the 1980s, a period of rampant housing cost increases, the median home values grew only 40 percent as fast as the national figure. In large part, this was due to modest population growth--Omaha in the 1980s grew only two-thirds as fast as the national rate of population growth.

The table at the top of the following page lists key demographics and market conditions.

Holy Name's Target Areas: Poor and Blue Collar

The neighborhoods of North and South Omaha saw development early in the city's history; South Omaha was the first part of the city to be settled. By the late 1970s, however, both of these areas had seen significant decline. Homeowners moved out, leaving dilapidated homes and vacant lots--conditions that increasingly hosted vagrants, gangs, and drug users. The deterioration and social problems are worse in North Omaha. Many middle- and higher-income families left these parts of the city for West Omaha and the western suburbs.

Since the founding of Holy Name Housing Corporation in 1982, some

	Omaha	USA
City population:	335,795	
Population growth, 1980s:	.2%	12.6%
Percent African American:	13%	12%
Percent Hispanic:	3%	9%
City median income:	$26,927	$30,056
Metro median income, 1996:	$45,900	$41,600
Unemployment rate:	3.2%	6.7%
Poverty rate:	12.6%	13.1%
Median home value:	$54,600	$79,900
Home value increase, 1980s:	59%	67%
Median monthly rent:	$386	$447
Homeownership rate:	59.2%	64.2%

U.S. Census, 1990; 1996 median income from HUD.

turnaround in these negative trends has occurred, even in the most distressed areas. In North Omaha, for example, other non-profit groups such as the New Community Development Corporation, United Ministries of Northeast Omaha, Habitat for Humanity, and Omaha Economic Development Corporation also are involved in the effort to revitalize the area.

The population of North Omaha is primarily African American and the unemployment rate is 12 percent, over twice the national average. Median incomes in the targeted census tracts in North Omaha range from $7,000 to $23,000 (1990 census data). For the combined census tracts, the median income is about $17,000.

The population of South Omaha is largely Hispanic or white. While most households have incomes below 80 percent of the median income, incomes are somewhat higher than those in North Omaha. The unemployment rate in the South Omaha target area averages 6.5 percent. Median incomes of the targeted census tracts range from $12,000 to as much as $41,000, while averaging about $24,000.

Operations and Financing

Marketing

According to a survey conducted by Holy Name, 90 percent of its clients come to the program via word-of-mouth referrals. Waiting lists for new or renovated homes are so long that little advertising is needed. Occasionally, newspaper ads are placed. Sometimes, open house events are used to market the program. And social services agencies are periodically notified of the availability of homes for sale.

To make house hunting easier for low-income families in Omaha, Holy Name Housing Corporation intends to publish an affordable housing directory, which will list recently renovated or newly built homes available from its program and all the other nonprofit-developed homes for sale in Omaha. The directory will be made available to both clients and real estate brokers. The format of the directory will be similar to the Multiple Listing Service. Each listing will include photographs of the house, its address, price range, and possible financing scenarios.

The home buyer training programs run by Omaha 100 also act as a marketing mechanism. Typically, trainees sign up before they have a specific home in mind to purchase. In the training, they learn that Holy Name and other nonprofits are offering new or rehabilitated homes that are the most affordable in Omaha.

Financing of Homes

The purchase of homes through both Holy Name Housing Corporation's and Holy Name Affordable Housing's homeownership programs is made possible through tandem loans offered by Omaha 100 and the City of Omaha.

For income-qualified clients, the City of Omaha offers a tandem loan at zero percent interest with all payments deferred until sale of the property. Holy Name and the other nonprofit home sellers in Omaha each get annual allocations of these subsidies and, in effect, act as brokers for the City's financing. Unlike programs in some other cities, the nonprofits never receive the funds or the eventual loan repayments.

The City offers second mortgage loans of up to $25,000 for new homes and up to $15,000 for renovated homes. The actual amounts of these loans are based on the financial gap that needs to be filled for each client.

On rare occasions, Holy Name Housing Corporation has made a gift of part of its equity in a home to assist buyers who would not otherwise qualify for a purchase.

On a typical newly constructed home, about $50,000 to $60,000 in construction financing are provided by either Omaha 100 or individual lenders through a first mortgage, while the City of Omaha provides about $20,000. With the permanent financing, Omaha 100 provides slightly less financing--$45,000 to $55,000--while the City typically provides $25,000 to the home buyer through its deferred payment loan.

On a typical rehabilitated home, the City of Omaha provides all the construction financing--usually $35,000 at zero percent interest. The permanent financing package typically consists of $25,000 from Omaha 100 and a $10,000 deferred payment loan from the city.

Rates for home purchase loans from Omaha 100 are adjusted frequently and pegged to the lowest prevailing rate offered at the time among all the participating lenders. Loans are all made on a participation basis--that is, each participating lender funds a percentage of each loan based on a predetermined formula. As of late 1996, none of the loans has been sold in the secondary market.

Qualification for Assistance; Underwriting Criteria

To be eligible to buy a home from Holy Name, a prospective buyer has to meet typical credit criteria--a stable employment record, adequate income, and an acceptable credit history. If a client has no credit history, he or she must provide a satisfactory history of payments for rent and utilities.

Eligible applicants may earn a maximum of 80 percent of the median income. In the past, a small percentage of the new homes were sold (without the second mortgage subsidies) to clients with incomes up to 120 percent of median income, but this is no longer the case.

Omaha 100 always provides the first mortgage financing. Its underwriting criteria are as follows: 1) a maximum 33 percent of the applicant's verified monthly income may be applied to the monthly mortgage payment; and 2) a maximum 42 percent of income for total installment debt.

Nominal down payments for the homes are three percent, and closing costs range from $500 to $2,500. However, up to $3,000 in down payment and closing costs may be financed with a grant from the Federal Home Loan Bank Board that is administered by Holy Name. Omaha 100 requires that buyers make a minimum cash investment of two percent of the first mortgage amount to ensure that they have some stake in the home purchase. The actual amount of cash-to-close ranges from about $500 to $1,500 for Holy Name clients.

When a buyer is approved by Omaha 100 for its first mortgage loan and is proven to meet the income criteria, approval of the city's second mortgage loan and the down payment assistance loan is sought, and in almost every case, received.

Intake, Screening, and Counseling

Holy Name Housing Corporation and Holy Name Affordable Housing have application processes that include a prescreening and application, then a personal interview.

Holy Name provides in-depth counseling to prospective purchasers who need to clear their credit record and develop a budget-- steps that help clients meet the underwriting criteria of the Omaha 100 consortium lenders. Holy Name also provides counseling to purchasers throughout and after the purchase process, helping new homeowners stay on top of their expenses and learn to maintain their new homes.

From April 1995 to March 1996, counselors with Holy Name Housing Corporation and Holy Name Affordable Housing worked individually with 255 applicants.

In addition, after prequalification by one of the Holy Name organizations, each client receives about an hour and a half of one-on-one counseling from Omaha 100.

Homeownership Training

Originally, Holy Name Housing Corporation offered its own training workshops, but discontinued them when Omaha 100 began to offer this service. Applicants are referred only if they appear very likely to be approved for a first mortgage loan. Thus, in the past year, only about 60 of 255 applicants were referred to training.

Omaha 100's homeownership workshops incorporate information from the Fannie Mae homeownership training manual with information specific to the housing market and financing opportunities in Omaha. At first, one three-hour workshop was offered, but this was expanded to multiple sessions totaling nine hours.

Home Selection

The homeownership programs of Holy Name Housing Corporation and Holy Name Affordable Housing both focus exclusively on selling and financing homes that were rehabilitated or newly constructed through their respective programs. Consequently, neither organization helps clients with purchases of existing homes in their markets--Omaha 100 fills this niche.

Counselors working for Holy Name Housing Corporation and Holy Name Affordable Housing help clients inspect and select their homes.

Housing Development Activities

In addition to rehabilitating scattered-site homes and developing two rental housing properties, the two Holy Name organizations have managed the following new construction projects involving homes for sale.

North Omaha:

Kountze Park: 18 homes built on vacant lots; an additional 80 to be completed over the next three years, priced from $75,000 to $86,000.

Monmouth Park: 40 new single-family homes on an 8 1/2 acre site, priced from $75,000 to $86,000.

Fontenelle Estates: 10 new homes being built on vacant lots, priced from $80,000 to $90,000.

South Omaha:

Riverview Meadows: 33 homes priced from $75,000 to $110,000 and aimed at encouraging moderate-income families to move back into this area of the city.

Loan Collections and Post-Purchase Counseling

Holy Name Housing Corporation and Holy Name Affordable Housing provide post-purchase counseling to new homeowners, educating them about home maintenance and assisting them in the event that they find it difficult to follow their budgets. Counselors work with clients on an individual basis and also make referrals to other private and city agencies if more specialized help is needed.

Omaha 100's loan delinquency rate is fairly high, at 15 percent of its portfolio. There has been only one foreclosure to date, but four are pending. While these statistics include borrowers who are unaffiliated with the Holy Name organizations, they are still somewhat indicative of their experience.

The largest identifiable group of delinquent borrowers in mid-1996 were buyers of new homes in Holy Name's Monmouth Park subdivision. Not coincidentally, this project includes some of the highest-priced homes sold by Holy Name in North Omaha. According to the executive director of Omaha 100, it is not the lowest-income borrowers, but those with higher incomes who are becoming delinquent--presumably because of less disciplined spending and higher installment debt.

While the causes of this problem have not been pinpointed, the staff of Omaha 100 suspects it may have something to do with the program's high underwriting ratios. Also, partly in response to this problem, Omaha 100 tripled the length of its home buyer training sessions.

Home Maintenance Program

Funded by grants from the local Lozier and Community foundations, Holy Name Housing Corporation is able to offer its buyers a handyman service at $5 per hour. The handyman tells homeowners how to make repairs, get estimates, and select contractors, or he performs the minor repairs himself.

The purpose of the program is to encourage residents to maintain pride in their homes and to assure that the houses sold will remain safe and attractive. However, because it has been difficult to raise ongoing funds for this program, its continuation is in jeopardy.

Long-Term Affordability Controls

Neither Holy Name Housing Corporation, Holy Name Affordable Housing, Omaha 100, nor the City places any long-term affordability controls on homes sold through the program, other than the minimal resale controls required when federal HOME funds are used. Only the South Omaha subsidiary uses HOME funds.

Assistance to Neighborhood and Homeowners' Associations

Because many of their homes have been developed on scattered sites, the Holy Name organizations have had limited involvement with neighborhood associations or homeowners' associations. When homes were built in one inner-city subdivision, Holy Name Housing Corporation did organize a homeowners' association.

During 1995, a volunteer intern provided by the Sisters of Mercy served as a grassroots organizer for new neighborhood associations in some of Omaha's low-income neighborhoods. The intern served as a liaison between residents and the City, nonprofit housing developers, the police department, and Neighborhood Courage (an umbrella group of Omaha neighborhood associations).

Partners

The key partners in the program are the City, the 11 lender members of Omaha 100, and (for development in South Omaha), its nonprofit affiliate and the for-profit NuStyle Builders.

Holy Name Housing Corporation also provides technical assistance to other nonprofit community development organizations. For example, in 1993, it assisted the United Ministries of Northeast Omaha in developing a plan and financing to renovate and sell 30 homes.

Administration

Management and Staffing

The staff of Holy Name Housing Corporation consists of 12 fulltime staff members and various volunteers. The fulltime staff positions are as follows:

Executive director
Construction manager
Financial manager
Secretary/Receptionist
Housing counselor
Manager - Leo Vaughan Manor

(rental property)
Rehabilitation specialist
Construction supervisor
Construction crew members (4)

Holy Name Affordable Housing currently shares its executive director with Holy Name Housing Corporation; it also employs a property manager and a homeownership counselor. Until Holy Name Affordable Housing can hire more fulltime employees, its staff is supplemented by assistance from the employees of NuStyle Development. NuStyle employs the following people:

Construction supervisor
Job foreman
Carpenters (3)
Project coordinator
Part-time bookkeeper

Board of Directors

Holy Name Housing Corporation is governed by a three-person board of directors consisting of priests of the Redemptorist order. The corporation also has a 12-person advisory board that includes local lenders, businessmen and women, professionals, the state government official in charge of apprenticeships and training, and one person listed as a resident of North Omaha.

The South Omaha organization, Holy Name Affordable Housing, has a 16-person board of directors that has a similar make-up. The director of Omaha 100 sits on this board and the parent corporation's advisory board. This board is approved as a "community-based housing development organization," or "CHDO" as defined under · the federal HOME program--a status that

gives the organization priority for certain funding under that program.

The board of Omaha 100 includes representatives of its member-lenders, nonprofit developers, and neighborhood residents.

Administrative Costs and Funding

The core operating expenses for Holy Name Housing Corporation for the fiscal year that ended March 31, 1996 were approximately $272,000, according to its financial statements. These expenses broke out as follows.

Salaries	$154,328
Benefits and payroll taxes	35,549
General insurance	14,675
Professional services	13,775
Handyman expense	12,171
Shop and tool expense	4,064
Rent	6,000
Telephone	7,799
Postage and office maintenance	3,582
Office supplies	3,643
Travel and mileage expense	2,580
Staff development	1,707
Equipment maintenance	1,531
Printing	351
Total	$261,755

Salaries shown are exclusive of construction crew members, but include the construction supervisor. The salary figure also includes the in-kind cost of two staff members (including the executive director), valued at $36,600. The following revenues were reported for the same period. These were used to cover administrative costs and generate a surplus that was reinvested in the organization's housing development projects.

City of Omaha grant	$47,554
City of Omaha project grants	29,037
Lozier Foundation grant	30,000
Omaha 100 grant	37,500
Hope 3 grant (HUD)	15,272
John Heinz grant (HUD)	10,500
Development grant	58,187
(performance-based grant from Omaha 100)	
Donation of salaries	36,600
Net income--rental housing	12,915
Chubbs Finer Foods grant	11,204
Other grants	958
Individual contributions	12,759
Total	$302,486

These financials do not include activities of the subsidiary Holy Name Affordable Housing, Inc.

Financial Management

Both Holy Name housing organizations appear to be in good financial health, although, like most nonprofit housing organizations, they have a thin cushion for unforeseen problems.

Like other low-income housing organizations, the two Holy Name housing organizations have recognized the need to diversify sources of funding in light of the decrease of federal funds available for housing programs. Although the corporations still rely primarily on grants, their viability has been increased by profits from some home sales, net rental income, and production-based grants provided by lenders involved in Omaha 100.

Recent financial statements of both organizations showed slight surpluses of revenues over expenses: for Holy Name Affordable Housing, about $21,000 on an annualized basis versus about $525,000 in revenues, and for Holy Name Housing Corporation, about $8,300 in positive cash flow for the year ended March 31, 1996, against about $1.9 million in revenues.

In relation to the scale of their development activities, both organizations are very thin in cash reserves and net worth. In recent financial statements, Holy Name Housing Corporation's net worth was only about $31,000 versus $1.14 million in assets. Holy Name Affordable Housing's net worth was $17,000 versus $172,000 in assets.

Both corporations are now turning their attention to national organizations--such as The Enterprise Foundation and the Local Initiatives Support Corporation--to help them expand their funding sources. Holy Name's current business plan assumes that national organizations like these can generate interest for the program among national funders who support community development. In the view of the executive director, national sponsors would induce local businesses and philanthropists to invest yet more in the housing programs sponsored by Holy Name.

Lessons Learned

Strengths of the Program

Through its vision, longevity, and productivity, Holy Name Housing Corporation continues to be the premier neighborhood-based nonprofit housing corporation in its city and a good example for other, similar communities.

The program is arguably unique among neighborhood-based housing programs for having created two successful spin-offs operating outside its target area--one a citywide lending consortium and the other a community development corporation operating in a different kind of neighborhood across town.

The organizations' success appears to be due to their skilled staffs, involved boards, City support, lender support, and the effective leadership of their shared Executive Director, Sister Marilyn Ross.

Most intermediary organizations, such as Omaha 100 lending consortium, are established at the initiative of lenders, local governments, or national organizations such as The Enterprise Foundation or Local Initiatives Support Corporation. Often, these citywide nonprofit housing entities cause community development corporations to become concerned about losing control and having to share a limited pool of money from local grant sources with other organizations. In this case, the strong involvement of Holy Name Housing Corporation and other nonprofit housing groups appears to have alleviated these conflicts.

In an industry known for competition for funds and battles over turf, this concern for the success of *all* nonprofit developers in all of the city's distressed neighborhoods is unusually enlightened. The organization also proved that this broader vision has in no way detracted from its own successes and, in fact, has added to them. While the affordable housing industry in Omaha has expanded considerably in recent years, the output, staffing, and financial health of Holy Name Housing Corporation has grown as well.

Achievement of Goals

In early 1993, Holy Name Housing Corporation prepared a detailed business plan forecasting its operations through March of 1996 (an excellent example of planning beyond the next 12 months). At the end of this period, the corporation was almost on target with its production goals, having built or renovated 47 homes versus a goal of 50. Also per this plan, the home maintenance program was started.

Hopes and Fears for the Future

Holy Name has earned a good reputation in Omaha and throughout Nebraska and the nearby plains states. This has brought an ability to expand services, but it has also brought on more public scrutiny. Holy Name is sensitive to the possible pitfalls its very success can bring. One of its major concerns is battling misconceptions about the organization.

The most common misconceptions are that: 1) it is an arm of the Catholic Church; 2) it is attempting to "take over" neighborhoods by swamping current residents with new housing; and 3) as it grows, it is less involved with the very community it was formed to serve. Holy Name stresses in its public relations efforts that it is a local community development organization that was founded to serve all low-income residents regardless of religious affiliation.

The board is also concentrating on increasing its visibility in the neighborhoods it serves and in gaining greater representation from the neighborhood residents on the board of directors and board of advisors. Holy Name also continues to try to increase the number of African

Americans on the predominantly white board.

As it has evolved, Holy Name Housing Corporation has learned to trust its own experience and abilities rather than always looking for outside expertise, according to its executive director. In this regard, its move into being its own general contractor was a good one. Having survived 14 years, the organization believes it knows its market better than any outsider and is better able to control quality.

Two major concerns not directly under the corporation's control are the continued presence of drugs and crime in the neighborhoods it serves and, aside from its housing program, in getting new private investment to occur there. Holy Name is working with other groups to figure out ways of addressing these broader social issues. But as of this writing, no major new initiatives had been decided upon.

Nonetheless, in its original target area and elsewhere, Holy Name has played a key role in filling the gaps in Omaha's affordable housing delivery system.

If the past is any predictor of the future, Holy Name Housing Corporation will find the vision, leadership, and partners to solve some of these underlying problems--most likely through another spin-off or a coalition effort. While keeping a global view of problems and solutions in the low end of Omaha's real estate market, the organization itself still focuses tightly on its original mission of renovating or building and selling affordable homes--a dual strategy that may well be the key to its success.

Information Sources

For more information, contact:

Sr. Marilyn Ross, R.S.M.
Executive Director
Holy Name Housing Corporation
3014 N. 45th St.
Omaha, NE 68104
Phone: (402) 453-6100
Fax: (402) 451-7187

Cynthia Swoopes, Director
Omaha 100
2424 Cuming St.
Omaha, NE 68131
(402) 342-3773

12

Jackson Metro Housing Partnership, Inc.
(Jackson, Mississippi)

Program Highlights

Jackson Metro Housing Partnership, Inc.

Target Area:	City of Jackson (population 196,637)
Program Goals:	Assist low- and moderate-income home buyers Revitalize inner city neighborhoods
Major Elements:	Financial counseling and home buyer training Below market rate first mortgage loans from lender consortium Low-interest second mortgage loans Single-family housing development
Average Client Income:	$17,000
Typical Home Price:	$40,000 (existing)
Year started:	1992
Other Programs:	Land bank managed for the City of Jackson Rehabilitation of rental properties Loans and grants to other nonprofit organizations
Staffing:	4 fulltime staff members
Annual Output: (1995-1996)	240 clients trained 73 clients received financing 17 homes acquired and rehabbed 0 homes sold
Funding:	City of Jackson Federal government Local banks and businesses

Overview

Jackson Metro Housing Partnership, Inc. is a private, nonprofit organization created in 1992 for the purpose of helping low-income Jacksonians gain safe, decent and affordable housing.

The strongest early support for the concept of the Partnership came from the City of Jackson planning and housing officials, Mayor Kane Ditto, a group of city council members, and a few concerned private citizens, all of whom wanted to see a new citywide nonprofit-sponsored housing effort that would work closely with city government. There were several motives:

▶ While the City operated (and still operates) a home repair loan program, it wanted more expansive programs; particularly ones that would increase homeownership and improve blighted neighborhoods.

▶ There was a particular interest in revitalizing the distressed Mid-Town neighborhood just north of downtown.

▶ It was felt that a private, nonprofit entity involving local lenders could operate more efficiently and leverage more private funds than an expanded City-run program. Despite the City's strong roles in forming the Partnership and providing ongoing funding, it is not represented on the board. Board members primarily represent lending institutions, utility companies, businesses, and neighborhood interests.

The formation of the Partnership was a direct result of a strategic planning process facilitated in 1991 by The Enterprise Foundation. Several planning sessions involved local government officials, lenders, community advocates, and representatives of nonprofit housing organizations. The outcome was a preliminary plan to form the Partnership. Enterprise also provided start-up technical assistance that was funded by the City of Jackson and the U.S. Department of Housing and Urban Development.

With the local government, nonprofit organizations, and private businesses committed to starting the Partnership, it has achieved success within a relatively short period of time. The Partnership sponsors homeownership counseling and training, acts as a liaison between its clients and lending institutions throughout the purchase process, and provides 20 percent of the homeowners' financing at below-market rates.

The Partnership also inspects homes chosen by clients, helps find contractors for needed renovations, and provides post-purchase counseling.

Lender Consortium

Mississippi's four biggest banks--Bank of Mississippi, Deposit Guaranty, Union Planters Bank, and Trustmark--provide below-market-rate loans to first-time home buyers in tandem with second mortgage loans from the Partnership.

The Partnership's core activity is making low-interest second mortgage loans in tandem with conventional first mortgage loans. The Partnership loans make up about one-fifth of the home purchase financing. Since the loans are amortizing (as opposed to having payments deferred and due only on sale), the mechanism is a shallow subsidy. This approach can work in Jackson because home prices are relatively low. The average price of a Partnership-financed home is $40,000.

Between the program's first loan closing in August 1993 and March 1996, the Partnership had closed 147 second mortgage loans. It has directly lent $1.7 million and leveraged $5.3 million in home purchase financing from private lenders. Most of these loans have been made in older, suburban-like neighborhoods on the south and west sides of the city, areas with some stability, modest housing prices, and high or increasing proportions of African American residents.

The Partnership also plays a role in affordable residential real estate development throughout the city, helping other nonprofits and undertaking its own developments. The Partnership's focal project, announced in 1994, seeks to rebuild a block of houses on Manship Street in Mid-Town Jackson, a neighborhood near downtown that is one of the city's most distressed residential areas. The Partnership assembled the land and a few buildings suitable for rehabilitation. Habitat for Humanity is building 50 new homes that will be sold to low-income families.

Ironically for an organization focused on encouraging homeownership, the Partnership's most aggressive real estate development activities are aimed at renters. The Partnership's motive for these projects is primarily neighborhood revitalization, not homeownership. Furthermore, prospective buyers in these areas are expected to have very low incomes--so low that they could not afford even the most minimally-priced decent home financed through the Partnership. As evidence of these market realities, the Partnership has not been able to finance any home buyers in the Mid-town area.

But in the Mid-Town scenario, the Habitat model of very low-cost financing, volunteered labor, and donated materials works very well. And since the target neighborhoods have renters, and a certain amount of existing housing needs to be rehabilitated as rental homes or apartments, the Partnership has accepted the landlord role more or less as a developer of last resort.

The Mid-Town project has other interested partners. The City of Jackson will build new curbs and gutters and install new water and sewer lines, while Mississippi Power & Light will improve area lighting.

City officials and other civic leaders see this project as a model for revitalizing declining urban neighborhoods in Jackson. The Partnership and Habitat for Humanity plan to move on to other blocks in the Mid-Town area when the Manship Street project is finished. To date, 11 homes and apartment units have been completed and occupied.

Lease-Purchase Program

As an adjunct to its neighborhood redevelopment efforts, eight existing homes that were purchased and rehabbed by the Partnership have been leased by very low-income renters with an option to buy. At this point, the clients in these homes cannot qualify for home purchase loans because their incomes are too low, they lack funds for a down payment, and/or their credit is too impaired. They pay rent that averages $375 a month and are expected to qualify for a home purchase loan within six months to two years, depending on their circumstances.

A Land Bank

The Partnership has primary responsibility for managing a "land bank" set up by the Jackson City Council in 1994. The land bank is a mechanism for the City to dispose of blighted, tax-forfeited properties transferred to it by the State. The Partnership manages the properties and helps the City dispose of the vacant lots or dilapidated homes.

The land bank properties are either sold to local nonprofits at a minimal charge or deeded free of charge. Some of the better properties are sold to home buyers participating in the Partnership program. The Partnership has acquired, rehabbed, and resold or rented 12 of these homes to low-income families. The structures on the properties, however, are demolished to make way for new homes. At any one time, about 50 properties are available in the land bank.

One of the advantages of the land bank is that the nonprofits do not have to pay taxes, insurance, or maintenance charges on the properties while they are in the bank. They take title to a home or building lot only when they are ready to begin work on it. Five other nonprofit organizations take advantage of the land bank. Including land bank homes and others, Habitat for Humanity had constructed or renovated 63 houses as of 1995 and plans to build a minimum of 25 houses per year in the Jackson area. Voice of Calvary renovated 45 single-family units in West Jackson between 1987 and 1995. And the West Jackson Community Development Corporation, the Society Against a Violent Environment, and the Mississippi Trust for Historic Preservation have built or rehabbed six land bank homes.

Market Analysis

The City

Jackson, the capital city of Mississippi, has an economy built on state government, banking, and insurance. Recently, the cellular phone industry has become an important employer.

Particularly in its older neighborhoods and downtown area, Jackson has experienced a struggling economy, increasing poverty, and a low-cost but deteriorating housing stock. In recent years, a number of inner-city businesses have moved to suburban locations or closed their doors.

Along with population losses in the 1980s, Jackson experienced a sharp increase in the poverty rate, from 18 percent to 22 percent.

For key statistics on demographics and market conditions see the table on the next page.

▶

	Jackson	USA
City population:	196,637	
Population growth, 1980s:	-3.3%	12.6%
Percent African American:	55.7%	12%
Percent Hispanic:	>1%	9%
City median income, 1990s:	$23,270	$30,056
Metro median income, 1996:	$37,400	$41,600
Unemployment rate:	6%	6.7%
Poverty rate:	22.7%	13.1%
Median home value:	$54,600	$79,900
Home value increase, 1980s:	36.5%	67%
Median monthly rent:	$388	$447
Homeownership rate:	57.3%	64.2%

U.S. Census, 1990; 1996 median income from HUD.

A 1990 survey found that 8,000 dwellings in Jackson were substandard (about 12 percent of the housing stock), with that number increasing by about 400 a year. In neighborhoods with lower property values, a considerable number of single-family homes have been bought by investor-owners, a trend that typically results in deterioration of neighborhoods.

To counter these trends, the housing programs of the City, the Partnership, and other nonprofit groups place a strong emphasis on: 1) rehabilitation of owner-occupied and rental housing; 2) increasing homeownership; and 3) revitalizing small target areas through a combined strategy of rehabilitation and infill new construction.

On the positive side, home prices in older parts of Jackson--while more expensive than in a few other inner-city markets--are still exceptionally affordable by national standards. Almost every home financed by the Partnership has cost less than $46,000.

There is some evidence that Jackson is experiencing a turnaround. In mid-1996, new construction activity in the city was up by almost one-third in a year-on-year comparison. The city's deputy planning director credited the increase in development to better crime control and improvements in deteriorated neighborhoods.

The county tax assessor said recently that property values in depressed areas of Jackson have begun to increase. He credited the Partnership and other nonprofit housing groups with turning around some of these neighborhoods.

Inner-City Target Areas

The Partnership and its allies are battling difficult trends. Mid-Town, for example, had an unemployment rate in 1989 of 19 percent. The median income in that year was approximately $13,500. Eighty percent of the housing was renter-occupied, and 22 percent of housing units stood vacant. Today, there is still little racial or economic integration. Ninety-three percent of the population is minority, and almost three-quarters of the households have incomes under $15,000 a year.

The Partnership's target areas for revitalization are more distressed than the neighborhoods where most of its home purchase loans are made. In the areas where clients buy homes, homeownership rates, incomes, and the quality of housing are somewhat higher. Since the beginning of the program, incomes of home buyers assisted by the Partnership have ranged from a low of $7,800 a year to a high of $27,200, with an average of about $17,000 and an average family size of 3.2 persons. Eighty percent of the buyers have been female heads of households. Eighty-nine percent are African American and the rest are white.

Operations and Financing

Marketing

Jackson Metro Housing Partnership advertises its services to low-income Jacksonians with brochures and pamphlets describing the program and the homeownership training workshops. Staff members attend neighborhood meetings. But word-of-mouth advertising by assisted clients is the most effective marketing tool. When the program began, donated television advertisements were effective in bringing in the initial clients.

The Partnership also receives extensive media coverage of its homeowner program

and renovation projects, such as "Operation Restore Pride." Since the organization represents a working partnership among long-established local nonprofit, business and public entities, it is widely known in the Jackson area.

Financing of Homes

When the program began, the banks pledged to make up to $16 million in portfolio loans over a five-year period. This backing enables the Partnership to offer loans both to low-income buyers and investors in low-income housing renovation projects.

The Partnership works with the prospective buyers to obtain financing from the participating lending institutions. Lenders offer mortgage loans at about one percentage point below the prevailing rate for 80 percent of the amount financed. Borrowers pay typical closing costs and a $500 origination fee for the bank loan, although most of the closing costs can be financed with the tandem loan package.

To date, none of the lenders' loans has been sold in the secondary mortgage markets. While many of the loans could potentially be sold, the lenders have preferred to keep them in portfolio.

The Partnership--using federal funds passed through the City--provides the other 20 percent of the financing at two percent interest (fixed rate.) Both this second mortgage loan and the first mortgage loan are written for 25-year terms. The blended rate of the two loans was 6.5 percent in late 1995.

During fiscal year 1995, the Partnership invested nearly $248,000 in second mortgage loans, a substantial decline from a first year rush of nearly $1.5 million the year before that depleted its funds available for lending. Double the 1995 activity--nearly $500,000 in loans--is predicted for fiscal year 1996. That level is on target with the original business plan for the Partnership.

Most of the funding--a total of $231,000--for second mortgage loans in FY 1995 came from grants from the HUD HOME program that were passed through the City. Repayments of loans accounted for the rest. All repayments go back into what is, in effect, a revolving loan fund. In FY 1995, these repayments amounted to $62,620.

Qualification for Assistance and Underwriting Criteria

To receive financing from the program, borrowers must: 1) meet the income criteria; 2) have at least $1,200 in cash available for a down payment and closing costs; 3) complete the homebuyer training course; 4) have reasonably good credit and job stability; and 5) purchase a home within the city limits.

The program is marketed to households with incomes at or below 60 percent of the area median income, which in 1996 was $22,440 for a family of four. Most of the Partnership's funding sources would allow it to finance households with incomes up to 80 percent of median income ($29,900 for a family of four), but it has imposed these tighter guidelines on itself. The 60 percent-of-median standard is based on the belief that families with incomes above this level have reasonable opportunities for home purchases in Jackson's affordable inner-city markets and do not require subsidies.

Occasional exceptions are made for households with incomes just over the line or those with unusual financial circumstances.

The program encourages coapplications by any combination of parents, children, and grandparents, so long as the combined incomes are still within the guidelines.

The underwriting criteria used by participating lenders is exceptionally liberal. The ratios for borrower debt are a maximum 35 percent of income for housing debt and 42 percent for all installment debt. This compares to 28 and 36 percent respectively for conventional loans, while many special financing programs for low-income borrowers extend these to 33/40.

As a practical matter, clients' total installment debt is the limiting factor on home purchases, with many of them pushing the limit of 42 percent. On the other hand, the average monthly housing payment is very low--usually amounting to less than 20 percent of income.

A minimum $1,000 is required for a down payment, along with sufficient funds (about $200) to pay for the credit report, two month's property insurance costs, and one month's property taxes.

The lenders require no mortgage insurance, since their loan-to-value ratio is typically lower than the conventional 80 percent maximum.

Intake, Screening and Counseling

The Partnership has screened over 2,400 clients since the beginning of its program. After an initial telephone screening, clients arrange for a prequalification interview. Those with serious credit problems are referred to the local consumer credit counseling agency. If clients are turned down for mortgages, the Partnership offers them continued counseling to help them reach the stage where they can obtain a mortgage.

Homeownership Training

The Partnership sponsors a 12-hour homeownership training workshop for all of its prospective home buyers. Training takes place in two sessions on Saturdays or week nights and follows the Fannie Mae homebuyer training manual. Most of the training is done by staff members. The workshops also feature speakers from the banking and real estate industries, who discuss the home purchase process and responsibilities of homeownership.

Entergy Corporation, the parent company of Mississippi Power & Light Co., underwrote the costs of homeownership training classes for the first three years of the program and continues to fund them. In 1996, HUD and the National Association of Housing Partnerships made a $35,000 grant for the training program.

Home Selection

Clients can choose homes from among the Partnership's land bank houses or can choose a home with the real estate agent of their choice. The staff will inspect and evaluate homes that are chosen for purchase and helps the buyer find contractors for needed rehabilitation work. Inspection costs are paid by the Partnership.

The program has a purchase price limit of $46,000, an exceptionally low limit among the programs surveyed in this study. This criterion focuses the program on financing lower-valued properties in the city's older neighborhoods--homes that are affordable to low-income clients. Indirectly, this provides some reinvestment and economic stimulus in areas where real estate values are currently low.

A home being financed must have a termite certificate and may not be located in a flood hazard zone.

Housing Development Activities

The Partnership has been involved in housing development activities that, as described earlier, primarily involve rental housing development in support of targeted revitalization efforts that are being undertaken with such partners as Habitat for Humanity. It has received a tax credit allocation for renovation of 18 rental units in Mid-Town and is involved in demolishing and rebuilding uninhabitable houses in that area. Houses in the West Park and Farish Street neighborhoods have been purchased and will be rehabbed for first-time home buyers.

To date, the Partnership has rehabbed about 40 dwelling units, both singlefamily and multifamily.

Long-Term Affordability Controls

When using HUD HOME program funds (as is the case with most clients) the Partnership imposes minimum provisions for long-term affordability associated with

HUD's HOME program financing. If assisted home buyers resell their homes, these provisions require that efforts be made to find purchasers with incomes below 80 percent of median income. In addition, the Partnership retains a right of first refusal to repurchase the homes at a formula resale price.

Assistance to Neighborhood Associations

The Partnership helped to establish a neighborhood association in the North Mid-Town community and is working closely with Christ United Methodist Church's outreach minister in Mid-Town to provide ongoing support.

The Partnership is also helping the Jackson police department establish a community policing program that will initially target the Mid-Town and Bailey Corridor areas and will include housing police officers in the targeted areas.

Loan Collections and Post-Purchase Counseling

Jackson Metro Housing Partnership boasts an on-time collection rate of 94 to 96 percent, compared to about 94 percent for all home purchase loans in Mississippi. To date, there have been no foreclosures. The Partnership stays in touch with the buyers after purchase, providing post-purchase counseling and help with practical issues, like finding a contractor for after-purchase repairs or setting up community organizations.

Partners

The Partnership's closest partners are the local government, its participating lenders, other nonprofit housing groups, and utility companies.

When it was formed, the Partnership was anointed by the City as an intermediary organization passing through HOME funds in the form of grants and loans to other nonprofits, like Habitat for Humanity, Voice of Calvary Inc., and the West Jackson Community Development corporation. Since the Partnership is primarily focused on its own housing programs, this is not always a comfortable role. Most of the other nonprofits would prefer to deal directly with the City.

The underlying reason for this arrangement appears to be a practical one. City officials prefer to have a single nongovernmental intermediary make allocations of funds for nonprofit housing activities to lessen the potential for political machinations and red tape.

The funds are used for various purposes. Habitat uses grants to buy house lots. Voice of Calvary uses the funds to write down project costs. For the West Jackson Community Development Corporation, the Partnership has provided 12 first mortgage loans to clients selected by the CDC who were not bankable enough to qualify for the Partnership's regular loan program.

Administration

Management and Staffing

Jackson Metro Housing Partnership is run by four fulltime staff members. The program coordinators direct the homeowner training and counseling and help out as needed with other Partnership activities. The staff roster is as follows:

Executive director
Program coordinators (2)
Administrative assistant

Three out of four staff members are minorities.

Board of Directors

The 19-member board of directors includes six representatives of the four participating lenders named in the program description. In addition, it includes representatives of Mississippi Power & Light, Mississippi Valley Gas, the Mississippi Municipal Association, and the local United Way. Six other members are neighborhood representatives, and three others are in business. Forty percent are members of minority groups.

Administrative Funding

The Partnership's general and administrative expenses for the fiscal year ended September 30, 1995 were just over $190,000, of which $104,000 was paid for "bare" salaries, $50,000 was paid for contractual services, and $35,000 was for other expenses, including employee benefits.

According to the organization's audited financial statements, the major sources of administrative funding and surplus revenues were as follows (rounded to the nearest thousand dollars).

Federal HOME program	$89,000
Federal CDBG funds	6,000
Lender contributions	65,000
Miss. Power & Light	25,000
Miss. Valley Gas	20,000
Entergy Corporation	17,000 (for homebuyer training)

An important piece of the Partnership's administrative funding was $438,000 in pledges of start-up funds from the corporations represented on the board plus a few other local sources. Most of these pledges covered a three-year period ending September 30, 1995, when they were renewed on an annual basis. Future annual renewals are expected.

The Partnership receives contributions of property from other private sources as well. An example is the donation in 1995 of an eight-unit apartment complex and two single family houses in the Mid-Town area.

Financial Management

The Partnership is a relatively healthy financial operation for a young organization. In the fiscal year ended September 30, 1995, it had an unrestricted fund balance (net worth) of over $92,000, representing mostly cash and real estate owned. Total assets were over $2.4 million. (The $1.7 million in loans made by the Partnership are shown both as an asset and a liability, due to the technical requirement that HOME funds be repaid to the primary grantee--the City. However, the City has pledged to recycle these funds back to the Partnership.)

Net revenues for the same period were nearly $29,000 for the same 12-month period, an improvement over a deficit of $98,000 in the previous fiscal year (a loss that was absorbed by a revenue surplus from the previous year).

Lessons Learned

Strengths of Program

When the Metro Jackson Housing Partnership could have chosen an easier path, it has held its hand in the fire to gain higher public benefits. As a program operating citywide, it could be working with higher-income clients in neighborhoods with higher-valued real estate. It could have avoided the tough neighborhoods and the extra work of rental housing development that revitalization of these areas demands.

Instead, the organization has chosen a tough self-discipline. Unique among all programs in this study it has capped client income levels and allowed home purchase prices at levels significantly below those imposed by its funders. The Partnership's income limits are 25 percent below the levels required by its HUD funding, and its home price limits are below half of

what some "officially" low-income buyers could afford. Similarly, it chose a target area--Mid-Town--that was one of the most distressed neighborhoods in Jackson.

A number of other programs in this study are limited to certain neighborhoods, rather than operating citywide. In the poorest of these neighborhoods, the market--rather than funders or another organization itself--dictates that client incomes and home prices will be low.

On the other hand, citywide programs (both those examined in this study and others) tend to work with clients representing a much broader band of incomes, including many who are close to the high end of low-income. Also, as a consequence, many citywide programs finance homes with values that are two or three times higher than those being financed in Jackson, a policy that tends to take programs into stable neighborhoods with no need for revitalization.

The Partnership home price limit is a particularly artful piece of program design. Of course, it reflects a very affordable home purchase market. But more importantly, it exemplifies three other things: 1) a tight focus on impacting low-cost (and more distressed) areas; 2) a recognition of what price ranges very low-income clients can really afford; and 3) a concern not to allow home buyers to use substantial subsidies to "buy up" to better homes. This guideline is so important to program outcomes that the Partnership actually lowered it from $50,000 to $46,000 after the first year of operations.

The Partnership has also made a pragmatic and apparently wise decision to pursue development of rental properties, rather than homes for sale, in the toughest neighborhoods. This works because the Partnership chose to build on pre-existing organizational strengths and join forces with Habitat for Humanity, whose program model for homeownership works better in these neighborhoods than the Partnership's. Rental housing development was obviously a niche that needed to be filled if these very distressed and very low-income areas were to be revitalized.

Another strength of the Partnership is the commitment of the City and four major lenders. The City--considering the other housing programs it funds--makes a substantial commitment of HOME and CDBG dollars to the Partnership's home purchase program and development activities. The lenders, for their part, make portfolio loans at one percent below market rates, and with very liberal down payment requirements and underwriting criteria. These concessions are above and beyond those found in the typical community reinvestment programs of private lenders.

Achieving Goals

Each year, the Partnership sets annual goals for its performance, and with minor exceptions, these have been achieved. In the fall of 1996, a board retreat is scheduled to develop a five-year plan.

Hopes and Fears for the Future

As with any community development organization operating on a citywide or areawide basis, the Partnership must consult with and satisfy a wide variety of clients, partners, and stakeholders.

Partnership staff members work regularly with the mayor, city council members, city officials, representatives of banks and other nonprofits, and community residents. While this juggling act has gotten results, it is difficult and time-consuming.

Looking toward the future, when the Mid-Town project is completed in a few years, the organization expects to select another distressed target neighborhood. In the view of Executive Director Phil Eide, the Partnership should continue to pursue what has worked to date--a mix of targeted neighborhood revitalization projects geared to manageably small geographic areas, and a home buyer assistance program that is less geographically targeted but is still tightly focussed on improving the fortunes of very low-income households and areas with relatively low property values.

For a city sitting on the divide between decline and revitalization, and with other important housing providers already at work, this young organization with a citywide focus quickly found a niche that works.

Information Source

For more information, contact:

Phil Eide
Executive Director
Jackson Metro Housing
    Partnership, Inc.
612 N. State St.
P.O. Box 22987
Jackson, MS 39229
Phone: (601) 969-1895

13

Liberation Community, Inc.
(Fort Worth, Texas)

Program Highlights

Liberation Community, Inc.

Target Area:	Fort Worth; Polytechnic Heights area (population 54,533)
Program Goals:	Assist low-income home buyers Revitalize inner-city neighborhoods Develop family self-sufficiency
Major Elements:	Financial counseling and home buyer training First and second mortgages Assistance in getting conventional first mortgage loans Single-family housing development
Average Client Income:	$14,000
Typical Home Price:	$35,000 (existing); $52,000 (new)
Year Started:	1985 (housing programs in 1988)
Other Programs:	Model Block--Polytechnic Heights YouthBuild--affiliated job training program Emergency assistance: food and clothing GED program; adult education English as a second language Legal aid
Staffing:	15 paid staff members; 4 fulltime volunteers
Annual Output: (1995)	140 prospective home buyers trained 5 newly constructed and sold homes 25 acquired/rehabbed and sold homes 20 clients receiving conventional mortgages 25 clients receiving down payment/closing assistance
Funding:	Federal Home Loan Bank Affordable Housing Program HOME and CDBG funds from local governments Private contributions Developer fees Net rental income

Overview

Liberation Community, Inc. develops, sells, and finances homes and operates other community improvement programs in Fort Worth's most severely distressed neighborhood. It is an offshoot of the Nazarene Compassionate Ministries, which established a mission and church in the neighborhood in 1985. In 1988, a ministerial student assigned to the mission began the housing program.

The neighborhood was named for the Polytechnic Institute, a small college that later became Texas Wesleyan University. Wesleyan is a respected Methodist-affiliated school that is alma mater to many business and civic leaders in Fort Worth. Surrounding the school is a once-prosperous blue collar residential neighborhood that experienced a major decline from the 1960s through the 1980s.

According to a recent study by the United Way, "Poly" (as the area is more commonly known) has the highest rates of unemployment and violent crime in Tarrant County (which includes Fort Worth and Arlington). About one-third of its households and half of its children live in poverty. About 40 percent of the area's homes were vacant when Liberation's housing program started, a number that has since been reduced to about 20 percent. Still, many vacant homes are boarded up and abandoned, and residents live in fear of random, drive-by shootings--one killed a child several years ago.

Given these negative factors and absentee ownership of 60 percent of the homes, Polytechnic in 1988 was one of the last areas a professional planner would have picked to start a homeownership program. In fact, in the early and mid-1980s, three nonprofit-sponsored community development programs failed in and around Poly. Two of the programs provided home renovation loans to owner-occupants, one rehabilitated and sold homes, and the third revitalized commercial buildings along the area's main thoroughfare.

Liberation Community has succeeded against these odds. The nonprofit organization started by offering food and clothing to the needy from a storefront location. At the time, it had an annual budget of $35,000. In 11 years, it has started a number of community development programs that now have combined annual expenditures of over $2 million. In affiliation with the national YouthBuild organization, Liberation Community combines a job training program with its renovation and construction of homes for sale.

Liberation's entry into housing development began in 1988. A local thrift institution had financed many investor-owners during a period of speculative buying in the 1980s. When the bubble burst in 1989, the lender foreclosed on scores of homes in Poly, many of them abandoned and boarded up. The lender donated 40 of the homes to Liberation Community. The then-director of Liberation Community, Brian Stone, saw an opportunity to begin an aggressive program of rehabbing homes and recruiting new homeowners to the neighborhood. (Mr. Stone was a Ph.D. candidate in divinity who has since returned to teaching.)

With financing from local foundations, businesses, and the City of Fort Worth,

Liberation began a successful program of renovating the donated homes using renovation contractors and crews of job trainees. Total costs of the homes ranged from $25,000 to $30,000, making them affordable to very low-income families. Ten of the homes were rented and later sold through informal lease-purchase arrangements, but most were sold outright.

Homes were made even more affordable through low-cost second mortgage loans from three federal programs supported by the City of Fort Worth: Community Development Block Grant funds, a $600,000 grant from the now-terminated federal Nehemiah program, and federal HOME funds. In many cases, buyers' first mortgage loans are as low as $15,000 to $20,000. About 60 percent of the home purchase loans have been funded by private lenders. Liberation funded the other 40 percent using its own revolving loan fund.

Occasionally, Liberation has also acted as a real estate agent, since its current director is a licensed broker. About 10 home sellers have come to Liberation, which found buyers and financed the purchase and rehabilitation of the homes. Liberation takes a commission on these sales.

The relatively low cost of homes and the flexibility afforded by having its own loan fund have allowed Liberation to finance buyers with incomes as low as $6,000 a year.

Liberation is also engaged in other housing activities:

Rental housing: At any one time, the organization provides four to six homes as rental units for families that wish to buy homes, but are not quite ready to qualify. Often, but not always, these renter families buy the homes they occupy after income or credit problems have been cleared up.

Transitional housing: Liberation provides six apartments and support services to single males who have completed drug/alcohol rehabilitation programs.

Home improvement loans: Liberation provides emergency home improvement loans to homeowners on a limited basis. Typically, these loans fall in the $1,000 to $5,000 range. About 50 of these loans have been made.

But housing is only part of a much broader effort to remake the Poly area. Since 1985, Liberation has provided emergency food and clothing to over 20,000 families, taught GED classes for nearly 1,800 adults, and provided legal aid to 5,000 individuals.

Liberation relies strongly on donated labor. Volunteers have logged over 50 person-years of work since the organization's beginning. Liberation is also strongly neighborhood-based, with half of its board of directors and half its staff living in its relatively small target area.

The organization started its operations in part of the Nazarene Church property. Now it occupies separate facilities nearby and has been spun off both legally and financially as a separate operation, although it still keeps close ties to the church congregation.

Model Block Program

In 1994, Liberation launched a model block program in a 15-block target area. The overall goal is to re-establish a safe and decent neighborhood. Toward this end, Liberation has targeted much of its acquisition, rehabilitation, and resale effort to this area of about 300 homes.

The City agreed to accelerate demolitions of vacant homes that were beyond repair. And on vacant lots, Liberation built five new houses beginning in 1995. The organization has also worked with residents to establish a neighborhood association and has sponsored weekly clean-ups of the vacant lots and alleys.

The donation of seven acres in the neighborhood by the Paulsel family has enabled Liberation to develop a neighborhood park that features a ball field and playgrounds for children.

For the time being, Liberation has taken its model block concept outside Polytechnic Heights. One new target area is across town in Como, where seven homes are being built or renovated. The other target area is a low-income neighborhood in East Arlington, where a 15-home subdivision is underway. Arlington is a prosperous and growing city located about 10 miles east of Fort Worth. Liberation's work in these new areas is seen as temporary. The organization hopes to spin off new neighborhood-based nonprofit housing corporations and then refocus on Poly.

Market Analysis

Citywide Demographics and Market Conditions

Fort Worth grew up in the late 1800s as one of the most important western railroad towns and cattle-shipping centers. While the stockyards eventually declined, the fortunes made in the city's pioneer days helped carry Fort Worth forward as a center of commerce, oil-related businesses, and finance. During World War II, it became a manufacturing center for military aircraft and home to Carswell Air Force Base.

From 1980 to 1990, the population of the city increased an average of nearly 1.8 percent a year, about 50 percent higher than the national rate of increase. This was based, in part, on increased defense-related manufacturing and the oil boom of the early 1980s. But more recently, the city's economy has been hurt by the closure of the Air Force base and cutbacks in defense-related manufacturing jobs. Between 1990 and 1993, an estimated 20,000 defense-related jobs were lost.

By 1993, the unemployment rate had increased to 10 percent, but it declined somewhat in the national economic recovery of the mid-1990s. Despite its major job losses, Fort Worth has seen diversified growth, especially in the airline, railroad, and computer industries. The city is headquarters to the major consumer electronics retailer, Tandy Corporation.

The poverty rate increased dramatically in the 1980s. In 1989, it was 17.4 percent, compared to only 13.5 percent 10 years before. During the same period, the number of persons on public assistance actually declined. These statistics indicate an increase among the working poor and a general loss of good-paying jobs. Clearly, Fort Worth exemplifies the national problem of downward mobility among blue collar workers.

The table at the top of the following page lists key demographic and market data.

	Fort Worth	USA
City population:	447,619	
Population growth, 1980s:	18%	12.6%
Percent African American:	22%	12%
Percent Hispanic:	19.5%	9%
City median income, 1990s:	$26,547	$30,056
Metro median income, 1996:	$47,500	$41,600
Unemployment rate:	8.1%	6.7%
Poverty rate:	17.4%	13.1%
Median home value:	$59,900	$79,900
Home value increase, 1980s:	86%	67%
Median monthly rent:	$403	$447
Homeownership rate:	54.5%	64.2%

U.S. Census, 1990; 1996 median income from HUD

By national standards, housing is plentiful and cheap. The median value of a single-family home in Fort Worth in 1990 was about 20 percent below the national median. Median rents were about six percent below the national median. As a result of over-building in the 1980s oil boom, vacancy rates, at 13.6 percent in 1990, were about 35 percent higher than the national average. The number of vacant units in Fort Worth more than doubled in the 1980s, from 12,000 units to 26,000 units.

But ironically, for a city with a surplus of relatively low-cost housing, the homeownership rate in Fort Worth fell dramatically, from 62 percent to 54 percent, in the 1980s. Housing cost burdens increased dramatically for homeowners, and the city had one of the highest rates of foreclosure and HUD-owned homes in the nation. One can only infer that homeownership and housing affordability were hurt by the softening of the job market and the resulting increase in poverty.

In such an economy, the most distressed neighborhoods, such as Polytechnic Heights, bear a disproportionate share of the problem. Where housing for sale or rent becomes cheaper and more abundant, families in the most troubled neighborhoods will tend to move to less troubled neighborhoods unless they have deep roots in these areas. That exodus occurred in Poly in the 1980s.

Characteristics of the Target Area

Polytechnic Heights is located in southeast Fort Worth, 10 minutes from the downtown area. About 9,000 people live in the neighborhood. The population is about 50 percent African American, 35 percent Hispanic, 10 percent Anglo, and five percent other ethnic groups. Many families are headed by single mothers. Nineteen percent of households included an unemployed adult, according to a United Way survey (cited earlier). In 1994, persons in seven percent of Poly households were victims of violent crime.

While conditions have improved in recent years, Poly in 1996 still had one of the highest concentrations of substandard housing in Fort Worth. And while housing costs are low in relation to other parts of Tarrant County, the prevalence of poverty-level incomes results in Poly residents paying the highest percentage of income for housing of any area in the county.

Virtually all of the housing stock is single-family. About 40 percent of the homes are owner-occupied, and 60 percent are investor-owned. About 20 percent of the homes are vacant, and most of these are investor-owned. Liberation targets this predominantly blighted, vacant housing stock for either rehabilitation or demolition.

The typical family involved in the Liberation home buyer program has two to five children, averages four persons, and has an income of about $14,000 per year. While some buyers were formerly renters in Poly, about three out of five are recruited from outside the area. Because of the prevalence of elderly residents, the transience of younger Poly renters, and their extremely low incomes, the neighborhood has a relatively small pool of potential home buyers.

About 50 percent of the buyers are Hispanic, 40 percent are African American, and 10 percent are Anglo. Incomes of clients are as follows:

Income Range	Percentage of Clients
$6,000-$12,000	15%
$12,000-$18,000	65%
$18,000-24,000	20%

Operations and Financing

Marketing

Liberation has many tools for advertising its programs, including brochures, fliers, folders of information, newspaper ads, and newsletters. The newsletter is abundantly supported by local advertisers, demonstrating Liberation's wide favor in Fort Worth.

Liberation's homeownership program is advertised in the metro area's Hispanic and African American newspapers. All advertising material is presented in English and Spanish. The program gets regular coverage in newspapers and on television news and feature shows. The organization has won awards not only locally, but nationally as well.

A half-time community organizer also helps market the program by opening up contacts with neighborhood residents, organizations, schools, churches, and social service organizations.

Still, referrals from past clients are the major source of prospective home buyers. About 20 to 30 families are always on the waiting list for new homes. In a sense, the homes sell themselves, because they are priced far below the value of comparable homes anywhere in the metropolitan area.

The low prices are due to the depressed value of vacant homes in the neighborhood, cost containment by Liberation, and the availability of subsidies for about 40 percent of the cost of each home.

Financing of Homes

Four forms of financing are available to clients: 1) first mortgages from conventional lenders; 2) soft second mortgages funded with HOME dollars; 3) direct first mortgages from Liberation's own revolving loan fund for non-bankable clients; and 4) amortizing second mortgages from Liberation's loan fund.

The program regularly works with the following lenders:

NationsBank
Bank United
Norwest Mortgage Co.
Judith Smith Mortgage Co.
Colonial Savings
Fort Worth Mortgage Co.
Woodhaven National Bank

Most of the lenders make concessions. Two, NationsBank and Fort Worth Mortgage, have regularly offered mortgages at one percentage point below market rates. Norwest Mortgage offers grants of up to $2,000 to help cover down payment and closing costs (funded in part by grants from the Federal Home Loan Bank). Other lenders waive fees or offer liberal underwriting.

Because of the use of second mortgages covering about 40 percent of the purchase costs of homes, first mortgages total only about $20,000. Because of the low loan-to-value ratios, mortgage insurance is not required. Still, FHA insurance is used occasionally because it enables the lender (Judith Smith Mortgage Co. is the primary FHA lender) to apply more liberal employment and credit standards. The cost of FHA loans, including the insurance premium, is about the same as conventional ones.

With about 95 percent of its home sales, Liberation offers tandem second mortgage loans averaging about $15,000 each and funded with HOME money that was set aside for Community-Based Housing Development Organizations (CHDOs) by the cities of Fort Worth and Arlington. With these soft seconds, all payments are deferred until resale of the property. If the homeowner stays in the home for five to 10 years (depending upon the amount of the second mortgage) the obligation is forgiven.

Liberation has taken issue with this loan forgiveness, which was required by the local governments. As a result, its newest $100,000 in HOME CHDO funding in Fort Worth will be used for second mortgages that are repayable at low rates. As opposed to being given away, the funds will be recycled to help future clients.

Liberation's Revolving Loan Funds and Loan Sales Program

Liberation's most successful financial tools are its own revolving loan funds. One was originally capitalized in 1989 and 1990 with $150,000 in grants from local foundations-- the Burnett-Tandy Foundation, the Amon Carter Foundation, and the Sid Richardson Foundation. Before Liberation received significant government funding, this was used to finance both first and second mortgages.

Even today, as many as half of Liberation's clients receive first mortgage loans directly from Liberation Community. Using its own funds, Liberation can take risks that lenders cannot, and can help clients who otherwise could not be financed.

In order to preserve the fund's capital, first mortgages are written at market rates. As with conventional loans, they are usually made in tandem with HOME-funded second mortgages.

A second revolving loan fund was capitalized with $100,000 in Community Development Block Grant funds from the City of Fort Worth. As with HOME monies, CDBG funds were used (primarily in the earlier phases of the program) to finance second mortgages that cover about 40 percent of the purchase price. These loans are not forgiven, and bear interest rates of zero to three percent, thus replenishing the loan fund over time.

Of the two funds, the first one is the most remarkable. Through a program of loan sales, the original capital of $150,000 has been recycled about four times to make approximately 40 loans totaling about $600,000.

Before selling loans, Liberation waits for six to 12 months to determine the

borrower's payment history. If payments have been prompt, the loan is sold. These four local banks have bought most of the loans:

Bank United
Summit National Bank
Bank of Commerce
Central Bank and Trust

The program offers lenders a trouble-free way of helping low-income families buy homes. No client processing or underwriting is required. Most of the loans are ultimately resold to Fannie Mae. And no lender has lost money. The one loan that went bad was immediately repurchased by Liberation Community.

Liberation services about 50 of its own loans and 30 of the loans that have been sold to lenders. Escrows for property taxes and insurance are always required.

In 1994, Liberation held just over $177,000 in second mortgage loans made with HOME funds and had made another $285,000 in second mortgage loans funded by the HUD Nehemiah program (which was discontinued).

As of the end of 1994, these were the primary sources of home financing that had been used by Liberation's clients:

	1994	1989-1994
Liberation Revolving Loan Fund:	$191,500	$1,085,580
City of Fort Worth CDBG:	37,500	588,210
HUD Nehemiah Program:	105,000	285,000
Tarrant County Housing Partnership:	115,000	187,000
Private lenders' first mortgages:	363,750	909,485
Buyers' down payments	26,000	70,000
Totals:	$838,750	$3,125,275

It is worthy of note that as of 1994, only about 30 percent of all home-purchase funding had come from conventional lenders. It is apparent that the use of federal and private grant money has been essential in making the rehabbed homes affordable and marketable to low-income families.

The $1 million-plus figure for revolving loan fund financing includes the value of donated properties.

Since 1994, HOME funds have become the most used source of subsidy financing. A total of $400,000 has been allocated by the City of Fort Worth and $225,000 has been allocated by Arlington.

Qualification for Assistance; Underwriting Criteria

To qualify for Liberation's homeownership program, applicants must have a household income of at least $1,000 a month. This can include SSI and Social Security income, but not public assistance. Applicants must be able to show a stable job history, proven credit, and stable residency, and they must participate in homeownership training and counseling.

Lenders' terms are typical of programs with liberalized underwriting. For example, NationsBank offers fixed-rate mortgages with a five percent down payment, or with a "3/2" plan--a three percent down payment with the other two percent coming from gifts, loans or grants. Most participating lenders allow a 38 percent debt-to-income ratio and a 33 percent housing expense ratio.

Bank United currently offers a three percent cash-to-close program with no mortgage insurance required and with a mortgage rate about four-tenths of a percent higher than its conventional mortgage rate.

As a result of these liberal terms, second mortgage subsidies, and low home prices, Liberation's buyers usually pay less than $1,000 out-of-pocket to purchase a home.

With its own revolving loan fund, Liberation is a little more conservative. Because many of its loans will be sold to Fannie Mae, Liberation follows that agency's 28/36 underwriting guidelines.

Intake, Screening, and Counseling

Prospective clients first must fill out a preapplication, either on their own or with help from one of Liberation's two loan counselors. Then a counselor conducts an intake interview. During the interview, an on-line credit report is obtained and reviewed. Based on the information, clients are then divided into three groups: 1) candidates for bank financing; 2) candidates for Liberation's financing; and 3) applicants who appear not to qualify for any financing.

People in the first two groups are referred to home buyer training classes. Applicants who don't qualify are told what is required to improve their income or credit standing.

Homeownership Training

Liberation provides between three and five hours of classroom training to each of its prospective buyers. The training takes place on Saturdays in one session and is taught by Liberation's personnel.

Most of the training is built around standard curricula developed by NationsBank. A banking basics curriculum covers such topics as budgeting, how to start a savings plan, how to open and balance a checking account, and how to resolve (and avoid) credit problems. The home buyer training addresses the advantages and disadvantages of homeownership, the mortgage process, the rights of a home buyer, the role of real estate agents, how to assess a house you are considering, and how to calculate whether mortgage payments will be affordable, among other topics.

In addition, Liberation requires clients to receive one-on-one credit counseling from Housing Opportunities, Inc., the major local housing counseling organization. This is more intensive than the home buyer training--involving two two-hour sessions a week for two weeks, and more if necessary.

Home Selection

Potential buyers may purchase any of the homes owned by Liberation or any other vacant house in the target area that falls within their budget. Most buy homes built or rehabilitated by the organization. The typical home has three bedrooms and averages about 1,300 square feet. All homes must conform to HUD's minimal Housing Quality Standards.

The average price of renovated homes is about $35,000, and the five new homes built so far were priced at $50,000. Liberation's staff shows the homes and closes the sales without the assistance of outside brokers. Included in the price of rehabilitated homes is a $200 to $300 landscaping allowance, which new home buyers can use for site improvements of their choice.

Housing Development Activities

To date, most of Liberation Community's housing development activities have focused on acquisition, renovation, and resale of scattered-site homes. Liberation buys and renovates about 25 homes a year, and as of the end of 1994 had an inventory of over 40 ready-to-develop homes. As of mid-1996, over 120 existing homes had been rehabilitated.

Early on, most of these homes were donated to Liberation. Today, Liberation pays an average of $2,000 per home for vacant buildings that need an average of $28,000 in rehabilitation. Transfer costs, holding costs, and other fees cost about $2,000. Liberation takes a $2,000 to $3,000 developer fee out of the sale of each home.

An $80,000 grant from the Dallas-based Meadows Foundation is used as a revolving fund for property acquisition, enabling Liberation to maintain a one-year pipeline of properties ready for development. Occasionally, the City of Fort Worth donates tax-foreclosed properties and forgives the back taxes, but this is a complex process involving sign-offs by multiple taxing jurisdictions.

Volunteers help trim about $3,000 off the rehab cost of each home by helping with demolition, painting, and other simple tasks. About 50 criminal offenders a week are referred for community service by the courts. Members of church congregations and corporate volunteers also help out.

Aside from its scattered-site program of acquiring and renovating homes in Poly for sale, Liberation also has undertaken some other real estate development projects. As of late 1996, this was their status:

New homes in Poly: Liberation built and sold five new homes on scattered sites for a total cost of $50,000 each. For each home, the City of Fort Worth gave Liberation HOME funds for $12,000 soft second mortgages and the Federal Home Loan Bank of Dallas contributed $3,000 in down payment and closing cost assistance through its Affordable Housing Program.

Como neighborhood, Fort Worth: In October, 1996, Liberation broke ground on four new homes being built on scattered sites for a total cost of $52,000 each. As with the Poly project, the City of Fort Worth contributed $12,000 in HOME funds for soft second mortgages and the Federal Home Loan Bank of Dallas contributed $3,000 in down payment and closing cost assistance. In addition, three existing homes on scattered sites will be acquired, renovated, and sold.

Arlington neighborhood development project: In nearby Arlington, in late 1996, Liberation began work on a 15-unit scattered-site project that included nine new homes, one existing home being rehabilitated, and five existing homes moved to vacant lots. The costs of the new homes were expected to be $65,000 to $75,000. The City of Arlington, using HOME funds, is supplying $15,000 per home for soft second mortgage loans.

Loan Collections and Post-Purchase Counseling

Since Liberation services about 80 first mortgage loans for itself and lenders to whom loans have been sold, it has better data on delinquencies and defaults than do most home buyer assistance programs.

Delinquency rates are as follows:

Days Late	Percent of Clients
30 - 60 days	10%
60 - 90 days	15%
Over 90 days	5%

While this 30 percent delinquency rate is alarming at first glance, Liberation finds it manageable. Its biggest worry is the three or four clients who are regularly 90 days or more overdue on payments. They receive careful attention, and if they do not catch up, must face foreclosures. If there is a good reason for the missed payments, Liberation will sometimes refinance the mortgage using its own funds.

Most of the delinquent loans are those held by Liberation. When selling loans, the organization chooses the loans with the best payment records.

Since 1989, Liberation and private lenders involved with the program have experienced five foreclosures and two other cases where homeowners gave a deed in lieu of foreclosure--representing about six percent of the loans made. Since Liberation has a revolving loan fund and a long list of qualified home buyers, this is not the problem it might be for other organizations.

In the one instance of outright foreclosure by a private lender, Liberation bought back the loan and resold the home. When it forecloses on its own loans, Liberation simply resells the home with few losses.

Still, delinquencies are a big concern. Until recently, Liberation's loan counselors provided post-purchase counseling. In 1996, the organization contracted with a professional credit counselor, a former employee of the local consumer credit counseling agency, to work one-on-one with clients.

YouthBuild Job Training Program

This program provides classroom and on-the-job training to youths between 16 and 24 years of age, most of whom are high school dropouts. The program teaches job, life, and academic skills over a two-year period. Modeled after a program in Harlem, the primary aim is to teach marketable job skills.

By its eighteenth month, 52 youths had enrolled in the program, and 12 of them had found jobs. Eighteen remained in the program, and about 20 had dropped out.

Participants spend about half the time in the classroom and half on Liberation's construction sites doing carpentry, plumbing, electrical, and heating work. They also work toward GEDs or high school diplomas. In the classroom, a number of volunteer professionals are brought in to expose the trainees to the entire process of building, selling, and financing homes. Volunteers include lenders, architects, insurance agents, bankers, and engineers.

The program is staffed with a director and two trainers. The annual budget of $350,000 is funded by a combination of private grants and state government sources. The local Tandy Foundation has been particularly supportive of the program. Classroom training and counseling services are provided by the City of Fort Worth and a private social service agency, Lena Pope Homes.

Ed Ellis, Liberation's Executive Director, said the job placement rate of participants is disappointing but not surprising in light of their numerous personal problems.

"The program gets them off the street and helps them get some education and get their lives in order," he said. "But they have so many problems, the program can't solve them all."

Long-Term Affordability Controls

Liberation Community has no special resale restrictions attached to its home sales or its financing, other than the standard HOME program requirement that homes be sold to low-income families if resold within a certain period of time.

Assistance to Neighborhood Associations

In the early stages of its program, Liberation helped its home buyers form a loose-knit organization, which has since faded away. Today, Liberation encourages homeowners to join neighborhood organizations. As a result, its buyers were catalysts for reorganizing the Polytechnic Neighborhood Association.

In the Como neighborhood, where Liberation is just starting its work, a strong neighborhood organization already exists. Future home buyers will be linked into it where possible.

Administration

Management and Staffing

Liberation Community Inc. has a staff of 15, plus four fulltime volunteers who work for its food and clothing bank. About half the staff lives in the community.

The fulltime staff for all programs, including housing, are as follows.

Executive director
Construction manager
Resource development director
Director of YouthBuild
Project director, Arlington
YouthBuild trainers (3)
Housing counselor/Loan processor (2)
Emergency assistance counselor
Community organizer
Bookkeeper
Administrative assistant
Custodian/file clerk

The staff is made up of almost equal numbers of African Americans, Hispanics, and Anglos.

Volunteers are also very important to Liberation's operations. In addition to the fulltime volunteers, many neighborhood volunteers assist with the food and clothing bank. As described earlier, many volunteers from outside the area work on rehabbing houses.

Board of Directors

The board of directors had 18 members as of the end of 1994. It has the usual officers, and also has an advisory board with nine members.

About half the members of the board reside in the organization's target area. Its composition is as follows.

Lenders: 2
Professionals: 7
Other business people: 2
Social service and church
     representatives: 6
Community residents: 10

Eleven members are African American, four are Hispanic, and 12 are Anglos.

The advisory board includes business people and past board members who have completed their maximum two terms on the board but still want to help. This group assists with business decisions, financial advice, and fund-raising.

Administrative Costs and Funding

In 1994, the program's administrative costs (excluding direct expenditures on housing development, rental housing, loans, interest on borrowed money, and family assistance) were as follows.

Administrative Costs

Administrative salaries	$147,226
Health benefits	11,188
Payroll expenses	15,513
General insurance	11,548
Professional services	13,346
Shop and tool expense	4,064
Rent	6,000
Telephone	5,786
Postage	4,230

Office expenses	6,563
Travel and mileage expense	9,331
Staff development	1,478
Utilities	3,722
Repairs and maintenance	7,774
Publicity	770
Printing	9,127
Total	$257,666

The aforementioned line items are not presented in the same fashion as in Liberation's financial reports. Rather, this summary is an attempt to separate overhead costs from direct program expenditures such as loan-making and construction. Readers should keep in mind that the 1994 numbers reflect only 11 paid staff members, rather than the 15 on staff in 1996. Also, while the expenses are mostly for housing work, they cover Liberation's social services programs as well.

Liberation has an exemplary system of financial reporting that breaks all expenses (including overhead, depreciation, and direct program expenditures) into functional categories. Some of the functional categories are not truly functional, but enable Liberation to report on activities paid for with restricted funding, such as HOME-funded work. Along those lines, the 1994 costs break out as follows.

Functional Area	1994 Cost
HOME--CHDO	37,000
Direct aid	53,000
HOME--Model Block	49,000
Revolving loan fund	49,000
Nehemiah program	60,000
YouthBuild program	8,000
Rental property	10,000
Housing under warranty	12,000

General and administrative	148,000
Total	$426,000

With its reporting system, Liberation allocates salaries and other overhead costs to each functional area. Thus, "general and administrative" represents indirect costs that were not allocated to programs and is considerably lower than our tally of administrative costs listed above. The revolving loan fund expenses do not include $206,000 in paper losses on homes that had been donated to Liberation and then sold at prices below the value of the donations.

Liberation listed the following sources of income in its 1994 financial reports.

1994 income sources

Federal grants	432,000
Other grants	148,000
Contributions	93,000
Food donations	24,000
Development fees	48,000
Rental income	14,000
Interest income	15,000
Other income	11,000
Total	$785,000

Liberation Community has attracted a remarkably large number of funders. In 1994, it had nearly 60 corporate, foundation, and government donors. Eleven church organizations contributed to the program, as did over 160 individuals.

Recent foundation supporters include the Sid Richardson Foundation, the Burnett/Tandy Foundation, the Amon Carter Foundation, the Meadows Foundation, the Hoblitzelle Foundation, the Fidelity Foundation, the Fannie Mae Foundation, the Katrine M. Deakins Trust, the William E.

Scott Foundation, and the Southwestern Bell Foundation.

Supporters among major regional and national corporations include Texas Wesleyan University, Southwestern Bell Telephone, Burlington Northern Corporation, and Allstate Insurance. About $35,000 a year is contributed by lenders, including Nationsbank, Texas Commerce Bank, Central Bank and Trust Co., Wells Fargo, and Bank of America.

Financial Management

The 1994 financials show a fund balance (net worth) of $1,093,803 against liabilities of only $26,000. At the end of 1994, cash amounted to $127,000. Loans receivable were $538,000. However, this net worth is somewhat overstated because of accounting methods chosen. Some of the loans receivable will be automatically forgiven over the years. Also, "property held for resale" is valued at $319,000. But during 1994, $206,000 of these paper assets were written off when they were sold, suggesting that by discounting its home prices, Liberation will not recoup much of this $319,000 in real estate value.

Nonetheless, the fund balance is very healthy for a neighborhood-based nonprofit housing corporation and a tribute to its support from government, foundations, and corporations.

Likewise, Liberation has a habit of generating excess revenues that are plowed back into the revolving loan fund and other community development activities. In 1994, the surplus was $154,000. In 1993, it was $143,000.

Liberation has audited financial statements that illustrate its financial situation very clearly.

Lessons Learned

Strengths of the Program

In an uncanny way, Liberation Community resembles the many successful local programs that sprang up with funding from the federal War on Poverty in the 1960s and early 1970s. Like them, Liberation focuses on helping low-income people in diverse ways to improve their lots in life--through education, employment, emergency assistance, legal aid, and better housing. And as with those organizations, federal funding has been critical to Liberation's success.

But the comparison ends there. Liberation Community did not need a federal program to get started. Rather than following a top-down blueprint, Liberation started through the bottom-up initiative of a church mission. It expanded because it quickly inspired volunteers and financial supporters from both inside and outside the neighborhood. One can only surmise that Liberation succeeded quickly because it was helping residents to help themselves, attracting new residents to the area, and improving Fort Worth's most distressed neighborhood.

The inclusion of neighborhood residents on its staff, board, and roster of volunteers also added to its effectiveness. This grassroots approach gave the organization high credibility with neighborhood residents, funders, and new home buyers.

The underlying philosophy is expressed by Executive Director Ed Ellis in Liberation's 1994 annual report: "Long lasting change takes place only when the environment allows the residents of a community to be the leaders."

One not-so-obvious asset of this program is Texas Wesleyan University. While the university is not a major financial supporter of Liberation, many business and community leaders in Fort Worth have a stake in the school, and therefore in remedying the deterioration of the neighborhood around it. This factor accounts for the strong support of Methodist churches and at least some of the local foundations.

Another asset is the very existence of the foundations that gave Liberation its critical early support. Fort Worth is particularly blessed with major foundations that have a commitment to community development in the city's low-income neighborhoods.

People familiar with Liberation Community also credit its founder, Brian Stone, with a hard-driving entrepreneurial spirit that quickly got the organization into high gear. Like many entrepreneurs, he was fortunate to be followed by managers who could reorganize and stabilize programs that were often started on a wing and a prayer.

Conventional wisdom would hold that neighborhoods such as Polytechnic Heights are too distressed to make a homeownership program feasible. But however tough the task, Liberation decided that finding new home buyers was a critical goal. Speculative absentee ownership was a major factor in the near ruination of the neighborhood, having left 40 percent of the homes vacant by 1989. That figure has since been cut in half.

Success in revitalizing the area was dependent upon getting people to settle there and stay, rather than leaving at the first opportunity. And Liberation found the people who would help pioneer a renewed Polytechnic Heights--mostly young families, both African American and Hispanic. In spite of the neighborhood's high crime rate and other distress factors, 60 percent of the buyers come from outside Poly, evidence of their trust that conditions will continue to improve.

Obviously, the low home prices offered by Liberation are a major factor in attracting new residents. Taking out the subsidies, many houses have been sold at an effective cost of $15,000 to $20,000. Even at those prices, many families willing to live in the area were not bankable in conventional terms. Therefore, early on, many of the homes had to be seller-financed. Responding to this reality, Liberation set up its own revolving loan fund.

The strategies required a massive amount of soft financing. Given the widespread skepticism about the probabilities of success in Poly, Liberation has been very successful in raising funds. Also, the organization has never been bashful about charging developer fees against its homes, charging market rates of interest, or selling loans. These internally generated revenues were critical to its survival and success.

In sum, anyone wanting to start a home sales program in a severely distressed neighborhood would be wise to study Liberation's program, funding strategies, and partnerships with the public and private sectors.

Achievement of Goals

Liberation's board of directors establishes annual goals that are framed by a business plan with a three-year planning horizon. In the current business plan, all major programmatic goals have been achieved, such as developing transitional housing and starting the YouthBuild program.

Liberation generally sets housing development and sales goals a little higher than it achieves. In recent years, the annual goal has been 40 homes, while 30 to 32 have been sold.

Hopes and Fears for the Future

Particularly in the past two years, Liberation has grown rapidly and spread out into new areas. It now operates nine different businesses: a food and clothing bank, legal aid, GED training, housing development, mortgage lending, a home repair program, management of rental housing, and job training. It has also expanded into two new geographical markets.

At the same time, Liberation is facing likely cutbacks because of reduced HOME CHDO funding for nonprofit organizations. The City of Fort Worth is encouraging additional CHDOs to organize and apply for HOME funds, dividing a finite pie into smaller pieces each year.

Ed Ellis now thinks it is time to trim the sails. He wants to spin off the housing development programs in Arlington and the Como neighborhood to new nonprofit organizations that would be sponsored and helped by Liberation. And because of the huge fund-raising demands of the job training program--around $350,000 a year --he wants to spin that off as well. The board planned to consider decisions in these areas in the fall of 1996 as it revisits its business plan.

"We must get leaner and meaner," said Ellis. "I predict we will slow down production a little and probably use more volunteers, more like the Habitat model. We have just tried to do too much."

But if Liberation's heart comes from its religious origins and its ties to neighborhood residents, its pragmatism comes from seasoned business people on its staff and board. Ellis is a former banker and real estate broker. Almost half of the board consists of business people or professionals. A former board member and key advisor is the owner of a manufacturing company. Another is a long-time investor in residential real estate, who at one low point made Liberation a substantial loan from his own funds.

Liberation's social ideals and its business brains seem to keep one another in balance and have achieved remarkable results against tough odds.

Information Source

For more information, contact:

Ed Ellis
Executive Director
Liberation Community, Inc.
3608 East Rosedale
Fort Worth, TX 76105
Phone: (817) 534-7185
Fax: (817) 534-2290

14

New Orleans Neighborhood Development Foundation
(New Orleans, Louisiana)

Program Highlights

The New Orleans Neighborhood Development Foundation

Target Area:	City of New Orleans (population 496,938) and Orleans Parish
Program Goals:	Assist low-income home buyers
Major Elements:	Financial counseling Homeowner training workshops Single-family housing development Landlord training
Average Client Income:	$22,398
Typical Home Price:	$59,000
Year Started:	1986
Other Programs:	Rental assistance
Staffing:	5 fulltime staff members Accountant retained on a contractual basis
Annual Output: (1995)	455 clients trained 209 clients bought homes
Funding:	Corporate and individual contributions Client-paid fees City of New Orleans Private lenders City and State housing finance authorities Private contributions

Overview

The New Orleans Neighborhood Development Foundation has never had a ground breaking or ribbon cutting. NDF does not build, rehab, or sell homes--nor does it directly provide home purchase financing. Nonetheless, the organization has proved that a well-designed and efficient program of counseling and training, working in cooperation with public and private financing sources, can help an impressive number of low-income families buy homes.

As of September 1, 1996, the day of its 10-year anniversary, this successful and widely copied home buyer assistance program had helped low- and moderate-income families obtain over $53 million in financing to buy 1,285 homes in New Orleans and New Orleans Parish.

The homeownership program qualifies potential home buyers and counsels and trains them in the responsibilities of homeownership and the process of purchasing a home. It helps clients get low-cost mortgages and payment plans that fit within their budgets. NDF staffers inspect houses chosen by clients, estimate the cost of needed repairs, and advise on negotiating the purchase contract. NDF also provides post-purchase counseling to help new homeowners avoid the twin pitfalls of over-indebtedness and delinquency.

NDF has trained and counseled nearly 2,600 clients. While only about one out of two trainees have bought homes to date, this is an excellent success rate for a program that offers no purchase subsidies. The typical family helped by the Foundation consists of three members, is African American, and is headed by a single mother.

Homes purchased through the program are located in many parts of the city.

The New Orleans Neighborhood Development Foundation is an affiliate of The Enterprise Foundation, which helped to establish the organization. Start-up grants for NDF came from John and Pavy DeBlois, a New Orleans couple who believed that one of the city's major problems was its low percentage of homeowners.

Initially, the program was intended to focus on real estate development--buying, rehabbing, and building homes for sale to low-income families. The initial development projects never gelled, but NDF's staff came up with a winning idea-- why not avoid the overhead, complexities, and expense of housing development and focus on giving low-income families the knowledge, skills, and self-confidence needed to become home buyers.

The NDF program quickly became a national model because of its success in creating homeowners without using any incentives, such as mortgage subsidies, or new homes offered at discount prices. NDF has served as a consultant to Enterprise-affiliated housing organizations that wanted to start similar programs in several cities, including Greensboro, NC; Topeka, KS; Fort Worth, TX; Orlando, FL; Chattanooga, TN, as well as in other cities and parishes in Louisiana.

Enterprise has used and adapted the program's policies, procedures, and model documents to help start home buyer assistance programs in other cities. In most instances, these other programs do not use the "pure" NDF model, but incorporate housing development and mortgage subsidies.

In a 1989 editorial praising the program for helping its 200th new homeowner, the *New Orleans Times-Picayune* summarized the program's self-help philosophy:

"The process of turning qualified low-income renters into property owners appears to be a practical way of helping people lift themselves by their own bootstraps."

Market Analysis

Citywide Demographics and Market Conditions

While New Orleans has experienced high poverty rates and other signs of economic distress for a number of years, there is some evidence of a recent turnaround. Both homeownership rates and the minimum prices of decent homes have increased in recent years. While the price increases have some negative effects on housing affordability, they are an indicator that inner-city neighborhoods are becoming more desirable places to live.

A former French outpost established in the 1700s, and queen city of the Mississippi riverboat trade, New Orleans has an old housing stock. A third of all housing units were built before 1939 (compared to 18 percent nationally). Most homes purchased with NDF assistance need minor or major repair.

The poverty rate in New Orleans is the highest of any city or county in this study and over two and a half times higher than the national rate. Nearly one-third of its population lives in poverty. Its overall housing vacancy rate--17 percent in 1990--was the second highest of any city in this study.

In part, these trends are due to the oil industry "bust" in the 1980s. New Orleans is one of the major support centers for oil exploration in the Gulf of Mexico. Although oil exploration has declined, the city's unemployment rate has been relatively low. Between 1992 and 1994, its population increased slightly.

Probably as a result of these economic improvements, the average price of a home purchased with assistance from NDF has risen noticeably. In 1994, it was $45,600. By 1996, it had risen to $59,272. In some neighborhoods, homes still sell in the $30,000s, but the supply of decent housing is relatively low. The city's ambience continues to attract newcomers and creates upward pressure on housing prices, despite the low-wage economy.

The homeownership rate in New Orleans in 1989 was the lowest of any city or county in this study. Troubled public housing--which accounts for about 10 percent of the housing stock--and thousands of abandoned houses have contributed to the decline of the poorest neighborhoods and a long-term trend toward investor-owners replacing owner-occupants. Fortunately, in the 1980s, there was a slight reversal in this trend. The rate of homeownership rose about four percent and probably continues to rise.

The population of New Orleans is 62 percent African American, three percent Hispanic, and about two percent Asian. In 1995, households assisted by the Neighborhood Development Foundation were 91 percent African American, one-half of one percent Hispanic, one-half of one percent Asian, and eight percent non-

	New Orleans	USA
City population:	496,938	
Population growth, 1980s:	-12.2%	12.6%
Percent African American:	61.9%	12%
Percent Hispanic:	3.5%	9%
City median income, 1990s:	$18,447	$30,056
Metro median income, 1996:	$35,500	$41,600
Unemployment rate:	6.1%	6.7%
Poverty rate:	31.6%	13.1%
Median home value:	$37,500	$79,900
Home value increase, 1980s:	37.5%	67.2%
Median monthly rent:	$379	$447
Homeownership rate:	43.7%	64%

U.S. Census, 1990; 1996 median income from HUD.

minority. Fifty-five percent of the households were headed by single mothers. The table above lists key statistics on demographics and market conditions.

Operations and Financing

Marketing

As with most home buyer assistance programs, the most important marketing for NDF is word-of-mouth advertising from satisfied graduates. In the early stages of the program, one of the most important marketing events was a television feature story about several of NDF's first buyers.

As an ongoing marketing strategy, NDF builds relationships with employers and reaches out to their employees. First, an NDF staff person meets with managers to explain the program and give them posters and brochures. Then, if management agrees, a staff member conducts informational meetings with one or more departments of the company or institution.

The focus on places of employment has brought in many clients and has led to active support of the program by some of the employers. As a result of these contacts, four colleges and universities now contribute to closing costs when employees buy a home.

NDF publishes brochures and fliers that explain the program succinctly. In line with the production-oriented approach of the program, the brochures list exactly those documents required at the interview.

The program has a clear vision of its target market--renters who are paying as much or more to rent as they would to own a home. The number of these households is roughly estimated at 17,000 --about 16 percent of the total number of renter households in the city.

The program's outreach specialist continually challenges his clients with these questions: "Are you tired of paying off someone else's mortgage? Why don't you pay off your own?"

To increase community visibility and help with fund-raising, NDF publishes an attractive semiannual newsletter publicizing its activities and successes and profiling successful buyers. The newsletter also lists donors to the program and "NDF homeowners giving back"--clients who have helped with training sessions or contributed other volunteer work.

Publicity materials focus on measurable results that speak for themselves--clients trained, clients purchasing homes, demographics of buyers, average incomes, average home prices. NDF has diligently tracked the numbers of new homeowners per year and the total number of people helped to date. The Foundation updates a fact sheet with this information on a monthly basis--a simple but effective marketing tool that weas made available by only one other program in the study.

NDF's fund-raising activities, such as an annual House Party, are well publicized. The Foundation has been featured on local television programs, including "The Angela Show" and "26 Minutes". It has its own theme song--"Jazzin' Up New Orleans"--and posters to go with it. The program is frequently reported on in the news, real estate, and business pages of the local print media.

Financing of Homes

Home buyers purchase homes with mortgages originated by local lending institutions. Cooperating lenders include First NBC Bank, Fidelity Homestead, Gulf Coast Bank, Hibernia Homestead, Liberty Bank and Trust, Union Savings and Loan, and Bank One. A program flier described three of the lenders as offering interest rates at one-half to one percentage point below market. A fourth, Union Savings, has offered loans at about three percent below market with a down payment of only five percent, no points, and no origination fees.

Much of the below-market-rate financing consists of loans that were originated through the New Orleans Home Mortgage Authority's tax-exempt bond program, which accounts for about one-third of all loans made to NDF clients. A much smaller percentage of loans were originated through a similar program of the Louisiana Housing Finance Agency.

Most of the cooperating lenders waive origination fees and charge no points. Homestead subsidizes closing costs so buyers pay no more than $135 and waives requirements for mortgage insurance even with low down payments. Gulf Coast Bank caps appraisal and legal/recording fees at a remarkably low $100 each.

Recently, community development corporations in New Orleans have teamed up with the city government and lenders to acquire, rehabilitate, and sell homes in distressed neighborhoods. The houses are subsidized with up to $25,000 in federal HOME funds, bringing the effective sale price down to an average of $24,000. NDF has helped prequalify and train 21 buyers of these homes.

Qualification for Assistance; Underwriting Criteria

To be eligible for NDF assistance, a prospective buyer must be able to make a down payment of at least $1,500 and must have a stable employment history. While perfect credit is not a requirement, the applicant must show a willingness to avoid credit problems in the future and to work within a prescribed budget.

Most cooperating lenders require down payments of only three to five percent. And most use liberal underwriting criteria, allowing 33 percent of income for housing payments, and up to 45 percent for all installment debt.

Intake, Screening, and Counseling

NDF has a well-defined and effective process for intake, screening, and prequalifying clients. Clients must bring copies of the following documentation to the initial interview--a step that in itself weeds out some half-hearted would-be home buyers:

- ▶ Three years' federal tax returns and W-2 forms
- ▶ Copies of installment loans and other monthly bills
- ▶ Louisiana driver's license or other state ID
- ▶ Recent paystub
- ▶ Proof of $1,500 in savings toward a home purchase

The initial telephone contact is with the outreach assistant who gathers the preliminary information. Then the prospective client meets with the outreach assistant and outreach specialist. After the meeting, the two staff members decide on the applicant's eligibility, based on credit history, debt-to-income and housing-to-income ratios, and the applicant's potential for accepting the responsibilities of homeownership.

In the initial interview, the NDF staffers usually obtain an on-line credit report and help the client fill out an application. They also counsel the client about the appropriate next steps. Clients who meet most of the program's criteria are then scheduled for the home buyer training course.

In the interview, which is about 45 minutes long, the client is actively counseled about how to overcome minor credit problems. The NDF staffers explain, step by step, how to clear up erroneous or outdated information. People with more serious credit problems are referred to credit counseling by an outside agency. And those with major credit problems, insufficient income, or other serious barriers to becoming homeowners are given advice in writing about how to overcome these obstacles--a "plan of action".

The program maintains a tight discipline about not sending clients on to a training course unless they meet most criteria for obtaining a home loan. The program's philosophy might be characterized as "tough love" rather than "we are here to help you." A brochure advises: "You will not be scheduled for training until you have provided proof that the plan of action is completed."

Clients are also advised not to look for a house until they have completed the training course, because one goal of the program is to make the clients more intelligent shoppers. It shows them how to find a home within their financial means, determine needed repairs, and drive a hard bargain.

Clients who complete all training sessions receive a prequalification letter at the last session. These letters have come to be recognized by local real estate agents and the lenders as the agency's seal of approval. A client who has qualifying problems receives a status letter spelling out the credit issue that has yet to be resolved.

Once prequalified, clients work closely with NDF staff members in every aspect of the home purchase process, including inspection of homes, relations with realtors, arranging financing, the final closing, and budgeting to allow for timely mortgage payments.

Homeownership Training

All clients approved for the homeownership program are required to attend a 12-hour course in family budget management, working with realtors, home selection, home financing, home maintenance, and the rights of home buyers. The two-hour classes are held twice a week, on Tuesday and Thursday evenings.

NDF publishes an exemplary home buyer's training manual covering all of the above topics. The manual includes examples of all financial and legal forms used in the purchase process. It also provides a clear and simple explanation of the procedures NDF advises clients to follow in the purchase process. A 15-page form for conducting a home inspection contains useful price guidelines for a number of common repairs and replacements.

Compared to manuals of similar home buyer assistance programs, NDF's has a minimum of narrative, an attractive layout, and for the most part, plain English--three characteristics that make it useful and attractive to the trainees, some of whom are semiliterate. For example, the succinct section on homeowner's insurance reads in its entirety:

"The lender requires that you have a homeowners' insurance policy prior to the Act of Sale. This protects both the Lender and the Borrower/Purchaser. Be sure to get price quotes from different i n s u r a n c e companies before making a final decision on any one company."

The NDF training course follows the participant's manual but makes certain that everything is explained verbally, with inspirational messages where they are appropriate. In the initial session, buyers are reminded that the information they are about to learn will make them much more skillful purchasers. The benefits of building assets for the family are strongly underscored. Those who have seen one of the lead trainers in action might think they have heard a good sermon, not a lecture.

Post-Purchase Maintenance Training

Since some NDF clients have been in their homes for as long as 10 years, the organization has become more concerned about home maintenance. As a result, it has started offering workshops on home repairs at both the basic and the advanced level. The training uses many building components as props and emphasizes hands-on skills.

The schedule of individual workshops is announced through NDF's newsletter, which is received by most of the people who have graduated from the program.

Citywide Certification of Training Program

In 1996, NDF helped establish a citywide program to certify home buyer counseling and training programs. Since NDF was formed 10 years ago, six other nonprofit organizations have gotten into the business, albeit on a much smaller scale than NDF's.

Recognizing the need to maintain high standards, NDF worked with the Chamber of Commerce and nonprofit counseling agencies to create a certification board. To review a program for certification, lenders, real estate agents, and builders volunteer to sit in on training courses, interview clients, and review client files. When deficiencies are found, the experts give advice on how to fix them. Soon, this citywide effort is expected to include training for counselors and classroom trainers.

Home Selection

More than most home buyer assistance programs examined in this study, NDF tries to help clients through virtually every step of the home selection process. When a prospective buyer has completed the training and receives a prequalification letter, he or she is encouraged to find a buyer's agent and search the market for a suitable home. When a client has found a good candidate for purchase, he or she is advised to complete a physical inspection of the property using the NDF forms and procedures described during the training course.

Next, the completed inspection forms are turned in to NDF, and the staff rehab/maintenance specialist schedules another inspection of the home. Based on the report and repair cost estimate from this inspection, the client decides whether to make an offer on the home, and how much to offer. Sometimes, the report is used to get a lower price. Other times, sellers are willing to make some or all of the repairs. In either case, NDF staff members are active in the negotiating process.

Before an offer is made, clients are advised to get two or three comparables-- sale prices of similar homes recently sold in the same area--to help them make informed offers. Then, if an offer is to be made, the client is advised to come to the NDF office to literally write out the agreement to purchase on an NDF-approved form. This level of assistance with purchase contracts is unique among home buyer assistance programs in this study.

At any one time, NDF has access to listings of 200 to 300 homes for sale in New Orleans at prices affordable to its clients. The average home purchased has three bedrooms; the average price is around $59,000. When the Resolution Trust Company was still disposing of bank-foreclosed homes, NDF worked closely with the federal agency to market the lower-priced homes in its inventory, some of which were being sold at a discount.

Loan Collections and Post-Purchase Counseling

Since NDF is not a direct lender to its clients, it has no formal ways of knowing when and if they have defaulted on their mortgages. However, NDF does stay in close contact with the major lenders used by its clients, and it has heard of just one foreclosure in 10 years. NDF's executive director said the organization hears about missed monthly payments about four times a year.

When NDF hears about a loan delinquency, an outreach staff person contacts the homeowner and, if invited, meets with him or her to help work out the problem.

NDF recognizes that a low foreclosure rate is one of the ultimate quality measures of the program, and steps have been taken to get more reliable information. In 1994, a student from the University of New Orleans conducted a random sample survey of NDF clients who had purchased homes. In checking the public real estate records, no foreclosures were found. In addition, a detailed database has been developed for all clients who bought homes from 1993 on, so tracking results will be easier in the future.

Landlord Training Class

Starting in the fall of 1996, NDF was scheduled to begin a landlord training course. About one-third of NDF's home buyers have purchased duplexes and rent out the second unit. While the rent can help pay the mortgage, many of the homeowners need coaching on how to be a landlord.

The new program will consist of four two-hour evening sessions. Volunteer professionals will talk about budgeting, bookkeeping, fair housing, leases, evictions, marketing, and Section 8 rent subsidies.

Administration

Management and Staffing

NDF's staff consists of five members:

Executive director
Office manager
Rehab/Maintenance specialist
Outreach specialist
Outreach assistant

The executive director oversees the operations of the organization and the other staff members, and serves as a liaison to the local and government institutions that are partners in NDF's activities. The outreach specialist promotes the Foundation's work in the community and recruits potential clients. The outreach specialist and the outreach assistant then guide the prospective home buyers through screening, counseling, and training, and form the link between the buyer and real estate agents and lending institutions. The rehab/maintenance specialist deals with the physical aspects of home rehab and maintenance.

Because of the small size of the staff, there is some overlapping of duties and responsibilities. The entire staff participates in planning and reporting. NDF contracts with an accountant to handle bookkeeping, payroll, and accounts receivable.

Since the program's inception, a majority or all of the program's staff members have been members of minority groups, reflecting the clientele.

Board of Directors

There are 21 members of the board of directors, a biracial group of business owners and professionals. As of April 1996, there were five bankers on the board. Other professions represented included accounting, public relations, law, finance, low-income housing, for-profit commercial development, and social services. John DeBlois, who with his wife gave the program its initial funding, sits on the board. NDF's first executive director is also a member.

Administrative Costs and Financing

To meet its annual budget of approximately $300,000, NDF relies on funding from the City of New Orleans, private grant-makers, HUD, and individual contributors. One of the program's first major benefactors was the First National Bank of Commerce. First NBC and other lenders continue to make annual grants in the range of $10,000 to $25,000.

The city has consistently supported about one-third of the program budget with Community Development Block Grant funds. And recently, NDF was approved by HUD as a certified housing counseling agency, a designation that should result in another predictable stream of annual funding (the average grant under that program is about $40,000 a year).

In addition to those funding efforts, the board of directors sponsors an annual House Party, a social event featuring entertainment by notable musicians, dining, dancing, and door prizes. The House parties are cosponsored by many local businesses and have proven to be a successful fund-raising venture, both from the $35 per person tickets and contributions that result from the event.

Lessons Learned

Strengths of the Program

NDF has accomplished what many others have thought of but few have achieved, a relatively low-cost program that empowers low-income people to become home buyers through education and skilled counseling. The program offers no mortgage subsidies, although tax-exempt financing has been helpful to some clients. And because NDF is not involved in real estate development, its overhead is relatively low and its need for development capital is nil.

Naturally, a program focussing only on training and counseling has its limitations. It works best in areas--such as New Orleans' blue collar neighborhoods--where there are low-priced homes on the market that do not require extensive rehabilitation. Since the program has no source of funds for mortgage subsidies, it cannot help the poorest families, however credit-worthy they may be. And since the homes purchased are not in a targeted area, the program has little immediate effect on revitalizing any specific neighborhoods.

Yet, by cooperating with other organizations, NDF has begun to overcome those limitations. One of its more recent strategies is to work with community development corporations (CDCs) that renovate dilapidated homes. With subsidies from the HOME program, the homes can be made affordable to very low-income families. The CDCs are the developer, and the NDF qualifies and trains the buyers.

There are important lessons to be learned from NDF. In the mid-1980s it invented a system of screening, qualifying, and advising low-income buyers that worked amazingly well--so well that many other organizations have copied it.

In many cities, nonprofit groups, housing agencies, and lenders sponsor programs that on the surface are very similar. Many of these organizations struggle to find the best approach to these tasks, and the results are not always so impressive. Some offer training as the point of entry and try to provide one-on-one counseling at the training session or later. Others take a soft approach to screening, and as a result get mired down in working with tough-to-help clients rather than beating the bushes for more qualified clients.

The following appear to be the major strengths of the NDF program.

▶ A careful, step-by-step process of intake, screening, credit counseling, training, and purchase counseling--in that order-- seems to make sense in almost any market, with any type of client. Clearly, tasks are done effectively and in the right sequence.

▶ A "tough love" approach identifies clients with major deficiencies at early stages and challenges them to overcome their problems before more services are offered by the agency. Clients must be close to prequalifying for a loan before classroom training is even offered.

▶ NDF tries to not just provide information, but also inspire clients to better their lives. Having a training room full of mostly prequalifying clients undoubtedly makes these exhortations more powerful than preaching to a less focussed and less motivated audience.

▶ NDF is closely involved with the negotiation and offering of purchase contracts--a step that is often left to clients and real estate brokers. While some sellers' brokers take their clients' interests to heart, many others simply want to close sales. NDF helps assure good decision-making at this critical stage.

New organizations faced with "reinventing the wheel" should study the fundamentals of the NDF program. Its model has transplanted well in many different regions and types of housing markets.

Another key to NDF's success is its tight focus. NDF operates just one coherent business, home buyer training and counseling. Many other organizations offering home buyer assistance programs are in two, three, four or more businesses, training, housing development, direct financing, rental housing management, and other endeavors--each requiring different operating systems, financing sources, and staff skills.

Not every housing organization can or should narrow its range of products and services as much as NDF, but NDF clearly has benefited by doing so--in terms of depth, quality, efficiency, and effectiveness of its client services.

Achievement of Goals

The hallmark of NDF's management is its goal-directed view of every aspect of its operations. Performance for each month is tracked by six different measures. During calendar year 1995, NDF exceeded its goals in every category except one. Following is a summary.

	Goal	Actual Clients
Intake/screening	500	761
Clients trained	400	455
Clients prequalified	400	568
Home inspections	150	190
Homes purchased	150	209
Clients training in home maintenance	75	36

In part, NDF can do this refined tracking of its progress because of its tight focus. Counseling and training are activities that make for a fairly predictable flow of work. With these tasks, staff members' skills and persistence can make a difference. In contrast, organizations that are focused on building or rehabbing homes have a much less predictable flow of work because they are subject to many outside constraints. And for developer organizations, tracking projects often becomes more important than tracking clients.

Hopes and Fears for the Future

NDF faces new challenges in the future. Executive Director Rosalind Magee-Peychaud is concerned about cutbacks in federal funds. At the same time, there is increasing competition for funds from an expanding number of nonprofit housing groups and social service providers who are getting into the housing counseling business.

Despite these challenges, NDF wants to expand its efforts. It plans to branch out in several new areas:

▸ Possibly spinning off a nonprofit housing development corporation that would take advantage of the city's relatively new HOME-funded program for acquiring and rehabbing homes.

▸ Stepping up its home maintenance training to include training on home repair financing that is available from such programs as HUD's Title One mortgage insurance--this, in light of the fact that some assisted home buyers have already owned their homes for 10 years.

▸ Continuing to improve the citywide certification and training program for the home buyer counseling programs.

Whatever its new endeavors, NDF will likely break new ground in the home buyer counseling business for years to come.

Information Source

For more information, contact:

Rosalind Magee-Peychaud
Executive Director
New Orleans Neighborhood
Development Foundation
Liberty Center, Suite 200
2051 Senate Street
New Orleans, LA 70122
Phone: (504) 282-4855

15

NorthRiver Development Corporation
(Toledo, Ohio)

Program Highlights

NorthRiver Development Corporation

Target Area:	Toledo; North River area (population 11,797)
Program Goals:	Assist low-income home buyers Revitalize inner city neighborhoods
Major Elements:	Financial counseling and home buyer training Assistance with first mortgages Second mortgage subsidies Single-family housing development
Average Client Income:	$22,895
Typical Home Prices:	$25,000 (existing); $75,000 (new) before subsidies
Year Started:	1981
Other Programs:	Home renovation loans Owner/manager of rental housing and commercial space Microenterprise loan program (for businesses) Housing/resource center for the disabled
Staffing:	5 fulltime staff members
Annual Output: (1995)	23 clients trained 17 received home purchase loans 4 homes acquired and renovated 5 homes newly built 6 homes sold
Funding:	Federal and state grants Loan repayments from a project funded with an Urban Development Action Grant Community Development Block Grant and HOME funds from the City of Toledo Corporate contributions

Overview

Program Description

NorthRiver Development Corporation is a nonprofit community development corporation dedicated to revitalizing neighborhoods in North Toledo through homeownership assistance, home renovations, construction of new homes, job training, and the development of a prosperous business community.

The neighborhood is bounded on the east by the Maumee River, which flows into Lake Erie a short distance away. NorthRiver was established through a joint effort of the City of Toledo and Riverside Hospital, which is located in the neighborhood. In 1980, the City received a federal Urban Development Action Grant of $948,000 to start up the organization--$798,000 for grants and loans to fix up the neighborhood's housing stock, and $150,000 in administrative funds.

Riverside Hospital sponsored NorthRiver's start-up and, in addition, was a recipient of a UDAG-funded loan for facilities expansion. Repayments of this loan continue to support the NorthRiver program, and are expected to provide revenues of $48,000 a year for the next 18 years.

NorthRiver operates the following homeownership programs:

- The Home Loan and Home Improvement Loan Programs provide low-interest financing for home purchases and renovations of existing homes. With home purchases, the program works in tandem with conventional first mortgage lenders. Financing the purchases of existing homes in tandem with conventional first mortgage loans is NorthRiver's primary activity-- accounting for 17 of NorthRiver's 22 loans in 1995 (the five other loans were for home renovations).

- Through a "HOME 4 Program," NorthRiver acquires, renovates, and sells vacant homes. Four were completed in 1995 and two were sold.

- Modest new homes are being built on vacant lots in the neighborhood--five were completed in 1995, and four were sold.

Since the organization's inception over 16 years ago, it has made 209 loans and grants for home purchases or repairs in projects with a total of over 800 dwelling units. In the early days, a major focus was small multifamily properties owned by investors. Owner-occupants were given grants as well as loans for home repairs. Today, the program exclusively focuses on owner-occupants, and makes only loans.

Early in its history, NorthRiver was involved in some direct development-- acquiring and renovating residential properties. Recently, after abandoning that activity for a number of years, the organization again assumed the role of developer.

Other Community Development Activities

Over the years, NorthRiver has also attempted to assist with commercial and economic development in the neighborhood, in a limited fashion. The organization believes that the revitalization of the area is dependent upon both housing improvements and the location of new businesses in North Toledo.

After an intensive strategic planning process in 1995, economic development efforts are being increased. A new microenterprise loan program offers loans of $50 to $5,000 for new or existing businesses. A three-year economic development plan is in the works. And another prime objective is to attract a full-service grocery store to the neighborhood, to replace the last remaining food market, which recently closed.

Last year, NorthRiver received a John Heinz Neighborhood Development Grant from HUD that is being used for various efforts to improve the appearance of the neighborhood and build a sense of community--such as clean-up campaigns, $500 grants to property owners for painting their homes, $250 grants for landscaping, and development of a pocket park.

NorthRiver's next initiative may be a construction job training program. This is being planned in cooperation with the Neighborhood Foundation of Toledo, Inc. and Lucas County. NorthRiver would provide the job sites, and may organize its own in-house construction company to facilitate that program and generate more fee income.

NorthRiver is also working with an experienced nonprofit child-care provider to create a day-care facility in the neighborhood.

Market Analysis

Toledo, located in extreme northwestern Ohio on the shores of Lake Erie, is unusual among older industrial cities for having maintained much of its manufacturing base. The city's major employer is Chrysler's Jeep assembly plant. Libbey Glass is headquartered here, and Owens-Corning is moving its headquarters to Toledo. The 1996 metropolitan area median income for a family of four was $42,800, a little above the national median of $41,600, while the city median income is about 20 percent below the national figure.

The North Toledo Target Area

NorthRiver Development Corporation serves the economically depressed area of North Toledo. This area of the city was a settlement--the town of Vistula--that preceded the present Toledo. It boasts some of the most historic homes and commercial buildings in the city. At one time, it was home to gracious Victorian mansions, more modest housing for factory workers, and a thriving business district. Since the 1950s, however, the area has witnessed a serious decline.

In the past four decades, North Toledo has seen a general population decrease, with a concomitant growth in the number of empty buildings. Homes were abandoned and boarded up. There has been a lack of visible policing of the area and landlords have not kept up property or evicted lawbreakers. Because of this vandalism, drug dealing, and prostitution became

	Toledo	USA
City population:	332,943	
Population growth, 1980s:	-7.1%	12.6%
Percent African American:	19.7%	12%
Percent Hispanic:	.4%	9%
City median income, 1990s:	$24,819	$30,056
Metro median income, 1996:	$42,800	$41,600
Unemployment rate:	9.6%	6.7%
Poverty rate:	19.1%	13.1%
Median home value:	$48,900	$79,900
Home value increase, 1980s:	29.4%	67%
Median monthly rent:	$378	$447
Homeownership rate:	60.7%	**64.2%**

U.S. Census, 1990; 1996 median income from HUD

significant problems for the area. It is these trends that NorthRiver Development aims to reverse with its housing and business incentive programs.

The table above lists key statistics for demographics and market conditions.

As of the 1990 census, the median household income in North Toledo was $7,138, compared to a median income of $29,246 for Toledo as a whole. Fifty-one percent of the households had poverty-level incomes, and over 70 percent of the households had incomes at or below 80 percent of the area median income.

The population of NorthRiver's target areas is largely made up of single adults, elderly people, and households headed by females. The population in 1989 was 70 percent white, 21 percent black, 7 percent Hispanic, and 2 percent other races. Fifty-three percent of the residents were unemployed.

North Toledo has a very high percentage of renters. Fewer than 28 percent of homes in North Toledo are owner-occupied, compared to 61 percent for the city of Toledo as a whole. According to a recent survey, there are over 175 blighted and/or vacant homes and 130 empty lots in the neighborhood. Eighty-five percent of these lots have been evaluated as unkempt. Added to this, over half the housing stock in the area was constructed before 1900, and is now in need of significant investments in updating and repair.

On the positive side, the neighborhood is located near downtown and includes some main traffic arteries and some areas that have potential for light industrial development. The nearby Libbey Glass plant is a source of well-paying jobs for neighborhood residents. A riverside park is planned by the City.

▶

Operations and Financing

Marketing

NorthRiver Development Corporation has a number of brochures, pamphlets, and fliers that advertise its programs. The organization also distributes a continually updated list of homes for sale in the neighborhood. The list includes homes developed by NorthRiver, along with other homes offered for sale. A recent list included 19 one-family homes and 10 two- to four-family homes.

As a leading and respected community development corporation in Toledo, NorthRiver also receives continual and positive press coverage. Limited paid advertising is placed in a local minority-owned newspaper. But as with most programs, word of mouth advertising is the major source of new clients.

New and rehabbed homes developed by NorthRiver are marketed and shown by the organization's loan officer. Also, signs are placed in front of each home both to advertise the homes for sale and to keep a high profile for the organization.

Financing of Homes

NorthRiver and a local bank provide mortgage loans, with NorthRiver providing 25 percent of the cost and the bank providing the other 75 percent. In some cases, NorthRiver's loan exceeds 25 percent of the financing. This can occur when the cost of a home plus needed repairs exceeds the after-rehabilitation appraised value of the home.

With most homes it finances, NorthRiver makes second mortgage loans for 30 years at an interest rate that is typically 6 percent. For some homes developed and sold by NorthRiver, the rates for NorthRiver's portion of the purchase financing may be set as low as 3.9 percent. Considering that these homes are generally more expensive than existing homes, this is seen as a necessary incentive to attract buyers.

In any case, most of these loans offer only a shallow subsidy in terms of reducing the carrying cost of the housing. The primary purpose of these loans is to make up for buyers' lack of cash, and to give the first mortgage lenders a margin of comfort by not requiring them to lend over 80 percent of the value of the homes. On the other hand, the grants used to write down development costs result in a substantial reduction of monthly carrying costs.

There is no set rate for the tandem first mortgage loans, but most of the participating lenders offer rates at or slightly below the prevailing market rates. Other lenders charge slightly more than market rates because of the perceived risks of these loans--related both to the distressed market and the lack of cash investment by buyers.

Even today, a major source of funding for the second mortgages is the UDAG grant obtained in 1980 by the City of Toledo. Initially, a portion of this grant funded 150 down payment loans for the NorthRiver area (the loans were paid for up to 50 percent of the purchase price of homes). This provided about a third of the capitalization of NorthRiver's present loan fund. Repayments of about $35,000 a year are returned to the fund to make future loans.

NorthRiver also receives about $48,000 a year in repayments of a UDAG loan used by Riverside Hospital in the early 1980s to construct a day surgery center. Restricted to the loan fund, these payments will continue through the year 2014. Also, federal HOME and Community Development Block Grant funds, passed through the City of Toledo, are used to fund loans. Repayments of all loans are used to replenish the organization's revolving loan fund. In some cases, NorthRiver takes out a small percentage of each loan repayment to pay for its administrative expenses.

In addition to keeping its loan fund adequately capitalized, NorthRiver must continually raise conventional and subsidy financing for its development projects. For example, an eight-home new construction project currently underway has these sources of funds:

University of Toledo (federal funds)	$4,250
City Community Development Block Grant	8,885
City HOME funds	169,896
State funds (non-federal)	109,522
Federal Home Loan Bank Affordable Housing Program	48,000
Net from home sales	278,261
Total	$618,814

In this project, a $246,000 line of credit from a local lender was used to partly finance the project pending the receipt of home sales revenues. Because of a goal to serve households with incomes between 35 and 60 percent of the median income, this is one of the most heavily financed projects undertaken by NorthRiver. About 55 percent of the financing came from subsidy sources. The remaining $35,000 is coming from first

mortgage financing obtained by the purchasers.

In addition, in this and other development projects, the City of Toledo has provided in-kind assistance. The City funds infrastructure such as curbs and sidewalks, and in some cases provides the land at no cost.

Qualification for Assistance

For purchase of existing homes, NorthRiver's qualifying guidelines are quite liberal. There is no maximum income level. Essentially, clients must qualify for the tandem bank financing and buy a home in the neighborhood.

In this regard, NorthRiver's goals are really two-fold: to help low-income households buy homes; and to attract home buyers with somewhat higher incomes into the neighborhood. Early in the program's history, there was a small surge of middle-income families buying and repairing older Victorian homes on a few streets. Today, there is little of that activity. In reality, almost all clients are low-income. Clients' incomes average around 60 percent of median income.

However, homes developed and sold by NorthRiver are subject to income guidelines because of the use of HUD funds to write down development costs. Purchases of NorthRiver's rehabbed homes and its most expensive new homes are restricted to households with incomes at or below 80 percent of median income. At this writing, one group of more heavily subsidized new homes was reserved for households with incomes at or below 60 percent of median income.

Of course, home buyers must have sufficient income to qualify for financing of specific homes. As a general rule, an income of $10,000 is approximately the minimum required to afford the lowest priced homes available in the neighborhood. For new homes NorthRiver is selling, the minimum qualifying incomes are listed in the advertising fliers for the homes. For two recent projects, these minimums were $14,000 and $18,800 respectively.

A remarkable feature of the program is that clients need very little cash to buy a home. When NorthRiver's financing is used, no down payment is required to purchase a home. Buyers must pay an application fee to NorthRiver, an application fee to the bank, one year's homeowner's insurance, and minor closing costs--representing cash out of pocket of about $280. Otherwise, closing costs (which average about $1,400) are all financed.

Intake, Screening, and Counseling

After an initial screening over the phone to determine basic eligibility, prospective home buyers make an appointment with the loan officer to fill out a loan application. During this appointment, an on-line credit report is obtained.

Clients are then referred to Housing Directions of Greater Toledo, an organization that specializes in housing counseling and training. Clients receive confidential one-on-one counseling, which focuses on family budgeting and cleaning up credit problems. A counselor reviews the client's income and expenses to help create a budget, and coaches clients through the home purchase process.

Homeownership Training

Housing Directions of Greater Toledo also conducts home buyer training classes. The topics covered include budgeting, home repairs, mortgage financing, lead paint abatement, and available neighborhood services. Five hours of training are offered in two sessions.

Loan Processing

If income and credit appear acceptable, forms for verifications of income, assets, rent payments, etc. are then sent out. Once all the paperwork is complete and in order, the organization's loan committee (which meets once a month) reviews the application for the second mortgage loan. If an applicant has already selected a home to purchase, the loan amount is equal to 25 percent of the purchase price plus closing costs. If a home has not yet been identified, the client is approved for a not-to-exceed amount based on a home price that he or she can afford.

If a second mortgage loan is approved by NorthRiver, the borrower then goes house hunting, if he or she has not already done so. Once a purchase agreement is signed, NorthRiver then schedules inspections by City mechanical code inspectors and NorthRiver's own rehabilitation technician. When a work write-up and cost estimates have been prepared, bid sheets are sent out to three licensed general contractors. When bids are received, the home buyer selects one of the bids.

After this process has been completed, NorthRiver assists home buyers in applying for a first mortgage loan at the lending institution of their choice. Once this has been approved, in some instances, the entire loan package must be sent to the City of Toledo for approval, depending upon the original source of funds.

Home Selection

Qualified applicants may choose any home within the boundaries of NorthRiver's target area which fits their financial resources. NorthRiver publishes listings of available homes for clients to choose from that can be purchased from the present property owner, through a real estate agent, or from NorthRiver Development itself. The listings include photographs, addresses, and financing information. Eligible applicants are not required to buy a home from the lists, but any home they choose must fit within their income guidelines.

According to listings compiled frequently by NorthRiver, existing homes in the neighborhood ranged in price from $1,500 to $40,000, with most homes being priced from $20,000 to $25,000. Homes must be brought up to housing code standards as a condition of NorthRiver's loan. The costs of rehabilitation can be (and usually are) included in the financing package.

Underwriting Criteria

NorthRiver uses a 28 percent of income housing payment ratio and a 36 percent total debt ratio in determining income eligibility for their homeownership program--the same ratios that are used in conventional home financing. Participating first mortgage lenders provide no more than 80 percent of the appraised value of homes, and thus do not require borrowers to obtain mortgage insurance.

For its portion of the financing, NorthRiver will lend up to 125 percent of the appraised value of a home. These liberal terms are allowed because the cost of a home plus needed repairs often exceeds appraised value. In these situations, NorthRiver may lend more than 25 percent of the purchase price in order to satisfy the first mortgage lenders' loan-to-value requirements. However, a few lenders will occasionally lend over 80 percent, still without requiring mortgage insurance. All loans are held in portfolio by NorthRiver; none is sold to the secondary market

Housing Development Activities

Despite some difficulties in acquiring suitable sites at the right price, NorthRiver's recent move back into housing development has been a success. Clients are eager to buy new or thoroughly rehabbed homes. Where the activity is concentrated, it transforms formerly deteriorated city blocks. And as an added benefit, it generates fee income for the organization.

NorthRiver is currently engaged in the following housing development projects:

HOME 4: This acquisition, rehab and resale program works on a scattered-site basis, and is expected to result in 10 home sales over two years. Subsidized with about $20,000 each in HOME funds, the houses sell for between $25,000 and $40,000 (reflecting the write-downs with HOME funds). The monthly payment on a recently offered $36,000 home was $265.

The School House Project: This features the construction of eight new homes in the neighborhood surrounding LaGrange Elementary School. Five units were completed in 1995 and three more are to be completed in 1996. These 1,080-square-foot, three-bedroom homes sell for $34,783 (after grant subsidies of about $35,000 per home) with monthly payments of about $315.

Riverside: A first, five-unit phase of this new home construction project began in 1996. These 1,248-square-foot, three-bedroom homes sell for $53,000 (after grant subsidies of about $30,000 per home), with monthly payments of about $455.

Properties earmarked for rehab or new construction are obtained in two ways: by purchases on the open market, and donation by the City of Toledo of tax-foreclosed properties. NorthRiver would like to accelerate this activity, but, unlike some of Toledo's other low-income neighborhoods where community development corporations operate, the North River neighborhood lacks large parcels of vacant land.

In 1992, NorthRiver completed its only rental housing project--the rehabilitation of an historic property that includes 4,000 square feet of commercial space and 19 studio and one-bedroom apartments. A property manager handles the residential rentals, which operate smoothly. However, an inability to rent the commercial space has led to negative cash flow.

Post-Purchase Counseling

Currently, NorthRiver's delinquency rate (for loans with payments over 30 days overdue) is 10 percent and the default rate is about three percent, about two to three times the rates reported in some other programs evaluated in this study. In the late 1980s, loan payment problems were much worse since the organization at that time had no regular system of sending out late payment notices or following up with phone calls. By 1991, new collection procedures had been instituted and the number of problem loans decreased dramatically.

Borrowers in trouble are referred to Housing Directions of Greater Toledo to receive counseling in mortgage default issues and financial management.

Long-Term Affordability Controls

Long-term affordability controls in NorthRiver's programs are limited to lending provisions that meet the minimum requirements of HOME funding, and apply only where HOME funding is used. In the loan documents, borrowers pledge to resell their homes at prices affordable to low-income households. These requirements typically have no restrictive effect since virtually every home sold in the neighborhood meets these requirements.

Assistance to Neighborhood Associations

NorthRiver has a close working relationship with the North Corridor Association, the only neighborhood association operating in its target area. Among other joint activities are the community clean-up and improvement activities described earlier. As this association is not incorporated, NorthRiver acts as its fiduciary, receiving and disbursing its funds.

With one group of new homes constructed, NorthRiver was required by the City to create a homeowners' association.

Partners

With regard to the day-to-day operations of its programs, NorthRiver's most important partners are the City of Toledo, private lenders that cooperate with the program, and corporate sponsors that help pay administrative costs. Riverside Hospital remains an important ally--it recently donated land for new home construction. The New York City-based Local Initiatives Support Corporation provides NorthRiver with some pass-through federal funds for administration, and helped it finance its single rental project.

NorthRiver also cooperates with other CDCs in the city. The HOME 4 Project, as an example, teamed NorthRiver with three other CDCs in Toledo in an effort to purchase and rehabilitate 40 homes in two years which were then sold to low-income people. Each CDC was responsible for ten homes in the two-year period.

Other partnership activities include:

▶ Working with the North Corridor Coalition on community policing, clean-ups, block parties, tree trimming, street lighting, nuisance abatement, and activities associated with the John Heinz grant (described earlier).

▶ Working with various Toledo social service agencies to plan for new day-care and transitional housing facilities in North Toledo.

Administration

Management and Staffing

NorthRiver Development Corporation's staff consists of five fulltime staff members:

Executive director
Assistant director
Project administrator
Project coordinator
Loan officer

In recent years, two or three of the five staff members (including the current director) have been members of minority population.

NorthRiver has requested additional funding in its CDBG application to hire more staff in the coming operating year.

Board of Directors

As of June 1996 listing, NorthRiver had 16 sitting members on its board of directors. Two members were appointed by the City, two by Riverside Hospital, and two by the American Maritime Office. Two members worked for lending institutions, one represented the Libbey Glass corporation, two represented Riverside Hospital, five were neighborhood residents, and the balance were business professionals or interested citizens. Four of the board members were African American and one was Hispanic.

Administrative Funding

According to audited financial statements made available for the year ending December 31, 1994, NorthRiver's core operating expenses were approximately $236,000 (all numbers have been rounded to the nearest thousand). This does not take into account a one-time write-off of $94,000 in loan losses (loan losses were only $11,000 a year earlier), $20,000 in depreciation, and $12,000 in real estate related expenses.

During that year, $146,000 was spent on salaries, $22,000 for benefits and payroll taxes, $27,000 for professional fees, and $41,000 for other overhead costs.

The major sources of income for operating costs were:

Federal grants	$135,000
Other grants	$98,000
Loan processing reimbursement from City of Toledo	$19,000

Corporate contributors include General Mills, Libbey Glass, Society Bank, National City Bank, Charter One Bank, and Capital Bank.

In 1994, development fees contributed very little to paying for NorthRiver's core overhead. But this is a growing source of support--providing $4,000 to $6,000 in cash per home developed once the homes are sold. These amounts are several thousands of dollars per unit below what private developers typically take out of similar projects.

Because of problems in renting the commercial space, NorthRiver's rental project does not yet help support overhead costs. The residential space taken by itself creates cash flow of about $5,000 a year, but currently this just offsets expenses associated with the commercial space.

Financial Management

Financially, NorthRiver is healthy. In 1994, it had excess revenues of $41,000, and in the previous year, $101,000. At the end of 1994, NorthRiver's net worth was $1,426,000--of which $997,000 was attributable to the value of loans made by the corporation, $348,000 was cash and cash equivalents (mostly, the balance available in the loan fund), and $94,000 was the net value of owned property (after depreciation). Liabilities totalled only $91,000.

NorthRiver is required by funding agreements to spend virtually all its loan fund assets only on making more loans. Some funding sources allow a small percentage of repayments to be taken out for administrative costs. Taking into account these restrictions, NorthRiver's unrestricted net worth (fund balance) was under $2,000-- a small financial cushion for operations. But restricted as they are, the loan fund assets give NorthRiver a very solid base for future operations.

Lessons Learned

Strengths of the Program

NorthRiver's homeownership program has enjoyed overall success and longevity in a daunting environment for a home buyer program--a physically deteriorated target area whose residents, on average, have extremely low incomes.

Remarkably, the primary product--a second mortgage loan of $10,000 to $20,000 at six percent interest--is a very shallow subsidy. Because this loan is amortizing and interest bearing (as opposed to the deferred payment loans offered by some programs), it replenishes a now-sizable revolving loan fund.

The key to NorthRiver's success is that it has been able to attract home buyers with household incomes that are several times higher than the median income for the neighborhood. While some buyers come from the neighborhood, many do not--a problem or a victory, depending upon one's point of view. Some neighborhood residents grumble that they cannot afford to buy homes even with NorthRiver's financing.

On the other hand, bringing in residents with slightly higher incomes can only improve the fortunes of the neighborhood, unless this leads to displacement of lower income residents. NorthRiver's staff sees little evidence of this occurring. As in many aging urban neighborhoods, newcomers just fill the places of elderly people and others who are selling their homes. Overall demand in the neighborhood appears very moderate.

One obvious keystone of NorthRiver's success was the huge infusion of guaranteed funding early on--a $698,000 UDAG grant that continues to be recycled as low-interest second mortgage financing. As described earlier, these funds were used to provide unusually large down payments for clients-- amounting to about 50 percent of the purchase price. And as opposed to today's practices, some of these loans had all repayments deferred until resale, and further, were forgiven over a period of years.

That earlier approach obviously offered a strong incentive to both home buyers and lenders to participate in the program. Lenders had to fund only 50 percent of the purchase price and thus would have a strong security interest in the houses in the event of any defaults. Normally, lenders fund between 80 and 95 percent of the purchase price of homes.

In the late 1980s, NorthRiver took the unusual step of tightening up its assistance guidelines. It reduced the maximum loan amount to 25 percent of purchase price--a change that stretched program dollars farther and increased the lenders' commitment to the program. Repayments of all loans were required from then on.

The earlier approach would have required constant new infusions of capital. The new approach stands a chance of becoming self-sustaining.

In part, the success of the program is due to some effective strategic thinking on the part of the City of Toledo some 16 years ago. The City, in effect, helped to create an endowment for the program--through both the initial UDAG funding and pledges of other UDAG loan repayments to NorthRiver's revolving loan fund. As the prime applicant for UDAG funding in the early 1980s (before that program expired) the City could easily have used the repayments for other purposes. As it is, the security of having a guaranteed future funding stream has added to the solidity of the program.

Clearly, though, this core program funding is not yet enough to run the program in perpetuity. Some of it was given away as grants and soft loans in the early stages of the program. And for new construction and acquisition/rehabilitation projects, deep subsidies are needed that the loan fund cannot provide and still be self-perpetuating.

Why are subsidies needed? As in many distressed inner-city areas, the cost of building or rehabbing homes in North Toledo is typically much higher than the market value of the properties. But investment in such projects can pay other benefits in terms of the overall revitalization of the neighborhood. Fortunately, the City of Toledo has continually provided write-down funds from federal sources to make these revitalization projects economically feasible. The City has also underwritten a significant part of NorthRiver's overhead expenses.

Hopes and Fears for the Future

One of the major problems still facing NorthRiver Development Corporation is the extent of empty lots and housing deterioration, which continue to dampen revitalization efforts. In response, NorthRiver is moving away from scattered-site development toward more geographically targeted projects designed to show more visible progress. For example, NorthRiver is aggressively targeting Census Tract 29, the area with the lowest incomes, oldest homes, most vacant lots, and highest number of renters. In part, the area was chosen because it had available land for development.

The organization is also increasingly becoming involved in coalition efforts to improve the neighborhood in areas besides housing--such as community policing, new day-care facilities, development of parks, etc. The current business plan calls for more involvement in the issues that affect the residents of the community: crime, trash dumping, lack of youth services, and lack of other city services.

Since the early days of the organization, one of its goals has been to encourage new business startups and expansions. Past efforts have been somewhat frustrating. However, a strategic planning process in 1995 helped to establish new goals and directions for economic development programs--one sign of which is the new microenterprise loan program started in late 1995 by NorthRiver. Historically, few neighborhood-based community development corporations have successfully straddled both housing and economic development--but NorthRiver is among a growing minority of CDCs that is trying to do both.

Among some neighborhood residents, there is a concern that NorthRiver does not help the majority of residents because the cost of renovating many of the old houses in the area is high, and sale prices cannot be made affordable to many residents of the neighborhoods. NorthRiver has to fight the impression that it is more interested in helping "yuppies," and more closely allied with City Hall than it is with longtime residents of the neighborhood. The reality is that many clients come from outside, but most have low or very low incomes, and displacement is not an issue.

In part, this impression of gentrification is a holdover from the early days of the organization when a few middle-class families moved in to buy older homes with historic architectural features. But in part, it is a natural consequence of NorthRiver's making homeownership, rather than rental housing, its priority and taking a shallow subsidy approach when it finances purchases of existing housing.

In contrast, rental housing development typically serves lower-income residents, but

NorthRiver's board presently has no interest in purely rental housing. However, it has discussed starting a lease/purchase program as a way of assisting much lower income households.

NorthRiver's director is concerned about current national cutbacks in federal funding but thinks the organization is in a good position to survive them. The organization's loan fund offers some cushion against future funding problems. However, NorthRiver does have a heightened interest in any activities that will earn fees--such as increasing its development activities or starting up a construction company.

Some ancillary activities have not met expectations--such as the commercial space development and past efforts to spur business development. But NorthRiver's core activities--its homeownership programs--have over the past 16 years been tuned and then fine-tuned into two very different, complementary, and successful strategies--

shallow subsidies for existing home purchases from a well-endowed revolving loan fund, and a home development/sales program that, by necessity, is heavily dependent upon deeper subsidies from state and federal funding sources.

Information Sources

For more information, contact:

Cassandra L. Palmer
Executive Director
NorthRiver Development Corp.
725 La Grange Street
Toledo, OH 43604
Phone: (419) 243-3204
Fax: (419) 242-7918

16

Santa Fe Community Housing Trust
(Santa Fe, New Mexico)

Program Highlights

Santa Fe Community Housing Trust

Target Area:	Santa Fe County, population 112,598 (1996 estimate)
Program Goals:	Assist low-income home buyers Add to low-cost housing stock Assure long-term affordability
Major Elements:	Financial counseling and home buyer training Assistance in obtaining first mortgage loans Deferred payment second mortgage loans Shared appreciation through land trust or mortgages Single-family housing and land development
Average Client Income:	$23,565
Typical Home Prices:	$94,000 (new); $110,000 (existing) before subsidies
Year Started:	1993
Other Programs:	Rent deposit loans fund Rent subsidies for individuals with AIDS/HIV Management of trust funds for local governments Management of single-family bond issue Management of predevelopment loan fund Reverse mortgages for disabled people
Staffing:	6.3 fulltime equivalent staff members
Annual Output: (FY 1994-1995)	350 home buyers trained 180 home buyers assisted (without financing) 91 home buyer loans made 59 homes sold
Funding:	HOME program, passed through State government City general funds Private lenders (development financing and grants) Contributions from foundations, businesses, and others Home buyer training fees

Overview

The Santa Fe Community Housing Trust was established in 1991 with a broad mission of increasing affordable housing opportunities for low-income residents of Santa Fe County. It was formed as part of a coordinated effort to respond to increasing displacement of low-income families from this historic, predominantly Hispanic city that is famous for its arts and tourist attractions.

For a relatively young organization, the Housing Trust's activities are unusually diverse:

▶ It trains and counsels home buyers and helps them find affordable, existing homes and first mortgage financing.

▶ It subsidizes home purchases with deferred payment second mortgage loans.

▶ It acquires and rehabilitates housing for resale and builds new homes, using bargain purchases and project subsidies to write down the costs. In this process, it has also become a land developer and works with conventional builders to market and help finance their lower-cost homes.

▶ It operates a land trust--in essence, a device used to obtain low-cost land and then tightly control the future affordability of the homes.

▶ And unrelated to its homeownership programs, it administers two housing trust funds and a predevelopment loan fund that were set up to benefit all nonprofit housing organizations in Santa Fe. It also operates a rent deposit loan program for the homeless and a rent subsidy program for HIV/AIDS victims.

There were two driving forces behind the formation of the Housing Trust that explain the diversity of its programs. First, a citizens' group founded the organization and wanted to form a land trust. Second, existing nonprofit housing groups and the City saw a need for an "umbrella" organization that could help them get land, project financing, and other resources needed to accelerate affordable housing programs in Santa Fe.

The Road Map: A Communitywide Strategic Housing Plan

The Enterprise Foundation assisted with the Housing Trust's startup. In 1991, Enterprise facilitated a strategic planning process that involved City officials, the Housing Trust's initial board of directors, and representatives of existing nonprofit housing organizations. The resulting plan called for assisting 700 households over three years, over and above existing programs being run by the local City and County housing authorities. These were ambitious goals, given that only a handful of "net new families" were being helped in 1991.

The planning process helped to define future roles for the Housing Trust. Existing nonprofit groups agreed to expand their activities with renters, the homeless, and rehabilitating existing homes. But many other unfilled niches (defined during the planning process) were assigned to the as yet unstaffed Housing Trust.

The goals were nearly achieved. Over 600 families had been assisted by the end of 1995, and financing and housing development plans were in place that would assist an additional 700 households.

Throughout this process, the Housing Trust has had to wear two hats. First, it has been the entrepreneurial, rapidly growing operator of its own wide-ranging programs. Second, it has played important "intermediary" roles--managing trust funds and a loan fund capitalized with nearly $2 million.

The Housing Trust develops its own subdivisions, gets below-market or donated professional services, uses cost effective home designs, and declines to take any developer fees or profits. In addition, project write-down grants and soft second mortgage loans reduce per-home costs by $5,000 to $30,000. Subsidies for each home are tailored to the family's finances--in each case they are just enough to make the home affordable.

The resulting home costs, after subsidies, range from $58,000 to $99,000. Subsidies total between $3,000 and $30,000 per home.

In response to rapid inflation of housing costs throughout Santa Fe, the Housing Trust places strong controls over resale prices of the homes it builds, as well as homes it acquires, renovates, and sells. Through mechanisms such as land leases, shared appreciation mortgages, and land use restrictions, the Housing Trust pays much more attention to long-term affordability than any other program examined in this study.

From its inception through September 1996, the Housing Trust's home buyer program has done initial screening of about 4,000 prospective clients, counseled about 2,500 individuals, graduated 1,206 individuals from home buyer training, financed 170 home buyers, and assisted with an additional 240 home purchases without providing financing. In addition, it has sold 59 homes and has another 165 homes in various stages of development. Of the homes in development, six were under construction in October 1996.

Remarkably, in late 1996, 27 of these homes had been pre-sold sight unseen-- testimony to the Housing Trust's success and the severe shortage of affordable homes in Santa Fe County.

Market Analysis

Gentrification and Displacement

The gentrification of Santa Fe has caught the attention of the national media during the past few years. Its housing crisis is emblematic of growing housing problems throughout the Rocky Mountain states, where an influx of wealthy retirees and part-time residents is driving up housing costs. Long-time residents with low incomes end up paying too much for housing. High prices drive others away from their traditional neighborhoods or home towns.

In Santa Fe, it is not uncommon for an old adobe home that was built in the 1800s or early 1900s to sell for $500,000 to $1 million--while a few decades ago the property was considered simply a modest home of one of the city's old families. New house lots in the Rocky Mountain foothills that are within the city limits sell for as much as $300,000, while some homes in those areas sell for millions of dollars. This high-end market has inflated land and construction prices throughout Santa Fe County, even in the most modest villages and neighborhoods.

Wages from a tourist-oriented economy have not kept pace with housing cost inflation. While housing prices are 40 percent above the national average, wages are 22 percent lower.

The dynamics of Santa Fe's housing market have dismayed natives and newcomers alike. Many native Hispanic families, with roots in the city going back as far as the 1600s, see their children being driven out by low wages and high housing costs. Many non-natives feel the same effects, or at least are concerned with the loss of the city's mixed-income, multicultural lifestyle. Thus, housing costs are perceived as Santa Fe's number one problem--lending strong public and local political support to the Housing Trust's efforts.

Housing costs have inflated a great deal since the 1990 Census data was collected. Homes that are offered on the market sell for much more than the average home valuation in the chart above, which includes all owner-occupied homes, both for sale and not for sale.

The median sale price of a home in Santa Fe in 1996 was $230,000, and the lowest-priced new homes sold in the open market for a minimum of about $130,000. Only about 70 non-subsidized existing homes sold for under $100,000--many of these mobile homes or in substandard condition. Usually, the Multiple Listing Service includes only three or four homes priced below $100,000. Studies have indicated that there is a pent-up demand for over 2,500 homes in this price range.

The table below lists key population and market statistics.

	Santa Fe	USA
City population:	55,859	
Population growth, 1980s:	20%	12.6
Percent African American:	>1%	12%
Percent Hispanic:	47.5%	9%
City median income, 1990s:	$30,023	$30,056
Metro median income, 1996:	$50,600	$41,600
Unemployment rate:	4.2%	6.7%
Poverty rate:	12.3%	13.1%
Median home value:	$99,000	$79,900
Home value increase, 1980s:	51.8%	67%
Median monthly rent:	$496	$447
Homeownership rate:	59.6%	64.2%

U.S. Census, 1990; 1996 median income from HUD.

This city of 62,514 people (1996 estimates by the State of New Mexico) has the highest area median income of any city or county represented in this study. But that statistic masks the city's large segments of both wealthy and low-income households. The metropolitan area median income is pulled up by the concentrated wealth in nearby Los Alamos, a "company town" for the federal research laboratory that constructed the first atomic bomb. The median income in Los Alamos is in the mid-$60,000s.

By contrast, the median income within the city of Santa Fe is about $35,000 for a family of four. More than half of the city's Census tracts have median incomes below $25,000.

In its homeownership programs, the Housing Trust provides financial assistance to households with incomes between 17 and 80 percent of median income ($22,000 to $36,800 for a family of four in 1995), although individuals with higher incomes may attend home buyer training. Most clients' incomes fall in between 40 and 70 percent of median, and average 63 percent.

Citywide Efforts to Make Housing More Affordable

A major impediment to building affordable homes and apartments is the lack of reasonably priced land. Until 1995, the minimum price for a house lot with infrastructure was $35,000 to $50,000, and land in that price range was scarce. To counter this problem, the City of Santa Fe created a nonprofit organization--the Tierra Contenta Corporation (TCC)--in 1993 to develop an 850-acre tract of land that had been foreclosed on by a bank.

TCC is solely a land developer, but one with a strong social mission--it offers steep discounts on land prices and (a rarity in Santa Fe) virtually ready-to-build land as incentives for builders to follow strict affordability guidelines. One-third of the 3,600 homes and apartments built on the site over the next 20 years are expected to be affordable to low-income households.

As a result of the TCC project, and a 120-unit land development by the Housing Trust, some affordable building lots finally came to market in 1995. Costs of house lots in this development have been pulled down to the $20,000 to $30,000 range. At this writing, construction of low-cost homes by several for-profit builders had already started in Tierra Contenta. Four nonprofit builders, including the Housing Trust, were soon to break ground on nearly 200 affordable homes and apartments.

Problems with "NIMBY"

Despite the widespread support for affordable housing, Santa Fe, like most growing cities, has a vocal NIMBY ("Not In My Backyard") faction that has opposed some of the Housing Trust's projects--in one case, a 120-home development that was finally approved in early 1996, and in another case, a market-rate home development in which the developer offered to sell the Housing Trust 14 homes at a bargain price.

Most NIMBYites focus on "no-growth" arguments. But a few residents of wealthier areas have also expressed concerns about property values and the introduction of low-income people into higher-income neighborhoods.

The Housing Trust successfully countered the opponents of its 120-home development by consulting extensively with nearby residents and organizing support. The Housing Trust conducted three public planning sessions and a number of smaller meetings with residents living near the site. As a result of the input, the site plan and home plans were amended a number of times and an agreement was made to donate some land to neighbors with unusually small backyards. In the end, 1,400 residents signed petitions in support of the project.

Competing Efforts

There is another unusual factor in the Housing Trust's market--competition with another nonprofit organization. In 1991, when the Housing Trust was charged by the City and other nonprofit organizations to start Santa Fe's first affordable housing programs for home buyers, there was no such competition. But once the Housing Trust began offering home buyer training and financing, the local Neighborhood Housing Services began to expand into the same program areas.

Initially, there was some logical differentiation: NHS tended to work with shallower subsidies (amortizing second mortgages), and the Housing Trust with somewhat deeper subsidies through its deferred payment second mortgages and other grants to write down project costs. As a result, the Housing Trust was able to help families with somewhat lower incomes.

But recently, this distinction has begun to blur. NHS now offers deferred payment second mortgages. And in some ways, NHS's program has become more generous. With some loans, NHS is willing to forgive the indebtedness over time. All of the Housing Trust's loans must be repaid on sale, and with some resales, the Housing Trust will get some of the profits from appreciation to fund future clients. NHS's more generous policies could force the Housing Trust to change its policies.

But while competition for clients and funding has led to some friction between the two organizations, they also collaborate on some funding requests and keep lines of communication open. In combination, the two organizations help between 120 and 200 low-income families a year buy affordable homes, an exceptionally high number for a city of this size.

Operations and Financing

Marketing

The Housing Trust's first program-- started in early 1993 and its best marketing tool to date--is an eight-hour home buyer training course. The sessions attracted hundreds of potential low-income buyers in the first year. The Housing Trust's executive director, Sharron Welsh, credits the first home buyer program director, Ben Martinez, with this success. A lifelong resident of the city, he used his many social and professional connections to spread the word about the new program.

In 1993, the Housing Trust acquired 45 attractive condominium units in Santa Fe's gentrified downtown area at a bargain price. Six hundred people signed up for a lottery for the homes. The lottery marketed the condominiums and also provided a list of people who needed assistance with other purchases.

At this writing, the most-used marketing tools are:

▶ Word of mouth referrals from past clients and from lenders, real estate brokers, and builders that are familiar with the program.

▶ Nearly constant media coverage of the Housing Trust's development projects, in part due to strong "NIMBY" opposition to affordable housing construction, but also due to the media's interest in affordable housing programs.

▶ Referrals from the Santa Fe Civic Housing Authority, which encourages applicants for Section 8 and public housing with incomes over 35 percent of area median to seek home purchase assistance from the Housing Trust. (Four of these referred clients prequalified for new homes by late 1996.)

Financing of Homes

Qualified Housing Trust clients buying existing homes can borrow up to $15,000 in cash, secured by a soft second mortgage from the Housing Trust--which is used in tandem with conventional first mortgage financing from local banks, thrift institutions, and mortgage companies. The subsidy is generous but designed in a thoughtful way and administered with a tight-fisted approach. As described earlier, homes developed and sold by the Housing Trust use other kinds of subsidies and usually in larger amounts.

The goal is to serve a broad band of low-income families, not just the high end of the low-income market. Following that logic, the maximum amounts of the Housing Trust's second mortgage loans are calculated on a sliding scale going from $3,000 to $15,000, with larger families and the lowest-income families qualifying for the highest amounts.

Clients receive these maximum second mortgage loan amounts only if they are needed to make the home purchase work. If clients have cash assets in excess of two months' income, they are expected to invest them in the home purchase.

These program rules discourage the over-subsidizing of families that occurs in programs offering the same amount of second mortgage financing to clients regardless of income, assets, or family size.

In most cases the second mortgage loan --which averaged about $10,300 in 1995-- represents real cash put into the purchase by the Housing Trust. However, when the Housing Trust builds and sells houses, the land or construction has already been subsidized with grants. Because these homes are effectively priced far below market value, a deferred payment second mortgage is taken back from the buyer. These paper transactions are intended to forestall windfall profits from the resale of the property and to recapture subsidies.

The second or third mortgage loans require no repayments whatsoever until the house is resold. But the indebtedness is never forgiven. The loan must be repaid upon resale, or it may be assumed by another qualified family. In either case, the subsidy is recycled to another family.

Sources of these loan funds during the reporting year 1994-1995 were as follows:

City general funds	$150,000
Federal HOME funds	208,000
City Trust fund	62,000
County Trust Fund	110,000
McCune Foundation	50,000
Other sources	22,000
Total	$602,500

To qualify for a second mortgage, Housing Trust clients must obtain a 30-year, fixed-rate first mortgage at competitive or below-market rates. No so-called B-grade first mortgages with higher rates are allowed. The program tries to provide just enough second mortgage financing to make the home purchases work and does not want to be in the position of subsidizing shorter-term financing or above-market rates for first mortgages.

Most institutional real estate lenders in Santa Fe County work with the program. Clients select lenders of their choice. Several lenders--Norwest, Bank of America, First Interstate, and Sunwest--have offered rates discounted about one or one and one-half percentage points under market, through special agreements with the Housing Trust.

The Housing Trust's training program and second mortgage financing mechanisms were approved by Fannie Mae, which buys a majority of the first mortgage loans given to Housing Trust clients. This means that banks can make nonconventional loans to qualified program participants and then sell the loans to Fannie Mae.

HUD Special Purpose Grant

U.S. Rep. Bill Richardson helped the Housing Trust obtain a $1.5 million HUD special purpose grant for innovative and collaborative homeownership projects in Santa Fe. As grantee, the Housing Trust allocated $500,000 to write down the costs of home construction by other nonprofit housing groups, including NHS and Habitat for Humanity. It used another $455,000 to underwrite the costs of the $30 million City mortgage bond issue, and the remaining $545,000 to write down costs of a 120-unit home construction project.

Administration of Mortgage Bond Program

In 1995, the Housing Trust proposed that the City of Santa Fe issue mortgage revenue bonds to create a larger pool of low-cost first mortgage financing for low-income home buyers. The City agreed. This bond issue was seen as an important tool for marketing and selling the several hundred affordable homes that would be built in the Tierra Contenta project and in the Housing Trust's La Cieneguita project.

The last time the City had directly issued single-family mortgage revenue bonds was in the early 1980s, so it needed expert help. Because the Housing Trust's Executive Director Sharron Welsh had managed single-family bond issues for the city of San Diego, the Housing Trust was also asked to administer the $30 million issue on an ongoing basis. The Housing Trust used some of its grant sources to pay all the costs of issuance.

Since the funds were made available in early 1996, over 90 loans have been made or committed at an interest rate of about 6.8 percent--about one and one-half percentage points below market at this writing. The Housing Trust is recovering the costs of issuance through a one percent origination fee on the loans, so the funds can be reused on other projects.

Discounts on Closing Fees

The Housing Trust continually presses professionals in the real estate industry to make in-kind contributions to the program. Because of their concern about the affordable housing problem, many professionals agree to do so. Appraisers routinely give program participants a 50 percent discount, and most local title companies give $150 to $300 discounts for title work. The home inspector used by the Housing Trust charges only $95 for $350 in inspection services.

Intake, Screening, and Counseling

Interested persons call for information, and the office manager conducts an initial screening over the phone. The office manager asks potential clients to fill out applications, get verification of their employment, and obtain copies of their credit reports before prequalifying interviews are scheduled.

Fannie Mae has provided the Housing Trust with computer hardware and software so that staff can obtain instant, on-line credit reports for a charge of $17 to $20. When a client's financial data is entered, a modified version of Fannie Mae's software helps

determine if the family prequalifies for a loan.

Then, during a scheduled appointment, the home buyer director or home buyer counselor meets the client for about an hour to determine the client's eligibility for homeownership training. If it appears that the client can qualify for a bank loan (and the Housing Trust subsidy loan) within a year and a half, they are signed up for training.

Most clients who are found ineligible for the homeownership training have the following problems:

- ▸ Excessive debt
- ▸ Bad credit
- ▸ Lack of employment
- ▸ Insufficient income, even with subsidies
- ▸ Too many assets

For clients with excessive debt or bad credit, the Housing Trust helps to establish a plan for credit clean-up, savings for a down payment, and eventual homeownership. Some are referred to Consumer Credit Counseling in nearby Albuquerque. Clients with incomes too low to afford a home are helped to set goals and improve their financial standing so that they can eventually buy a home.

Approximately three out of four persons (or couples) who are interviewed end up attending training. But, to date, only one out of five who were interviewed have actually purchased a home. The attrition is mainly due to three factors: 1) continued bad credit or employment history; 2) inability to save cash for a down payment; and 3) the scarcity of affordable homes in the market.

But given the serious barriers to homeownership in Santa Fe, the success rate is higher than one might expect. The staff attributes this to the resourcefulness of the clients. Large extended families--unheard of in other parts of the country--are a major resource, helping younger couples get land for construction or cash for closing costs.

Clients who end up closing on home purchases receive, on average, about 10 hours of one-on-one help from Housing Trust staff members. The scope of this counseling includes help with prequalifying for the program, resolution of credit problems, arranging for home inspections, and referrals to first mortgage lenders. Advice is given on negotiating purchase contracts. The staff is also willing to work with banks' loan processors and loan officers when problems occur with loan applications.

Qualification for Assistance

The primary qualifications for financial assistance or purchasing a home from the Housing Trust are: 1) an income below 80 percent of median income; 2) being able to qualify for a first mortgage loan; 3) ability to pay a minimum of three percent of the purchase price in hard money, rather than grants, loans, or family gifts; 4) finding an affordable home in Santa Fe County; and 5) successfully completing home buyer training workshops.

The 80-percent-of-median standard applies to all existing homes that the Housing Trust has helped to finance and most new homes it has sold to date. However, the three land lease houses it built and sold, along with 35 more being built with land leases attached, will be restricted to even lower-income families. But in some projects, the Housing Trust sets its own targets that are lower. Prices are skewed to achieve these goals. About 40 percent of the homes being built are reserved for households with incomes below 50 percent of median income.

Cash requirements for down payments and closing costs are fairly high when compared to subsidized homeownership programs in other cities--in large part due to the relatively high cost of homes in Santa Fe. While the Housing Trust can subsidize part of these costs, the minimum cash-to-close for most buyers is about $3,000 to $5,000.

In a similar vein, clients with low incomes but large assets may be disqualified from the program or receive a reduced subsidy. Assets are "imputed" to income--that is, a certain annual percentage return is assumed for non-income producing assets such as stocks, real property, or personal property. In this regard, the Housing Trust follows the rules of the federal HOME program, whether HOME funds are being used or not. Another touchy problem concerns newcomers to Santa Fe--some of them temporarily or voluntarily poor--who want to take advantage of the Housing Trust's low-cost homes and financing. While the Santa Fe City Council and the Housing Trust's board of directors would like see a residency requirement for all housing programs it supports, the legality and constitutionality of this has been questioned by the City Attorney. However, the Housing Trust does require evidence of three years' local employment as a measure of borrowers' income stability.

It also puts strict limits on gifts of cash to buyers from family members, limited to 5 percent of the purchase price of a home, plus $1,000 per family member. (These rules were internally developed and not imposed by funders.)

The Housing Trust's loan committee is comprised of one board member, the executive director, and five private sector mortgage loan officers (who are not board members). The committee reviews and approves loan applications of home buyers during monthly meetings to assure fair treatment and adherence to funding requirements.

Loan Underwriting Criteria

Lenders cooperating with the Housing Trust use fairly lenient underwriting criteria. Most lenders allow up to 33 percent of income for housing payments, and up to 40 percent of income for all debt, as opposed to conventional 28/36 ratios. However, the Housing Trust prefers to qualify clients at 30/36 ratios, so the homes will be more affordable, and clients will be at less risk of default. In no case will the Housing Trust approve a second mortgage loan when the housing payment ratio is less than 25 percent--this is seen as using excessive amounts of subsidy.

Because clients need low down payments and ratios generally above the conventional 28/36, they must obtain mortgage insurance. With mortgage insurance, lenders will allow loan-to-value (LTV) ratios as high as 95 percent. Private mortgage insurance (PMI) is used for most of the loans, but does not add a significant cost because of the Housing Trust's soft second mortgages and the resulting lower loan-to-value ratios for first mortgage loans. PMI adds an extra cost to each monthly payment, but it is on a sliding scale based on LTV ratios. So for most Housing Trust clients, the cost is

minimal. FHA insurance is almost never used.

It was difficult to get banks to provide first mortgage loans for homes on the two land trust houses already sold (since the land is leased and only the improvements are sold). Currently, the Housing Trust is working with Fannie Mae to get its pending 35-unit land trust project pre-approved for first mortgage lending, despite the fact that the loans will be nonconventional because of the land leases.

Homeownership Training

Typically, the Housing Trust has a three- to four-month waiting list for its homeownership training classes. The typical class has 40 participants.

The training sessions are held once a week for three consecutive weeks. Professionals from related disciplines-- including a credit counselor, a lawyer, a mortgage banker, a housing specialist, an appraiser, the county tax assessor, a real estate agent, and a tax preparer--assist the Housing Trust staff in conducting the training.

The sessions teach buyers how to use a household budget to qualify for a conventional mortgage loan, shop for a home, repair poor credit history, and to maintain successful ownership after the purchase. The Housing Trust and The Enterprise Foundation developed the curriculum and training materials using a variety of sources, including Fannie Mae's home buyer training manual.

The Housing Trust requests a $250 fee for the training, home inspection, and other assistance it provides. This fee is collected at loan closings on an honor system. About 75 percent of clients voluntarily pay it or ask that it be paid out of loan proceeds. Those who do not pay are never billed.

Home Selection

Because of the difficulties of finding affordable homes in the Santa Fe market, most clients are not able to close on a home purchase until about six months after their training is completed.

Clients usually retain a buyer's broker. The Housing Trust keeps up-to-date lists of the few affordable homes that come on the market. The information comes from brokers and by word of mouth from a few sellers who want to see low-income families have a chance to buy a home.

Prospective buyers of older homes are encouraged to inspect them carefully. The Housing Trust will arrange for--and pay for --a professional home inspection. The Housing Trust's contract inspector follows standards that exceed HUD's Housing Quality Standards (HQS) and assure a life expectancy at least as long as the term of the first mortgage.

When existing homes are being purchased with HOME-funded second mortgages, the Housing Trust requires that they meet HUD's minimal Housing Quality Standards within six months of move-in. In other cases, the Housing Trust simply requires that homes be decent, safe, and sanitary, with a life expectancy at least as long as the mortgage term. In most cases, the homes do not need extensive repairs.

When a Housing Trust development project with new homes is being planned, the Trust puts together a focus group of prospective buyers to advise on designs and site plans. This input not only assures happier buyers, it builds public support for projects and gets buyers lined up before the homes are built.

As a result of the sporadic nature of the Housing Trust's development projects, it has no permanent staff position responsible for showing and selling the homes it has developed. For its largest project to date-- the 45-unit condominium project--two persons were hired for six months under contract to do the sales work and handle the closings for a set fee per month. This system worked well, and the Housing Trust plans to replicate it in the future.

Partnership with a For-Profit Builder

For-profit builders in the City-sponsored Tierra Contenta project have also begun to bring some affordable new homes to market --priced as low as $90,000 for attractive, semi-detached homes. The Tierra Contenta Corporation, also a nonprofit, gives builders price breaks on residential land in exchange for requiring that 40 percent of the homes be affordable to low-income buyers. To find qualified low-income buyers and certify their incomes, builders are encouraged to form alliances with nonprofits that are more experienced with this part of the market.

The Housing Trust teamed up in this way with one builder in Tierra Contenta, BT Housing Corporation, which developed a 158-unit subdivision. The Housing Trust trained, counseled, and prequalified over 55 low- and moderate-income families (mostly low-income) over a one-year period without having to provide subsidies. In effect, most of these buyers are subsidized by bargain land sales from Tierra Contenta, and reflecting that fact, Tierra Contenta takes back a soft second mortgage to prevent windfall profits. That second mortgage, unlike the Housing Trust's, is forgiven over a period of a few years.

Housing Development Activities

As of late 1996, the Housing Trust had completed three development projects and was set to start construction on two more:

Las Acequias: Fourteen homes were built in a conventional subdivision--two of them on land donated by the City of Santa Fe and sold on leased land (a land trust regime). Home prices ranged from $61,000 to $99,000 (after subsidies) for the outright sales, and $62,000 to $84,000 for the homes on leased land. Market values of the homes ranged from $90,000 to $110,000.

Pueblo del Rosario: Forty-five condominiums were acquired and resold with support from the City of Santa Fe, as already described. Effective home sale prices ranged from $58,000 to $112,000, while the appraised value of the homes ranged from $103,000 to $190,000. The difference--in effect a subsidy to buyers--is subject to a lien described in the section on Long-Term Affordability.

Scattered site rehabilitation: Five existing homes were renovated and one new home built on two sites near downtown. Effective sale prices will range from $65,000 to $100,000, while the appraised values will range from $85,000 to $150,000.

Arroyo Sonrisa: Thirty-five homes will be built in the City-sponsored Tierra Contenta development and sold in the land trust regime. Effective sale prices will range from $55,000 to $85,000, while the appraised values are expected to range from $105,000 to $135,000.

La Cieneguita: This is a 120-home infill land development and home construction project in one of the city's older neighborhoods, Agua Fria. Effective sale prices will range from $55,000 to $110,000, while the appraised values are expected to range from $110,000 to $145,000.

While the Housing Trust's activist approach to development has added greatly to the impact of the program, it has also been taxing for a young organization. Each project has required different staff skills, consultants, designers, builders, financing, and financing sources. Because of the great variations among projects, the Housing Trust hired one project manager and a construction manager on short-duration contracts. This allows more flexibility in shifting gears and saves money during downtime between projects.

Fortunately, financial packaging and fundraising is the Housing Trust's strong suit. In 1995 and 1996, the organization raised $1.8 million in grants and other subsidy financing and got $8.5 million in loan commitments for interim and construction financing.

Long-Term Affordability Controls

The Housing Trust's program operates along the lines of a land trust. Until recently, the term "land trust" has meant sales of homes on leased land by a nonprofit organization. Land trusts were created so nonprofit developers could have a sound legal means of controlling the price appreciation of the housing they produce, and thereby keep the homes affordable for a long term. At the Housing Trust, the term land trust is also used more loosely to describe other affordability controls unrelated to land leases.

The concept of land trusts, and especially the land lease mechanism, has been promoted since the early 1980s by the Massachusetts-based Institute for Community Economics (ICE). ICE advised the Housing Trust in its early planning stages.

When the Housing Trust develops and sells homes, it uses these three techniques associated with land trusts to control long-term affordability, as follows:

A land lease with resale restrictions: The City of Santa Fe bought three house lots that were leased to the Housing Trust for a nominal amount. Newly built homes were sold outright to the low-income families, but the land was subleased. Through the lease, the Housing Trust controls any resales of the home. The lease allows a reasonable amount of appreciation to the homeowner, but restricts resale to another low-income buyer and controls the resale price. Starting in 1996, 52 more homes were developed using this model.

Shared appreciation mortgages with land use restrictions: The Housing Trust acquired, renovated, and sold 45 condominiums in a high-cost area near downtown Santa Fe. A typical home was appraised at $66,000 more than the effective sale price. The Housing Trust placed a lien on each home equal to that added value and will share in any future appreciation. That share is roughly proportional to its original share of the entire financing package.

A deferred payment second mortgage: This is simply a zero percent interest loan with all payments deferred until resale of the property. This mechanism is used with all homes purchased on the private market and financed by the Housing Trust and all homes that it builds and sells that are not located in rapidly appreciating neighborhoods.

The Land Trust

Under the first arrangement, land is leased from the Housing Trust for 99 years. Unlike some land trusts that charge at least nominal lease fees to cover administrative costs, the Housing Trust leases the land free of charge. However, it does accept responsibility for perpetual management of the land leases (every time a home is sold, a new 99-year lease begins).

Through this mechanism, the lot cost is effectively removed from the price of the housing. As structured by the Housing Trust, the land lease is dormant until the homeowner decides to sell. Then, the Housing Trust has a right of first refusal on the purchase of the property and is entitled to repayment of a deferred payment second mortgage for the amount of the Housing Trust's original subsidy plus a portion of the appreciation.

The initial house lots for the land trust program were purchased outright by the City, then leased to the Housing Trust, and then subleased to the home buyers. In late

1996, construction was scheduled to start on a subdivision that was designed to contain 35 land trust homes. In this project, the land and the infrastructure were paid for by the nonprofit land developer (the Tierra Contenta Corporation) using a HUD grant.

The Housing Trust's homes on leased land are differentiated from other homes it develops in the following ways:

▶ They are the most subsidized and therefore have the lowest effective prices.

▶ They are reserved for the lowest-income clients--usually below 50 percent of area median income.

▶ Through the land lease, they have very strong controls over resale prices.

Trust Funds and a Loan Fund

In 1992, coinciding with implementation of Santa Fe's new strategic housing plan, the City of Santa Fe began to encourage market-rate developers to include a certain percentage of affordable homes in their developments. While the program was voluntary, developers sensed that they might get better treatment during the City's notoriously slow land development approval process if they followed these voluntary guidelines.

As a side effect of the City's "inclusionary" guidelines, some developers offered to pay cash in lieu of providing affordable housing. Because of limitations imposed by the state constitution, the City wanted these grants of cash to go into a housing trust fund administered by a nonprofit organization. The Housing Trust was selected to administer these funds, which as of late 1996 amounted to over $300,000.

Soon after the City trust fund began, Santa Fe County obtained a similar pledge from a developer to provide $1 million to a housing trust fund. So a second and similar fund was established by the Housing Trust.

While the Housing Trust has the fiduciary responsibility for these funds, allocation decisions are made by a committee of the Santa Fe Housing Roundtable. The Roundtable is an unstaffed coalition organization that includes the City, The Enterprise Foundation, the United Way, the Housing Trust, and representatives of 11 other local nonprofit housing organizations.

Having one of the most productive affordable housing programs in Santa Fe, the Housing Trust has been able to access about one-third of the trust fund monies for soft second mortgages.

Along the same lines, the Housing Trust administers a predevelopment loan fund that both it and other nonprofits use to borrow up-front capital for development projects. The fund was capitalized by a $750,000 grant from the local McCune Foundation--an amount that was matched by a pledge of $750,000 in low-interest loan funds from The Enterprise Foundation.

Assistance to Neighborhood Associations

To date, the Housing Trust has been responsible for establishing one formal homeowners' association--a condominium association for the 48-unit Pueblo Del Rosario property. The association previously existed as a shell organization controlled by the original for-profit development group, since only three units had been sold (the rest were rented).

During the development and sales phase, the Housing Trust's primary help was to:

► Finance and manage the acquisition, rehab, and home sales.

► Create a long-term operating plan and maintenance schedule.

► Organize a functioning association.

► Pre-fund replacement and operating reserves.

► Hire a property manager.

A few months after it was organized, the association took full charge. The two organizations stay in close communication, and the Housing Trust offers help or advice when problems arise.

In its first, 14-unit project, 14 homes located on one street in a conventional subdivision, the Housing Trust organized an informal homeowners' association, which remains active and in close communication with the Housing Trust.

Loan Collections and Post-Purchase Counseling

Since all Housing Trust loans are due only on the resale of properties, it will have no worries about loan collections except in the case of a default and foreclosure on the first mortgage--in which case the Housing Trust's investment could be lost. To date, no foreclosures have occurred.

The Housing Trust has been informed about only three delinquencies. When these have occurred, the Housing Trust has offered financial counseling. In all three cases, the Housing Trust and the family approached the first mortgage lender, who entered into a forbearance agreement allowing payments to be caught up over time. In one case, the Housing Trust also made an unsecured loan to cover some of the late payments. The loan was repaid over a one-year period.

During the prepurchase training, clients are urged to come back to the Housing Trust if they get into financial trouble after buying a home. As a result, homeowners have asked for counseling even before their loans became delinquent.

Partners

The Housing Trust's success to date has been due, in large part, to its ability to develop and sustain successful partnerships. These are its key partners:

City government: In its first few years, the Housing Trust received a major portion of its administrative funding from the City and was designated by the City to undertake certain activities--for example, management of the City's Housing Trust Fund and development of the condominium and land development projects mentioned earlier. In exchange, the Housing Trust has gotten some critically needed development funding, a small source of second mortgage money from the Trust Fund, and, when needed, political clout with federal agencies and to resolve administrative issues.

County government: When the County created its Housing Trust Fund, modeled after the City's, it selected the Housing Trust to manage it.

State government and HUD: The State Housing Division has been an important source of second mortgage money through the HOME program it administers on behalf of HUD. HUD's funding has been the major source of second mortgage money for clients.

Lenders: The Housing Trust's programs could not operate without the broad support of local lending institutions. A few have made remarkable concessions. For instance, Norwest offered permanent financing for the condominium project at seven percent financing with no origination fees, when market interest rates were 8.5 percent with a two-point origination fee. The Housing Trust is represented on two lenders' community boards, and one or more bank presidents are always represented on the Housing Trust's board.

Other industry professionals: As mentioned, professionals in the real estate industry contribute in a number of ways, including waiver of closing fees and volunteer help with training sessions.

Other nonprofits: The Housing Trust's cooperation with NHS has been described. The Housing Trust, NHS, and other nonprofit housing organizations are members of a Santa Fe Affordable Housing Roundtable, some of whose members collaborate on funding and public policy matters. For example, the Santa Fe Civic Housing Authority and Santa Fe Land Trust (not a true land trust) have both lent funds at low rates to the Housing Trust to facilitate earlier construction starts.

Builders: Santa Fe's few builders of affordable homes (mostly spurred into the business by the Tierra Contenta project and the City's inclusionary housing guidelines) are important allies. The Housing Trust refers qualified low-income buyers to them, and the builders, in turn, refer some prospective buyers who require the Housing Trust's subsidy financing.

National funders: The Housing Trust's relationship with The Enterprise Foundation has been described. Important funding was also received from the Pew Partnership for Civic Change. The Federal Home Loan Bank of Dallas has supported Housing Trust projects with capital grants, starting early on. And Fannie Mae has been an important ally, smoothing the way for acceptance of the Housing Trust's subsidies by local lenders and providing some administrative funds.

Congress and the State Legislature: The Housing Trust has received strong support from local legislators. For example, state legislators from Santa Fe helped to obtain the $30 million single-family mortgage bond allocation, an exceptional step given that no local government had received one for years. And as described earlier, Congressman Richardson helped the Housing Trust obtain a $1.5 million special purpose grant for homeownership programs in Santa Fe.

Clients: The Housing Trust identifies its clients as its most important partners. They help in many ways: publicizing the program, referring new clients, supporting requests for funding, and even testifying in favor of development approvals for new projects.

Administration

Management and Staffing

The Housing Trust had the following staff positions as of reporting year 1994-1995, amounting to 6.3 fulltime equivalent positions:

Executive director
Home buyer program director
Project managers (one fulltime;
  one part-time)
Housing counselor
Office manager
Receptionist/bookkeeper (part-time)

Board of Directors

The Housing Trust board has an average of 12 members. As of this writing, about half the board members were professionals and the other half were community or neighborhood leaders. Professions represented included lending, real estate sales, law, the clergy, and accounting. Over half the board members were Hispanic.

Administrative Funding

For the year ending December 31, 1994, administrative and program services costs for the Housing Trust, and the sources of funds used to pay for them, were as follows:

Uses of funds:

Personnel	$165,576
Employee benefits	29,638
Contract services	87,928
Supplies	8,610
Maintenance and repair	3,873
Travel	2,735
Board-related	2,117
Office rent	7,800
Other costs	20,975
Total	$329,252

Sources of funds:

Government grants	$112,374
Foundation grants	98,884
Project financing	87,928
Individual contributions	9,443
Gain on home sales	17,471
Other revenue	5,391
Total sources	$334,491

The Housing Trust notes that its "pure" administrative costs are only a small part of these expenses, which mostly cover program services (including some program services unrelated to the home buyer program).

As a matter of principle, the Housing Trust does not charge developer fees to projects, nor does it attempt to make profits on home sales. The "gain on home sales" shown was used to cover project-related expenses that were not capitalized. Project financing was used to pay the costs of contract personnel, and those costs were ultimately passed through to home buyers.

Fees paid for home buyer training show up in "other revenue." Even though a $250 fee per client is requested, the revenue in 1994 was not significant.

Financial Management

By most financial measures, the Housing Trust is in sound financial condition. After operating for just two years, it had a fund balance (net worth) of over $1.8 million. This is attributable primarily to its management of large sums of money in the City Housing Trust Fund, the County Housing Trust Fund, and a Predevelopment Loan Fund capitalized by a $750,000 foundation grant.

Even though the Housing Trust "owns" these funds in a strict legal sense, these are very restricted assets. Outside committees decide how they are spent, and while some of the funds are awarded to the Housing Trust for its own use, a half-dozen other nonprofit housing providers are loaned or granted a majority of the funds.

In addition, all the deferred payment second mortgage loans made by the Housing Trust show up as assets, even though they may not be collectable for years to come.

When these restricted funds and long-term investments are taken out of the equation, the assets available strictly for Housing Trust programs are much more modest. However, there is no doubt that its healthy balance sheet is a major factor in this young organization's ability to get $17 million in combined lines of credit in 1996 for land development, infrastructure, and home construction. The credit is being provided primarily by private lenders, augmented by low-interest loans from The Enterprise

Foundation, the McCune Foundation, and the Santa Fe Civic Housing Authority.

Information Management

Given the complex array of housing development and housing finance programs managed by the Housing Trust, information management is of major concern. Custom software has been developed to track clients, produce reports for funding agencies, and track multiple restricted funds. Proprietary software is used to track loans made with the mortgage revenue bond issue that is administered by the Housing Trust.

Lessons Learned

Strengths of Program

For an organization that has been operating for less than four years, the Housing Trust's programs have grown with remarkable speed and success. Over 400 families have achieved homeownership with the Housing Trust's help, 59 homes have been built or renovated, and 165 homes are in development.

But this is just part of the picture. The Housing Trust was launched by private citizens and the City government to fill gaps in the local affordable housing delivery system, which as recently as 1992 managed to help only three additional families. And fill gaps it has.

The Housing Trust administers a $30 million bond issue. It manages nearly $2 million in two housing trust funds and one predevelopment loan fund for the benefit of its own programs and those of other nonprofit housing providers. The organization has provided administrative and fund-raising services to an 11-member coalition, the Santa Fe Affordable Housing Roundtable. In three years, nearly 700 low-income families received housing assistance from this broader effort.

Harvard University and the Ford Foundation have given national recognition to the City of Santa Fe, the Housing Trust, and the other members of the Affordable Housing Roundtable, which includes local nonprofit housing providers, the United Way, and the Enterprise Foundation. In late 1996, representatives of the City, the Housing Trust, and Enterprise were scheduled to go to the White House to accept an Innovations in American Government Award. A $100,000 prize was awarded for addressing a major community problem by successful City-supported but privatized programs in the nonprofit sector.

In addition, the Housing Trust provides loans to the homeless for rent deposits and rent subsidies for individuals with AIDS/HIV.

The program has these obvious strengths:

▶ High output with low overhead.

▶ An ability to raise large amounts of grant money to undertake capital-intensive projects such as bond issues and land development, and conventional financing.

▶ An ability to build homes at costs at least 20 percent below market.

▶ A high regard for the big picture--exhibited by the Housing Trust's willingness to fill gaps in the delivery system (even difficult ones) and to provide other nonprofit groups with technical and financial help.

▶ Support from local and state government, in terms of operating grants, project subsidies, and assistance with federal agencies.

▶ Backing from local foundations such as the McCune Foundation, and national ones, such as The Enterprise Foundation, and the Pew Partnership for Civic Change.

▶ Support from clients and neighborhood residents, both in promoting the program and standing up against NIMBY forces.

Keeping Costs Down

What is most remarkable is that six staff people--along with all the professional volunteers they can muster--are responsible for all of this output. Hands down, the program could win any award for frugality and efficiency. How was this accomplished?

"We're cheap," says Executive Director Sharron Welsh. She gave these tips on keeping costs down:

▶ Shortcut bureaucratic processes--keep things as simple as possible.

▶ Keep a minimum core staff that is cross-trained for multiple tasks. Job descriptions are not neat and clean and are subject to rapid change.

- Use temporary staff and contract personnel to put together development projects, which come and go, and often are so dissimilar that they require different skills.

- Get as many pro-bono and discounted services as you can--both to help with administration and to reduce costs for clients.

- Network with other organizations to undertake cooperative projects, so some of the workload is taken on by the other organization. The AIDS service community, for example, does all of the screening and qualifying work for the rent subsidy program.

- Minimize developer fees taken out of projects. While this may seem self-defeating from the standpoint of the organization, the Housing Trust believes that the actual delivered cost of homes must be kept as low as possible.

That last operating principle--avoidance of developer fees--goes against current trends in the nonprofit housing industry. But so far, the Housing Trust believes this approach earns more respect from foundations, government agencies, lenders, and other funders--and thereby increases overall financial support.

Most of the Housing Trust's core expenses are paid for with grants from the City, foundations, and businesses. This is a gutsy strategy, since the organization has no certain sources of support from year to year, although the City and the McCune Foundation have been steady supporters of the program.

Santa Fe is a tough place to raise money. It has one large foundation, no major businesses, a relatively small population, and nearly 400 nonprofit organizations competing for grants. The arts and New Age organizations are still more popular with donors than community development projects.

Hopes and Fears for the Future

The Housing Trust has just gotten over some major humps. Two projects with 155 new homes are about to start construction, after a bruising two years of obtaining development approvals and spending scarce cash on predevelopment expenses. The Housing Trust learned that land development is a much more difficult and capital-intensive business than home construction.

In order to be affordable in this high-cost market, these projects depended on cost-cutting, and they were completely dependent on subsidy money. Most of the subsidies are federal funds in one form or another, and it is uncertain how much of this funding will be available in the future.

Another factor that will affect future strategies is the housing market. Due to over-building and to hyper-inflation in housing prices, the middle and high end of the market are now in a recession. This could result in distress sales of house lots that would obviate, at least temporarily, the need for more land development.

For-profit builders are starting to offer affordable homes in the city-sponsored Tierra Contenta land development. It remains to be seen how much this new production will meet the demands from low-income buyers.

Because of these trends and because the Housing Trust has two years of home construction ahead of it, no new land development projects are being planned. The organization can afford to take a wait-and-see position and look for opportunities when they come along.

With a small staff and a proven history of being adaptable, the Housing Trust is positioned to quickly readjust its priorities. In those respects, it bears an uncanny resemblance to the successful for-profit real estate developers and entrepreneurs who have made Santa Fe a boom town since the 1960s.

But instead of marketing homes to the wealthy, the Housing Trust found a way to sell them to low-income families, thus filling a void that had been growing for several decades.

Information Sources

For more information about the Housing Trust, contact:

Sharron Welsh, Executive Director
David Vlaming, Operations Manager
Santa Fe Community Housing Trust
P.O. Box 713
Santa Fe, NM 87504
Phone: (505) 989-3960
Fax: (505) 982-3690

For more information about other affordable housing programs in Santa Fe, contact:

James Duncan III, Housing Planner
Community Services Division
City of Santa Fe
P.O. Box 909
Santa Fe, NM 87505
Phone: (505) 984-6562

GLOSSARY OF AFFORDABLE HOUSING TERMS

[Portions of this glossary are reprinted from *Affordable Housing Yearbook* with permission of the publisher.]

Acquisition-Rehab Program - A colloquial term for program, usually run by a nonprofit group or local government, that purchases abandoned or substandard properties, rehabilitates them and sells them, typically to low-income home buyers.

Amortization - The gradual repayment of a mortgage by installments.

Amortizing Loan - A loan for which equal payments are due on a periodic basis, usually monthly. The payments include varying amounts of principal and interest. These loans are sometimes called "level payment" loans, as opposed to deferred payment loans (due only on resale) or loans repaid with unequal periodic payments of principal and interest.

Affordable Housing Fund - A subsidy funding program of the Federal Home Loan Bank Board, the official governing body that oversees savings and loan institutions.

Area Median Income (AMI) - A term used by some federal programs to describe published income standards for various areas of the country that are used as benchmarks for determining households' eligibility for federally-funded programs. For example, home buyers assisted with HOME or CDBG funds generally must have incomes at or below 80 percent of the area median income. AMIs are calculated and published annually by HUD (see "HUD"). "Median" means that half of all households in the area are estimated to have more that this amount of income, and half less are estimated to have less.

Capacity Building - A term currently used to describe technical assistance (and sometimes staff grants) given to nonprofit organizations to increase their organizational and staff capacity to undertake community development activities.

Capitalize; Capitalization - Has several meanings as used in the low-income housing industry. The most common is "capitalizing a loan fund," i.e. raising grants or low-interest loans for a fund from which loans are made to third parties. In real estate development, the term can also mean characterizing certain expenses such as loan interest and professional fees as capital costs, not ordinary operating expenses.

Cash-to-Close - A colloquial term used in the single-family lending industry to describe the total amount of cash to be provided by the home buyer at the real estate and loan closing. This cash is applied to pay the down payment, appraisal fee, and other loan-related fees, recording costs, and pre-paid real estate taxes and insurance.

CHDO - (Pronounced CHO-DOE) A HUD term for a Community-Based Housing

Development Organization in relation only to the federal HOME program (see "HOME"). HOME reserves 15 percent of its funds for CHDOs. A CHDO must have on its board at least one-third low-income people, their specially elected representatives, or residents of low-income census tracts.

CDBG Entitlement - The amount of money a city, state or urban county gets annually from HUD on a formula basis through the Community Development Block Grant program.

Closing - The occasion where the sale of real estate and/or the making of a loan is finalized. Sometimes called "settlement."

Community Development - A term broadly used to describe any efforts to improve housing, infrastructure, education, social services and employment in lower income areas.

Community Development Block Grant Program (CDBG) - This is a HUD (federal) program that provides grants to cities and states to undertake community development efforts. Affordable housing is a common use, and many cities subcontract with nonprofits to run the programs. Generally rural areas and cities smaller than 50,000 population must apply on a competitive basis annually or bi-annually to a state government agency administering the Small Cities CDBG program.

Community Development Corporation (CDC) - A loosely defined term for a nonprofit organization that undertakes commercial or residential real estate development. It usually, but not always, indicates some targeting of efforts to a low-income neighborhood.

Conventional Financing - In the low-income housing industry, a term often used to refer to any loan made with non-subsidy sources. Among private, single-family lenders, a term to describe a loan that is made with a minimum 20 percent down payment and conventional underwriting criteria, which include a maximum 80 percent loan-to-value ratio and maximum 28/36 underwriting ratios. See "loan-to-value ratio" and "underwriting ratios."

The Community Reinvestment Act (CRA) - A federal law that encourages lenders to make residential and commercial loans to low-income and minority people, and/or in low-income areas.

Debt Ratio - See "installment debt ratio."

Debt Service - Principal and interest payments on a loan, usually paid monthly.

Deed In Lieu of Foreclosure - The transfer of title of a mortgaged property from the owner to a mortgage lender to avoid foreclosure and further collection actions.

Deed of Trust - See "mortgage loan."

Deferred Payment Second Mortgage Loan - A nonamortizing loan, usually at 0 percent interest, on which no repayments are due until sale or some other point in the future. They are usually made by a public or nonprofit agency to a lower income home buyer or a developer of low-income housing. Sometimes called a "deferred payment loan," a "DPL," or "soft second mortgage."

Down Payment Assistance - Grants or low interest loans given to lower income home buyers to help fund down payment and/or closing costs--usually in the range of $2,000 to $5,000. Less commonly, the term is used to refer to any second mortgage financing in any amount.

Entitlement Jurisdiction - In the affordable housing world, a city or county entitled to receive Community Development Block Grant funds directly from HUD--usually with a population exceeding 50,000.

Extremely low-income household - As widely defined by governmental and nonprofit organizations, a household with an income at or below 30 percent of the area median income. See "area median income."

Fannie Mae - The most common term for the Federal National Mortgage Association (FNMA), a publicly chartered corporation that buys residential mortgage loans from loan originators, typically local banks and thrift institutions.

Farmer's Home Administration - See "Rural Housing Service."

Fee Simple Ownership - Outright ownership of real estate, as opposed to leasing, lease-purchase arrangements, and buying a home on land leased from a land trust.

First Mortgage Loan - For a home purchase or a real estate project, usually the largest loan and one that gives the lender the most security. In case of foreclosure and sale, the first mortgage lender gets their money before any other lender is paid off. Also called a "first deed of trust" loan in some areas of the country.

Fixed-Rate Mortgage Loan - A mortgage loan for which the interest rate does not change over time.

Forbearance Agreement - An agreement in which a lender postpones foreclosure on a mortgage loan to allow the borrower time to catch up on overdue loan payments.

Foreclosure - The process by which a mortgaged property may be sold when a mortgage is in default.

Forgivable Loan - A loan that requires no monthly payments, which is due only on resale, and for which the debt is forgiven over a certain period of years. This mechanism is used by nonprofit or governmental organizations to subsidize low-income home buyers and to recapture some or all of the subsidy if the home is resold within a certain period of time, usually between five and 15 years.

Freddie Mac - A commonly-used name for the Federal Home Loan Mortgage Corporation, a publicly chartered corporation that buys residential mortgage loans from loan originators, typically local banks and thrift institutions.

The HOME Investment Partnership Program (HOME) - a HUD program that grants housing subsidy funds on a formula basis to cities and states. Smaller cities must apply to states for funding. Funds may be used for property acquisition, housing rehabilitation, rent subsidies and (in some places) new housing construction. Subsidies can be in the form of low interest second mortgages, "forgivable" loans, grants, interest subsidies, and rent subsidies. The program requires local nonfederal matching funds. HOME will fund reasonable developer fees and administrative costs of programs (up to certain limits).

Home Buyer Training - Workshops conducted for groups of prospective home buyers. Participants receive training on the pros and cons of buying a home, credit issues, home searches, mortgage financing, special financing (if available), loan closings, home maintenance, and other responsibilities of homeownership.

HOPE - A series of HUD programs that provide grants to local governments, housing authorities, or nonprofit organizations to convert unused or HUD-owned rental properties to homeownership opportunities. Properties must be public housing or government foreclosed housing. The grant pays for some administration, but requires a local match. Applicants compete for funds in periodic requests for proposals.

Housing Payment Ratio - In single-family lending, the percentage of a borrower's income that will be spent on the housing payment after a home purchase, refinancing, or home renovation financing. This ratio includes payments of loan principal, interest, real estate taxes, and insurance (called PITI). See "housing payment ratio."

Housing Trust Fund - A loosely defined term covering various types of public and nonprofit-controlled funds from which loans and grants are made for affordable housing. These trust funds are variously capitalized with public revenue, dedicated taxes, grants and payments from market-rate developers.

HUD - The U.S. Dept. of Housing and Urban Development. See definitions of the Community Development Block Grant Program, HOME, HOPE, Low Income Public Housing, Section 8 and Section 202.

Infill Housing - New homes or apartments built on smaller tracts of land, often in older neighborhoods, urban renewal areas or inner cities.

Installment Debt Ratio - In single-family lending, the percentage of a borrower's income that will be spent on all installment debt after a home purchase, refinancing, or home renovation financing. The conventional ratio is 36 percent of income. Some community reinvestment loan products and insured loans allow a higher ratio. See "housing payment ratio."

Land Trust - In the strictest sense, a nonprofit organization that sells affordable homes but retains ownership of the underlying land in order to control, through the leases, the long-term affordability of the homes. The leases ensure that homes are resold to low-income families, sold at a below-market price, and/or sold with shares of the appreciated value going to the nonprofit. The term is used more loosely to describe programs that subsidize fee simple home ownership for low-income families and impose similar kinds of long-term affordability controls.

Layered Financing - Financing for an affordable housing project that includes several subsidy sources (for example, HOME, CDBG and Tax Credits).

Lien - A document recorded in public records that represents a debt owed on the property. Examples of liens include: a recorded mortgage deed, a lien for unpaid taxes, and a mechanic's lien representing construction work on a property that was not paid for.

Leverage - In low-income housing, this means using one source of funds in a project to encourage investment by another source. As in "our funding was leveraged five times in that project."

Loan-to-Value Ratio - The ratio between the proposed loan amount and the appraised value of a property that money is being borrowed for. For instance, if a proposed loan equals 85 percent of appraised value, the loan-to-value ratio is 85 percent. For community reinvestment programs, lenders will sometimes lend up to 95 percent or 97 percent of appraised value, typically only if mortgage insurance is provided. The maximum ratio for conventional loans is 80 percent.

Low-income household - As widely defined by governmental and nonprofit organizations, a household with an income at or below 80 percent of the area median income. See "area median income."

Median Income - See "area median income."

Moderate-income household - As widely defined by governmental and nonprofit organizations, a household with an income between 80 percent and 120 percent of the area median income. See "area median income."

Mortgage Insurance - Insurance provided by a private institution or public agency that insures a lender in whole or in part from losses due to a default on a loan. Lenders typically require mortgage insurance only for loans that are considered conventional (see "conventional financing:). Borrowers pay the premiums. The Federal Housing Administration (FHA--part of HUD), provides many kinds of mortgage insurance, as do the Veterans Administration (VA) and many private insurers, who provide what is called "private mortgage insurance (PMI)."

Mortgage Loan - A loan secured by a mortgage deed, meaning the property owner has agreed to give the property to the lender if monthly payments are not made, so the property can be sold to pay off the loan. First deed of trust loan means the same thing.

Mortgagee - The lender of a mortgage loan.

Mortgagor - The borrower of a mortgage loan.

Nonamortizing Loan - See "deferred payment loan."

Origination - Once a loan has been underwritten, the act of processing the loan through closing, providing the loan funds and setting the loan up for servicing.

Participation Loan - Usually, a first mortgage loan made on a larger real estate project such as an apartment acquisition, where two or more lenders provide the funds. In a few affordable lending programs, single-family loans are subject to participations. In proportion to the funds each lender provides, it shares risk, repayments, and any proceeds of sale in the event of a default.

PJ - Either what you wear late at night, or a Participating Jurisdiction under the HUD HOME program. A PJ is a local or state government eligible to contract directly with HUD for HOME funds. Smaller cities must subcontract from state government agencies.

PMI - See "mortgage insurance."

Prequalification - The process of assisting a home buyer in determining if they qualify for conventional and/or subsidy loans. This process typically involves a credit check, verifying income and asset information, and evaluating debt, income, and credit information in relation to lender underwriting standards. The process typically determines: 1) if a borrower has good enough credit to borrow, and 2) approximately how much can be borrowed at certain interest rates and loan terms.

Purchase-Rehab Program - See "acquisition-rehab."

Qualifying ratios - See "underwriting ratios."

RTC - Resolution Trust Corp. - A quasi-public, federally chartered corporation that was charged in the early 1990s with selling off assets acquired by the government from bailed-out lenders that were federally insured.

Rent Subsidies - Term typically used to describe HUD's Section 8 program, which subsidize the rent of low-income tenants in privately owned apartments. They are typically administered by local housing authorities. There are two types of subsidies with only slight technical differences-- certificates and vouchers. Generally, tenants pay 30 percent of income for rent and utilities and HUD pays the rest directly to the landlord. Some other HUD funding programs for supportive housing and special needs housing can be used for rent subsidies. Some local governments sometimes provide rent subsidies or stipends with their own funds.

Rural Housing Service - A division of the U.S. Department of Agriculture that provides housing grants and loans to housing projects in small cities and rural areas, similar to programs of HUD in urban areas.
.
Section 8 - See "rent subsidies."

Section 502 - A program of the Rural Housing Service that provides low-income borrowers with direct low-interest loans or loan guarantees to buy a new or existing home. The guarantees are used as an incentive for private, institutional lenders to make home purchase loans at interest rates slightly below market. Section 502 loans are also sometimes originated as low-interest second mortgage loans made in tandem with first mortgage loans from private lenders.

Secondary Market - Collectively, the companies and government institutions that buy mortgage loans from lenders that originated them. A large number of single-family mortgage loans and some multifamily loans are sold to the secondary market, even though originators may still service many of the loans (see "servicer").

Secondary Financing - As used in this book, a term used to describe any financing used in conjunction with first mortgage loans from conventional financing institutions--for example, a down payment grant, a deferred payment loan, or an amortizing second mortgage loan.

Self-Sufficiency Programs - A loosely defined term used to describe various programs that assist the homeless, people on welfare or public housing tenants in getting training, day care and employment. HUD funds or promotes several self-sufficiency programs for public housing tenants and tenants with HUD rent subsidies.

Servicer - Or "loan servicer." A company that collects payments due on a mortgage loan, often the lender that originated the mortgage loan, even if the lender sold the loan to another entity.

Servicing - The act of collecting loan payments, accounting for them, making reports and managing escrowed funds for taxes and insurance.

Settlement - See "closing."

Soft Costs - A jargon term for non-bricks-and-mortar costs of a real estate development project. Includes architectural costs, surveys, appraisals, other fees, holding costs, etc.

Soft Money - A jargon term for subsidy funds from public or charitable sources used in a real estate development project. There are degrees of "soft." The softest funding consists of grants and deferred payment loans. Less soft are low interest, amortizing loans.

Soft Second Mortgage - See "deferred payment second mortgage."

Special Needs Housing - A loosely defined term for affordable or no-cost residential facilities for people with special medical problems, the homeless or people enrolled in self-sufficiency programs. In the broadest sense, it includes emergency shelters, longer-term shelters, transitional housing, half-way houses and group homes.

Subordinated Loan - In single-family mortgage lending, a second or third mortgage loan with a lien that is subordinate to a first or second mortgage loan. In the event of default and foreclosure, a subordinated loans are repaid only after other debts with a higher claim have been satisfied. (See "mortgage loan" and "lien.")

Subsidy - In housing, money put into a deal to lower the monthly debt service on an individual home or in a larger project. Low interest second mortgage loans are the most common source of subsidy. Tax Credit investments can also act as a subsidy. Rent subsidies are given to landlords to reduce rents paid by tenants.

Tax Credits - See separate section at the end of this section.

Three/Two (3/2) Option - Underwriting guidelines that allow home buyers to make a three percent down payment with their own funds, coupled with a gift from a relative or a two percent grant or unsecured loan from a nonprofit or government-sponsored program. For example, Fannie Mae will purchase loans from approved lending programs that use this option, if the borrower's income does not exceed 115 percent of the area median income.

Transitional Housing - A loosely defined term covering a number of housing facilities that serve the formerly homeless, people trying to get off welfare, or people released from institutions. Usually the term of stay is restricted to one to two years. The most common form is apartments or shared living facilities for the formerly homeless or single female parents with children. When treatment and supervision is involved, a facility is usually called a halfway house or group home.

Underwriting - The process of evaluating a loan application to determine if it meets credit standards and any other special requirements (as with special loan products for low-income borrowers). The underwriting process determines whether or not a loan will be approved, and on what terms and conditions.

Underwriting Ratios - Criteria used by lenders to determine how large a loan a prospective borrower can afford. The housing payment ratio (or "front" ratio) is the maximum percentage of monthly household income that can be paid for principal, interest, taxes and insurance (PITI). The installment debt ratio (or "back" ratio) is the maximum percentage of income that can be paid for total installment debt (including PITI, car loans, etc.). Ratios for conventional loans are 28 percent for PITI, and 36 percent for all installment debt, often expressed as 28/36. Many special loan products allow ratios of 33/38 or even higher--increasing the amount of the monthly payment and, thus, the amount that can be borrowed.

Variable-Rate Mortgage Loan - A mortgage loan for which the interest rate may change over time in relationship to some index such as the market price of long-term U.S. Treasury obligations.

Very low-income household - As widely defined by governmental and nonprofit organizations, a household with an income at or below 50 percent of the area median income. See "area median income."

Vouchers - Or Housing Vouchers. See "rent subsidies."

Write-down - A colloquial term used to describe a grant from a public or private source used to pay for part of the costs of a real estate development project. The grant is called a write-down because it makes the housing more affordable for tenants or home buyers.